QUEEN OF SPEED

Mildred Mary Petre Bruce: 10 November 1895–21 May 1990
(Courtesy of Julia Driver)

"She found unlimited new destinations in distance divided by time—the infinitely renewable frontier of speed. Her life sends a message to all of us. Don't believe it when they say you can't. Go ahead and give it a try. There are no barriers for those who simply will not quit trying."

Peggy Whitcomb, *Oregon Magazine*

Queen of Speed

The Racy Life of Mary Petre Bruce

Nancy R Wilson

ELSP

Published in 2012 by ELSP
11 Regents Place
Bradford on Avon
Wiltshire   BA15 1ED

Origination by Ex Libris Press
www.ex-librisbooks.co.uk

Typeset in 10.5/14 point Minion Pro

Printed by CPI Anthony Rowe
Chippenham, Wiltshire

ISBN 978-1-906641-42-9

All enquiries and correspondence relating to this
book should be addressed to the author:

Nancy R Wilson
Petaluma, California, USA 94952
Email: queenofspeed@sonic.net

www.queen-of-speed.com

For my family

Contents

Foreword

by Carey Chapman

I arrived in Bradford-on-Avon an hour before my appointment with the estate agent to view Priory Steps. Well before he arrived with the key I had already decided that this was where I wanted to live.

As we walked from room to room my mind was looking to the future, when Diana and I would own the house . . . wall down there, bathroom here—oh, and a new door would brighten this room up so much. But gradually the house forced me to start looking back, at its past.

A faint scent of lavender showed this house had been lived in until recently: it reminded me of my grandmother's apartment in Putney. Clothes still hung in the open wardrobes; washed up pots and pans lay upside down on the draining board by the old-fashioned kitchen sink. In the living room a card table pushed up against the wall held rather more empty bottles of champagne than one might regard as strictly necessary for a nonagenarian's bridge party.

I started to build a mental image of the last resident. I noticed what appeared to be a clock lying in the centre of the oak dining table. It wasn't a clock: it was a compass. The estate agent explained that the owner was the first woman to fly solo round the world and this was the compass that had been fitted to her plane.

He said it in such a nonchalant way that I asked him to repeat himself. Surely her name should be as familiar as Amy Johnson or Amelia Earhart. He gestured toward a silver cup on the mantelpiece and added she was also the first woman to win the Monte Carlo Rally. These two achievements alone, I thought, would make her name instantly familiar to me. I asked again, who was this lady? "Oh," he said, "Mary Bruce, The Honourable Mrs. Victor Bruce." It was the first I'd heard of her. "She has had to go and live in London with her son."

Six weeks later we returned to Bradford-on-Avon, picked up the key and let ourselves into our new home. The house had been stripped bare by the house clearance company: not a single sign of the previous owner remained. We began the major job of renovating Priory Steps so it could become an up-market bed and breakfast.

In my first months in Bradford-on-Avon I heard many stories and anecdotes about Mrs. Bruce from the neighbours. In a window seat, long sealed with layers of paint, I found an old newsreel in a sealed can, some dusty papers and a silver plaque from the Swedish Automobile Association commemorating her "Fairytale trip to the Arctic." This just fed my hunger to find out more about her exploits and to reacquaint the world with this remarkable woman.

In May 1990 Mrs. Bruce died, and a few days later, at about four in the morning, I was woken by the phone. It was an American journalist tasked with writing Mrs. Bruce's obituary checking facts. I answered a few questions as best I could before I mentioned it was actually, in England, the middle of the night. I asked her to phone back later when I could lay my hands on all the facts: after a moment's silence the journalist apologised for phoning so early and hung up. It was the last I would hear from her but soon after, far away in California, Nancy Wilson was reading the completed obituary in her morning paper. This sparked her interest in the remarkable Mrs. Victor Bruce and led directly to this book being written.

Many months later, Nancy phoned from America to find out more. I was delighted as even in England very few people know anything about the Honourable Mrs. Bruce. Her remarkable achievements have, for some reason, faded from common knowledge: her pioneering past is being forgotten. Interest from overseas was welcome. It seemed natural Nancy should stay in Mrs. Bruce's own house so I booked her in for one night – in the end this became three.

When Nancy arrived at Priory Steps we spent hours talking about Mrs. B. Since we moved in to Priory Steps I'd been collecting anything relating to Mrs. Bruce and my collection of memorabilia and ephemera was, even then, substantial. We delved deeper and deeper into her life. Then I remembered an old cardboard box which was stuffed with miscellaneous newspaper cuttings from papers around the world. We opened it and found there were thousands. It was like a lucky dip as we plunged our hands into a Pandora's box. Each clipping brought news of some new, long-forgotten Mrs. Bruce adventure in which she'd pop up unexpectedly in yet another far-flung part of the world with another record shattered. Nancy asked if she could sort the cuttings out: it was late in the evening so I readily agreed. At Priory Steps we pride ourselves on providing a good night's sleep but I don't think Nancy got one. By the next morning the box's entire contents had been carefully sorted into subjects and Nancy had made copious notes which proved the foundations of this book.

Through the last 20 years I have been fortunate to be asked to talk about Mrs. Bruce on many occasions and members of the audience have often shared priceless anecdotes and memories: many of these have found their way into this book. Talks about Mrs. Bruce on BBC Radio 4's "Women's Hour," Nick Barratt's "Secrets in the Attic" and BBC1's "Antiques Roadshow" have brought forth even more glimpses of her life. Specialist organisations such as the Blackburn Aeroplane Company and the Bentley Drivers' Club have provided precious information from their archives. Nancy has made many research trips to England over the years and I've been able to share all this new information.

Rather like assembling a jigsaw puzzle without knowing the picture or how many bricks it has, Nancy has pieced together the story of the life of a remarkable woman. This is the tale of a pioneering woman who drove, rode, sailed, flew and – above all – partied all around the world.

The suffragettes may have succeeded in throwing off the patriarchal cloak of Edwardian Society, but Mrs. Bruce showed the world that anything men could do, she could do. Not only just as well, but better.

Introduction

In May 1990, a chance reading of a San Francisco newspaper's small obituary of a British woman ignited two decades of fascination with The Honourable Mrs. Victor Bruce. The headline read 'Mary Victor Bruce: She Broke Records'. I tore it out and carried the scrap of newspaper in my wallet for years.

What was that spark in that small obituary? What made her story so compelling? Mary Bruce was adventure personified: fearless, headstrong, stubbornly determined. Nothing seemed impossible to her, and she allowed nothing to come between her and her goals. She was impulsive but doggedly single-minded; extravagantly self-indulgent yet lavishly generous to her friends; a shrewd entrepreneur with a razor-sharp mind for business but with curious lapses of judgment which led, in some cases, to conflict and disaster.

The more I learned about this complex and contradictory woman, the more I wanted to know. The search for answers to what made Mary tick provided a look into a way of life that has vanished.

She was a teenage law-breaker, an unwed mother, and a record-setting speedboat and racing car driver; a pioneer round-the-world flyer, an author, and an innovative airline executive; a fearless adventurer, a free-spending, luxury-loving millionaire and an eccentric curmudgeon. The Honourable Mrs. Victor Bruce titled her autobiography *Nine Lives Plus*, and she lived every one of them to the fullest.

The only daughter in the family of an English squire, Mildred Mary Petre Bruce led a life of adventure equaled by few. Mary's speed records on land and sea, her newspaper columns offering motoring advice for women, and her career in a flying circus kept her name constantly before the British public in the 1920s and 1930s. Her improbable solo flight around the world, undertaken after only a few weeks of experience as a pilot, set aviation records and made international headlines.

Born in the closing years of the nineteenth century, Mary enthusiastically embraced the dazzling technology of the twentieth. From early childhood she loved speeding and flirting with danger. "Going slowly always makes me tired," she once claimed. There were very few times in her life when she did that!

Mary exemplified the flat-out, full-steam-ahead spirit of the Jazz Age, an era of unprecedented expansion and innovation. The peaceful and prosperous decade following the Great War saw spectacular advances in science and industry, as well as a tidal wave of record-setting feats. There were marathon dances and long-distance flights; sports legends set impressive new marks in stadiums and on race tracks. Records fell nearly as soon as they were set; new challenges arose constantly.

Bright as her star was, it has faded until few remember her now. Mention "the first woman to fly around the world alone" and puzzled looks follow. "Amelia Earhart? Geraldine Mock?" The former never completed her flight; the latter was the first to make the entire circuit by air, in 1964. Yet decades earlier, newspapers everywhere followed Mary's progress as she flew eastward across Europe and Asia to America and back to England, folding her plane's wings and crossing the oceans by ship.

That she slipped so soon into obscurity is regrettable. Her odyssey coincided with the onset of the Great Depression. Financial disaster, political upheaval and warfare in Europe, spreading worldwide by the 1940s, diverted attention from what must have seemed, in contrast, her somewhat frivolous adventures.

Mary wasted no time regretting the absence of the limelight; bent on accumulating wealth and enjoying every penny of it, she energetically careened through the remainder of the twentieth century at top speed. She was fiercely determined to live life on her own terms, and to a remarkable extent she was successful.

A powerful woman long before 'women's lib' became a catchphrase, iron-willed and farsighted, Mary maintained her independent lifestyle into her 90s. Her fearless race through life, her sheer determination, and her ability to cope with a series of personal and business calamities shaped a fascinating life. She wrote five books, including a very selective autobiography. Here is the entire story.

Chronology

1895	10 November: Born Mildred Mary Petre in Essex
1911	Cited for speeding on brother's motorbike
1920	Son Anthony born
1926	Marries Victor Bruce in Menton, France
1927	January: Wins Monte Carlo *Coupe des Dames,* places 6th overall
	February–March: Mediterranean circuit in AC
	July–August: Arctic run
	December: Ten-day endurance run at Montlhéry
1928	Sets record for double English Channel crossing
1929	June: Sets 24-hour endurance record at Montlhéry
	August: Retakes Channel speed record
	September: Sets 24-hour motorboating endurance record
1930	25 May: Takes first flying lesson
	27 July: Gets pilot's licence
	25 September: Takes off from Heston on world flight
1931	20 February: Arrives Croydon airfield, completing world flight
1932	August: Mid-air refuelling record
	September: Earns commercial pilot's licence
1934	Establishes Air Dispatch and Commercial Air Hire
1937	September: Mary and Victor separate
1941	Eric Noddings dies
1947	Buys *Fantasia*
1950	Buys The Rise (Priory Steps) in Bradford-on-Avon
1974	Speed trial at Thruxton in Ford Ghia Capri
1977	*Nine Lives Plus* published; loops the loop over Bristol
1985	Moves to London
1990	21 May: Dies at age 94

1 Growing Up

Summer, 1911. It is a warm afternoon in the village of Hounslow, west of London. A collie named Laddie sits quietly in the sidecar of a sleek and shiny eight horsepower Matchless motorcycle parked in front of the Police Court of Hounslow. Patiently he awaits the return of his mistress, a fifteen-year-old speed demon who has been cited for causing a public nuisance and disturbing the peace.

Mildred Mary Petre had no licence to operate the motorcycle, which did not belong to her. Her older brother Louis had purchased it at a motor show for £120. He laughed at Mary when she asked to ride it, declaring, "Don't be childish! You're a girl!" Some months later he left it in her care when he went abroad, asking her to look after it by keeping it polished. Mary felt, however, that a motorcycle needed the same kind of 'looking after' that a pony required—frequent exercising. As soon as Louis was out of sight, Mary enlisted the help of a young man at the village garage, who gave her a half hour's instruction on motorcycle care, maintenance and riding technique.

She was a natural, and soon was racing around the family tennis court, with Laddie in the sidecar. Her mother Jennie, arriving home to find Mary and Laddie riding in circles, had launched into a theatrical speech about the dangers of speeding and the certainty that Mary was flirting with disaster. Volatile as her mother was, however, she quickly accepted Mary's invitation to go for a spin. Lifting Laddie out of the sidecar, Jennie climbed in. They circled the tennis court, then hit the open road. By the end of the ride her mother was won over and offered no further objection to Mary's new obsession. In an interview years later, in fact, Mary complained that, once her mother got a taste of the sensation of speeding along in the sidecar, she always wanted to ride with her; "I couldn't get rid of her!" Mary exclaimed.

Mary, headstrong and willful, had been accustomed to getting her way since her earliest days. She was a spoiled child, no doubt about that: the only daughter born to an upper-class Englishman, Lawrence Joseph Petre, and Jennie Williams, an American actress from Indiana. Mary always claimed that her mother was a prominent Shakespearean actress touring England in the 1880s; however, the London theatre where Jennie performed, the Gaiety, was a burlesque house. Lawrence, grandson of the Earl of Wicklow, saw Jennie on stage one night and was smitten. He courted her, married her, and took her home to Coptfold Hall, his splendid manor house in Essex. Set amid gently rolling hills, the estate boasted acres of woods and meadows full of pheasant and rabbits—an idyllic setting for children. Jennie later described her husband as a gloomy man, but she could not resist the glamour of a marriage into the Petre family, with its close ties to nobility and a firm place in the upper class of nineteenth century England.[1]

Mildred Mary Petre
(Courtesy of Wiltshire Swindon Archives)

Lawrence and Jennie produced six children in 11 years; three sons died in infancy. Mildred Mary, born 10 November 1895, was raised with two brothers: Louis, four years older, and Roderick, six years younger. Mary was clearly the princess of the family, and her mother encouraged her headstrong and adventurous ways. From her earliest days, this adored daughter of the Petre household was a thrill-seeker. At the age of two, Mary fretted when her donkey wouldn't pull her cart fast enough. At age six, she delighted when her Shetland pony Dinky bolted. At nine, she owned a spirited Welsh pony with a propensity for wrecking governess carts by hurling them—with Mary in the basket—into ditches. After the second crash, she later claimed, the insurance company no longer would cover her.

Her mother viewed these escapades with a theatrical eye; after each episode she would declare that Mary was like a cat with nine lives. Her father, dour and far less indulgent, always worried about the financial consequences of his headstrong daughter's mishaps. In spite of the family's social position, money was a perpetual source of worry for him. He had inherited Coptfold Hall from his mother, but as the result of a legal tangle of no fewer than 12 codicils to her will, she had left him no money with which to maintain the estate or to pay the requisite staff.

Mary's childhood home, Coptfold Hall

The Petre family moved several times, and Mary attended a succession of convent schools. She made no claim to scholarly success, admitting to a particularly dismal showing in arithmetic. Nevertheless, when her mother asked her once what she wanted to be when she grew up, Mary answered, "A millionaire." Her mediocre showing in school did not keep her from accomplishing this goal.

In 1910 the family was living in Osterley Park, west of London. With her brother Louis away, the adventurous Mary loved racing his Matchless over the narrow lanes around her home, usually with Laddie in the sidecar. Big red ribbons festooned Mary's brown braids, flying in the air as she clocked speeds between 55 and 60 miles an hour—far in excess of the 20 miles per hour national speed limit. Mary discovered she could increase the speed and lighten the weight of the bike by removing the baffles from the muffler; she found the resulting roar of the engine exhilarating.

However, Osterley Park was a quiet haven for the other residents. The wife of the Seventh Earl of Jersey, who resided in the grand manor house at the center of the park, described it: 'As Sunday evening draws in, the peals of distant church bells are the only sounds which come to break the quiet of a home so near the town and yet seemingly so secluded from the world; then these cease, and the song of the nightingale alone disturbs the slumbers of Osterley Park.'[2]

The young Mary (Courtesy of Wiltshire Swindon Archives)

Complaints from the neighbours (including, no doubt, Lady Jersey) had brought Mary to Police Court where she set her first record, becoming the first female in England to be cited for a motoring violation. Keeping the news from her parents, she rode the Matchless to court. The magistrate listened to the evidence against Mary, and then asked her how old she was. "Fifteen and three-quarters, Sir . . . nearly," was her reply. Had she a licence? She had not—although, she volunteered, she did have one for Laddie, waiting patiently outside. The magistrate dismissed the charges against her, but assessed her court costs of six shillings and banned her from riding the motorcycle until she was sixteen and old enough to get a licence. She and Laddie walked home from court; the young garage mechanic retrieved the motorcycle.

By the time Mary had served her 'sentence' and celebrated her sixteenth birthday in November 1911, her brother Louis was home again. Much to Mary's delight, he'd lost interest in the Matchless and purchased a car. The motorcycle was hers.

She painted it red to match her hair ribbons, and she and Laddie resumed riding. To avoid a repeat run-in with the local constabulary, she ventured farther from home. In London, motor vehicles were still outnumbered by horses, and she was greeted with waves and approving looks in her travels. She made a trip to the convent school she had attended in Herne Bay, several miles east of London, to visit her favorite nun. Sister Sacre Coeur resisted only briefly when Mary invited her to climb on behind her for a ride around the tennis court. Assured that the Reverend Mother was not watching, Sister gathered her robes, sat sidesaddle on the pillion, and rode into history as the first nun to travel on a motorcycle.

Mary's parents separated while she was a teenager. They lived apart, but there would be no divorce; their strong Catholic faith forbade it. Louis, already in his 20s, was on his own. Roderick, mentally slow, lived with his father in London's fashionable Kensington. Mary and her mother lived in a caravan park on the outskirts of Shoreham-by-Sea, on England's south coast.

The open road called to Mary constantly, and she was always ready to explore new territory. In the seaside resort of Brighton, she collected another dubious honour by becoming the first woman to crash a motorcycle. With a friend in the sidecar, she was cruising down the main promenade when the sight of a beautiful car parked at the curb mesmerized her. Distracted by the sight, she sideswiped a passing taxi and the motorcycle tipped over. No one was injured, but the rear wheel flew off the Matchless. A crowd gathered quickly, helped right the cycle and reattached the errant wheel. The girls went on their way amid cheers from the bystanders.

Mary loved the attention she attracted when riding the Matchless. In pre-war England motor vehicles were still a novelty, especially when driven by attractive young women. On the road, friendly smiles were the rule rather than the exception, and Mary was her mother's daughter when it came to basking in the spotlight. Years later, when asked by an interviewer what she had enjoyed most in her life, she answered with no hesitation, "The fuss! Oh, I did love the fuss everyone's made of me!"

The advent of war in Europe brought a petrol shortage and other hardships; Mary's days of carefree joyriding came to an end. Her father insisted she stop riding, thinking it in very poor taste for members of the leisure class to 'lark about' on motorcycles during those trying times. Mary reluctantly agreed; her father sold the motorcycle.

Although Mary had never excelled at academics, she had a real talent for art. Painting was one activity that occupied her time during those difficult wartime years. It became a lifelong hobby, although only one of her paintings is known to have survived: in 1914 she completed an oil painting of an Arabian street scene and gave it as a gift to a boyfriend, an officer in the British Army.

Another interest was the opposite sex. Stephen Easter was a wealthy landowner in Shoreham-by-Sea. His extensive holdings included the caravan park where Mary and her mother lived, and the teenager quickly caught his eye. Easter was 21 years Mary's senior. He had married at the age of 19; he and his wife, Alice Gibbings—by all accounts a stern and humorless woman—were childless. The petite and lively young Miss Petre enchanted the middle-aged Easter. Vivacious and bright, Mary was not like the girls he had courted in the 1890s. She was clearly a twentieth century woman, and he was thoroughly smitten. Stephen Easter had qualities that appealed to Mary: he was sophisticated, mature, and successful—and he was quite wealthy. She had expensive tastes; he longed for the excitement of youth. They began a love affair that lasted for several years.

Britain struggled through the dark war years with determination. Plans and dreams were put on hold in anticipation of peacetime. Predictably, Mary's dreams centered around speed. She read every bit of motoring news she could find, studying statistics and specifications. She saved her money for a car, and decided just what she wanted to buy at the earliest opportunity. "I told my father that I wanted a car with a big leather strap around the bonnet, just like they had on the race tracks. I got one, too," she said, "because I was a spoiled brat. It was a Vauxhall 30/98, the fastest car of its day. You were in a shiver of dust from the moment you moved."[3]

By the time the Armistice was signed on 11 November 1918, Mary was ready; she had saved £75, and with some financial help from her father and mother (or, more likely, from Stephen Easter), she was on the road again. She quickly realized that times had changed. Automobiles were no longer a novelty, nor were they received with waves and smiles of approval. Many people found them objectionable: noisy, smelly, and somewhat menacing, they frightened horses and raised great clouds of dust. Policemen, charged with enforcing traffic regulations, viewed automobiles with similar scepticism, if not hostility. The restrictions embodied in the new speeding regulations came as a rude shock to Mary. She considered road racing great sport and revelled in speed.

She often stayed with her father in Kensington, and raced her car down to Brighton. A policeman whistled her to a stop one day in Bayswater Road and announced with glee that he and his colleagues had been watching her speeding and had tried for weeks to apprehend her. Timed with a stopwatch over a measured distance, Mary distinguished herself by becoming the first female motorist ensnared by a speed trap. She claimed that most of the time she could beat the traps by driving so fast that there was no time to start the watch, but eventually she became a regular in London's Bow Street Police Court, once appearing three days running for separate speeding offences. On the third day the magistrate scolded her soundly and fined her ten shillings.

Mary celebrated the return of peace with frequent jaunts in her sporty car as everyday life in Britain slowly resumed. Thousands of soldiers came home; food rationing was phased out; manufacturing plants retooled from war production to peacetime pursuits. For most Britons, life returned to a familiar pre-war normalcy.

In the summer of 1919, however, Mary found herself involved in a completely new undertaking: a baby was on the way. Marriage was not an option; Stephen Easter would not divorce his wife. It may have been a case of financial prudence—a scandalous affair and a divorce might have ruined him—or perhaps genuine affection or comfortable history kept him tied to Alice. Certainly the spirited and headstrong Mary, pregnancy notwithstanding, knew that marriage to the older Easter was not what she wanted.

To Easter's great credit, he provided very generously for Mary. He set her up in a beautiful house, Lyndale Hall, on Finchley Road in north London. She was kept in luxury. When their infant son was born on the first of March, 1920, Easter's name appeared on the birth certificate as the father of the child. His occupation was given as 'Landowner', with an address of 36 Great Tower Street in London. Mary's name was recorded as 'Mildred Mary Easter formerly Petre'—no proof of marriage was required. The baby's name first appeared as 'Anthony Billy', later amended to 'Anthony Billy Stephen Petre'. 'Easter' was not included in the baby's name on the certificate, although Anthony always used that surname.

It is not clear just when the relationship between Stephen and Mary cooled. Surely Stephen's wife Alice was aware of the baby's birth, and she may have agreed to cooperate with Easter's financial support of the baby on the condition that his emotional involvement was curtailed. Perhaps Mary resented the way her life had been changed by the pregnancy. While there was a nurse to care for Tony and plenty of money to provide for both of them, her freedom was limited by the demands of motherhood.

In any case, by the time little Tony was five, the romance was a thing of the past. Mary and Stephen remained friendly, and Stephen continued his support of Tony and his mother. He paid for Tony's schooling and Tony was included as a member of Easter's family, sometimes celebrating Christmas with his father in Shoreham.

Unburdened by the mundane, day to day responsibilities of parenthood, Mary turned her attention to her first love: speed. She always had an eye for sleek, stylish, and speedy vehicles, and she followed motoring news avidly.

Auto companies prospered in postwar Britain. Manufacturers maintained company racing teams, typically comprising young men of the leisure class who had the resources to indulge in driving as a hobby, and whose employment by the auto companies provided them an outlet for their enjoyment of the sport.

Mary's future husband, Victor Austin Bruce, was a professional competition driver with Auto Carriers, Ltd., in Thames Ditton, Surrey. The fourth son of the second Baron Aberdare, Victor was raised with six older brothers and sisters. His lifelong passion for cars began in childhood, when his eldest brother, Lyndhurst, owned a 'rather splendid' car, a De Dietrich.

Like vast numbers of his contemporaries, Victor had spent years in military service, joining the Buffs[4] in August 1914. Back problems rendered him unfit for active duty; he was stationed in Cardiff, working as an army filmmaker. He was hospitalized, and eventually discharged from the Army, but within months he was able to join the Royal Marine Forces as a second lieutenant; he served until the end of the war.

During the war, Auto Carriers had suspended production of their sporty little cars and switched to manufacturing war materiel, but in 1919 they retooled and once again were in the automotive business as AC Cars. In the 1920s, under the leadership of motor racing pioneer Selwyn Edge, AC developed a prestigious automobile racing reputation. Superb performance and attractive body styling were characteristic of the extremely popular AC cars.

Besides regular competition in road rallies, hill climbs, and time trials, which showed off their skills and their employers' products, racing team members were on call   for publicity events. The annual British International Motor Show was an opportunity for carmakers to introduce their new models to the public and demonstrate new features. Eager auto enthusiasts like Mary Petre flocked to see the array of vehicles. At the 1925 Motor Show she met Victor Bruce.

2 Gearing Up

British automobile racing really began in 1902 in the resort of Bexhill-on-Sea, when the eighth Earl De La Warr organized a two-day meet that drew 200 competitors. Speeds of over 50 miles an hour were clocked as the smoke-belching machines thundered down the seafront promenades before thousands of curious spectators.

Well before 1907 there was a clear need for a venue dedicated to racing. Unlike the continent, where racing on public roads was allowed, mainland Britain forbade it, enforcing a speed limit of 20 miles per hour until 1930. The absence of racing facilities was seen as a deterrent to progress in British motorcar manufacturing, so Hugh F. Locke King, with the enthusiastic encouragement of his wife Ethel, constructed the world's first purpose-built motor-racing track, Brooklands, on his estate 20 miles south-west of London. His intention was to give the fledgling automotive industry a boost. He used horseracing as a model; drivers wore certain colors for identification, as jockeys do, rather than having numbers on their cars. The 2¾-mile course was an oval, but in the interest of greater speed and safety, he added high concrete bankings at the turns.

As construction of the track progressed, interest grew. In 1906, months before opening day, the Brooklands Automobile Racing Club was formed. Official Opening Day ceremonies took place on 17 June 1907. Following a luncheon, Hugh and Ethel Locke King proudly led a stately procession of cars (including The Honourable C.S. Rolls in a Rolls-Royce) around the track. Ethel, at the wheel of their 70 horsepower Itala, suddenly accelerated, speeding away from the other cars. Lord Lonsdale, president of the Brooklands Automobile Racing Club, was the first to take up her challenge, chasing after her. What had been a dignified parade turned into a wild race, with cars tearing around the track at breakneck speed.

Later that month, British auto racing pioneer Selwyn F. Edge established an auto endurance record at the new track, driving for 24 hours at an average speed of nearly 66 mph.[1]

S. F. Edge sets 24-hour endurance record; Brooklands, 1907

Brooklands Paddock, July 1907
(Both photos courtesy of Brooklands Museum Photo Archive)

Racing at Brooklands was not limited to automobiles. The Club offered a grand prize of £2500 for the first person to fly an airplane around the track before the end of 1907. No one beat the deadline, but Brooklands quickly became a Mecca for fliers as well as racing car drivers. Early aviators like A.V. Roe began building biplanes, testing and revising their designs.[2]

In 1909 the future of aviation was full of promise. Louis Bleriot of France claimed a £1000 prize offered by the London *Daily Mail* when he became the first to fly the English Channel in a powered aircraft. One of the earliest airfields in England was constructed in the middle of the Brooklands track, and by 1910 several aircraft design and manufacturing concerns were operating on the grounds. Until war broke out in 1914, there was a constant hum of activity on the ground and in the air. Auto racing and flying records were set with regularity, and speed-demon Mary Petre was undoubtedly watching closely.

During the war, racing was discontinued and Brooklands was taken over by the military. Recreational activities were replaced by a training school for the Royal Flying Corps and by aircraft construction: Sopwith and Vickers were just two of the well-known manufacturers in production there. By the end of the war, the racetrack had been heavily damaged by military vehicles and their solid tyres; extensive repairs were needed. When Brooklands reopened in 1920, it ushered in a new era in British racing history.

Mary's future husband, the dashing Victor Austin Bruce, was making a name for himself in his capacity as racing team member for Selwyn Edge's popular AC motorcars. In 1923 he undertook two challenges designed to capture the attention of the British motoring public and enhance AC's reputation. In April he drove an AC roadster to Clovelly, described by Victorian poet Edward Capern as 'a village like a waterfall'. This cluster of gaily-painted cottages and shops clings to the side of a cliff on the north coast of Devon. Too steep for cars even today, the high street is a series of 4-inch cobbled steps rising from the harbour side. The whole village turned out to watch as Victor drove up the steps, his shiny aluminum AC two-seater 'bounding and bucking in the most alarming fashion' as photographers recorded the feat. (In a less photogenic but even more challenging accomplishment he had, of necessity, first reversed down the steps, since there was neither other access nor room at the bottom to turn around.)

Later that year Edge sent Victor on a mountain-climbing jaunt in which he drove another AC automobile up railroad tracks to the summit of 3,560-foot Mt. Snowdon, the highest point in Wales. The Royal Automobile Club was there to observe the widely publicized event, lending an air of official approval. Victor made the ascent in just two hours, as a crowd of onlookers cheered and, again, photographers recorded the stunt.

Victor's heavy schedule for AC continued in 1924 with road trials, hill climbs, and track racing throughout Britain and on the continent. In addition to his driving duties, Victor used his filmmaking skills to produce automotive films for the rapidly expanding motoring public. His topics covered the basics: passing, signaling, turning, cornering—as well as such titles as *Dealing with Horses on the Road* and *When to Use the Hooter.*

In January 1925, with several years of experience behind the wheel, the 27-year-old Victor Bruce became the first Briton to compete in the prestigious Monte Carlo Rally. First held in 1911, this annual winter competition eventually grew into the premier automotive touring event in the world.[3]

The Hon. Victor Austin Bruce: 8 April 1897–16 December 1978

The Monte Carlo tests both drivers and automobiles; its dead-of-winter scheduling is no accident. Originally each driver selected his own starting place for the race, and points were awarded based on the distance covered, average speed, and number of passengers carried. January's treacherous roads and freezing temperatures throughout much of Europe offered an extra challenge for drivers, adding a special edge of pressure as they set out from such distant points as Athens, Greece, and Stavanger, Norway—both over 2,200 miles from Monte Carlo. In 1925 Victor Bruce chose Glasgow as his starting point and, in a very respectable first-time showing, he and his passenger, T.C. Gillett, finished a respectable fourth out of 47 starters. Firmly intending to take first place the following year, Bruce spent the balance of 1925 honing his skills with dozens of races and speed trials at LeMans, as well as Brooklands and other courses throughout Britain.

That October, Victor met Mary Petre in London at the yearly Motor Show. The pair shared a common love of automobiles, fast driving and adventure. With Victor at the wheel of an AC car, Mary made her first circuit of the Brooklands track, and he introduced her to many of the best-known racing drivers of the day.

Victor's single-minded focus on the upcoming Monte Carlo Rally was only slightly diverted by the entry into his life of this captivating young beauty. The discovery of a woman who shared his passion for speed and competition intrigued him. Their courtship centered around the automobile; from October to January, Mary watched as he competed in speed trials and road rallies.

Victor Bruce triumphed in the 1926 Monte Carlo, elevating it to a truly international event by recording the first British victory in the Rally's history. Bruce drove a 2-litre AC touring car and captured the 25,000 franc first prize. He chose as his starting point the village of John O'Groats, at the northeastern tip of Scotland. The journey to Monaco—the first part of the Monte Carlo Rally—was a 70-hour ordeal marked by nearly constant blizzard conditions. Victor's passenger and navigator, W. J. Brunell,[4] was a well-known professional photographer whose reputation had been established by his images of Queen Victoria's funeral procession in 1901. After their Monte Carlo win, Brunell presented Victor Bruce with a handsome photograph album, a pictorial record of the event.[5]

Mary, Victor's most enthusiastic fan, was waiting for him at the finish line in front of the Casino. She was his navigator and timekeeper for the *Mont des Mules* hill climb and Alpine trial portions of the Rally. Three weeks later they were married at the British Vice Consulate in the popular seafront resort of Menton.

A wedding in France was a convenient way to avoid conflict with Victor's family, which took a dim view of their relationship. Mary was seen as an inappropriate bride for this privileged son of the aristocracy. Theirs had been a whirlwind courtship, and Mary's social standing was distinctly below Victor's. To the dismay of Victor's family, she was from a staunchly Catholic background and—worse yet—she was the unapologetic unwed mother of a five year old child.

After a honeymoon on the Riviera, they returned to England with the huge silver Monte Carlo winner's cup, trophies for the *Mont des Mules*, Alpine trial, and the Nice Automobile Club race. They settled in a cottage in Esher, near AC's headquarters in Thames Ditton. The newlyweds' activities revolved around automobiles as Victor participated in race meetings and speed trials at various venues in Britain and France. Brooklands, only minutes from Esher, was a frequent site for automotive events but there were also rallies in Cornwall and Scotland, speed trials on the wide beaches of Southport and Blackpool, and meets and races in France.

Married at Menton, France – 16 February 1926
(Courtesy of Wiltshire Swindon Archives)

Throughout the year, the determined and headstrong bride kept up a campaign of gently badgering Selwyn Edge, trying to coax him into lending her an AC automobile to drive in the 1927 Monte Carlo Rally. Edge was a canny businessman as well as a record-breaking racer. He saw the publicity value in having a woman drive one of his automobiles in the prestigious Rally. Even if Mary merely completed the course without an accident, it would be great advertising for his cars. Edge gave her the use of an AC saloon, and she began making plans.

As her husband had in 1926, Mary selected John O'Groats as her starting point for the 1927 Rally. She carried three passengers: Victor, engineer A.W. Pitt from the AC works, and Robert W. Beare, Motoring Editor for London's *Daily Sketch*. Carrying three passengers garnered more points for the entry, as each passenger was equivalent to five hundred extra miles travelled. (Clearly, however, there was a point of diminishing return with this scheme; one man started from Stockholm in a motorbus with 20 passengers. The heavily loaded bus slid into a ditch and could not continue in the competition. Had it completed the course, the bus might well have won.)

The course from John O'Groats to Monte Carlo was 1,700 miles. January weather was, as expected in the far north of Scotland, less than ideal for driving. The roads were icy; snow was everywhere. The night before the Rally, Mary came down with flu and a high fever. Undeterred by illness, she settled herself behind the wheel the next day and they were on their way. At the very first turn in the road after leaving the starting point at the gloomy Gothic hotel at John O'Groats, the car went into a skid on the icy surface. 'The way in which she dealt with this skid was really masterly,' wrote Bobby Beare in his *Daily Sketch* motoring column. 'The car wagged its tail like an exuberant puppy, but there was never a moment's doubt that it was completely under control. And I believe Mrs Bruce enjoyed it— or at least enjoyed putting the wind up her passengers.'

From that first skid onward, Mary needed every bit of driving skill she possessed to stay on course. The need for concentration hastened her recovery, and she was soon feeling fine. The first day's drive took them south over the imposing Grampian mountain range. A thick Scottish mist clung to the ground and drastically reduced visibility. The roads were nearly all under reconstruction, with tedious detours and haphazard temporary bridges. The foursome stopped only for a cup of coffee in Inverness, determined to get through the mountains before dark. At dusk they stopped for high tea at Blair Athol, at the southern edge of the Grampians, and soon were back on the road.

Later that evening they reached the first checkpoint in Glasgow, some 300 miles from their start, where they sat down as dinner guests of the Royal Scottish Automobile Club. The travellers had barely touched their bowls of soup when they were handed a telegram with a weather report: 'Thick fog 50 miles round Carlisle; mist on Yorkshire moors, heavy snow falling onwards London; frozen roads very dangerous.' Interest in nourishment evaporated. "Let's get on with it!" exclaimed Victor. They rose from the table with one accord, and in moments they were back in the car and on the road again, hoping to gain ground while the weather was still tolerable.

Fog and wind-driven snow cut visibility to practically zero as Mary drove through the Scottish Lowlands. They crossed into England in the dark and by early morning had reached the second control point at Doncaster, south of York. It was about then—after 16 hours of driving—that the subject of a relief driver came up for the first and last time. The original intention was that Mary and Victor would share the driving, each taking shifts of approximately 200 miles. The press, however, believing that Mary would drive the entire distance, had trumpeted this news in advance. Having enjoyed the challenge of the run down the length of Scotland, she determined to attempt the feat as sole driver.

After 24 hours, with Mary still behind the wheel, they were in London for another checkpoint at Leicester Square. Interest in the Rally had been stirred by Victor Bruce's win the previous year, and a crowd of spectators was eager to see this year's Bruce entry, especially since it was Mrs. Bruce at the wheel.

London check-in formalities concluded, they were soon on their way again, south to the English Channel port of Folkstone. They arrived a bare half-hour before the ferry to Boulogne sailed. The only other Channel crossing scheduled that night was going to Calais—a destination that would have added many miles and much precious time to their planned route through France to Monte Carlo. The boat trip was the longest break from driving Mary would have. She made a dash for their cabin, but she was too excited to sleep.

It seemed like mere moments before she was behind the wheel again, speeding down treacherous, icy roads toward the next checkpoint, in Paris. Victor served as navigator and the two backseat passengers took turns tapping Mary's head to keep her awake. They were in Paris at midnight, ahead of their schedule; no doubt recalling the bowls of soup they had abandoned in Glasgow, they took time to refuel themselves with sandwiches and strong coffee.

It was always easier, they learned, to get into a city than out of it. Paris, very much alive in the middle of the night, was a challenge as they headed south, searching for the route out of the city. Six hundred grueling miles lay between them and Monte Carlo—a potholed, mountainous route with dozens of hairpin turns unprotected by guardrails or parapets, to be negotiated in the darkness. Mary credited fast driving with keeping her awake and helping her cope with hallucinations of big black dogs crossing the road ahead of her. To the consternation of Bobby Beare, the one passenger who remained awake through the most treacherous part of the dash through the mountainous Esterel region, she amused herself by spinning yarns of frightful crashes and potential hazards on dark roads such as the one they were travelling.

The welcome lights of Cannes greeted them just before dawn on the fourth day. As the sun rose, the Mediterranean glistened before them; they followed smooth roads up the coast toward the principality of Monaco. A last-minute delay in the resort town of Antibes was a near disaster. Having found their way easily to the central square, they asked a pedestrian for directions to Nice. *Tout droit* they were told—or perhaps, Mary thought, it might have been *à droite*. In either case, the word *droit* was clear enough: 'right'. They turned to the right, once, twice, three times—and arrived back in the central square. Inquiring again, they got the same reply; assuming that they had somehow missed a turn, they exited the square and took several right turns again. Frustration was mounting as they entered the central square once more. The third time they inquired—upon reflection, Mary thought that it had been the same man every time—they were told again *tout droit*. She finally remembered a subtlety of the language from her schoolgirl French: there is a distinction between *tout droit* (all right, straight on) and *à droite*, (turn to the right). Scenic touring of Antibes thankfully concluded, they left the square for the last time and went 'straight on' up the road to Monte Carlo.

Mary crossed the finish line in front of the Monte Carlo Casino exactly on time, 70 hours and 20 minutes after leaving John O'Groats. As officials, fans, and reporters surrounded the car, Mary, completely exhausted, laid her head on the steering wheel and fell asleep.

At the Monte Carlo finish line – 21 January 1927

As always, she recovered quickly. The next day found her ready and eager for the Alpine reliability trial over a mountainous route high above the Riviera. Up over the Col de Braus, through the ancient village of Sospel, over another pass, and down through the seaside village of Menton: there were three checkpoints, and drivers had to arrive exactly on time. At one point, on the summit of the Col de Braus, they were met by a lady running toward them, waving her arms frantically. The roads were icy, and Mary dared not brake hard; instead she took her foot off the gas and allowed the automobile to slow naturally, hoping whatever the lady was trying to warn them about was far enough away that they could avoid disaster without hard braking and the loss of control that might result. They rounded several corners with no sign of trouble but around one last corner lay a hair-raising scene: five cars all over the road, with only a low parapet between them and a thousand-foot drop to the sea. Mary saw no hole to creep through, and hard braking would still be asking for trouble. At the very last second the drivers involved pushed aside one car just enough to allow her to steer through; they arrived at the next checkpoint dead on time.

The Monte Carlo Rally continued with the hill climb of the *Mont des Mules*, named for the massive rock formation on which Monte Carlo is set. Mary won her class in this competition, which tests both the skill of the driver and the power of the car.

Mont des Mules hill climb

The 'beauty pageant' for the competing automobiles, the *Concours d'Elegance*, ended the Rally Week competition, followed by a banquet at Monaco's elegant Hotel de Paris. As winner of the *Coupe des Dames*, awarded to the first female finisher, Mary was seated in the position of honour at the right hand of the president of the International Sporting Club of Monaco. The contestants, from all parts of the continent and Britain, gathered in the great square before the palace of Monaco for the grand finale: the distribution of prizes, which concluded the 1927 Monte Carlo Rally.

Mary was on top of the world that night. She had proven herself a worthy player in the world of automotive competition, besting all but five of Europe's top male drivers and capturing the *Coupe des Dames*. The fame and reputation she yearned for had become reality, but it was a constant hunger; she craved more. And with her customary determination, she set out to get it.

Winner of the Coupe des Dames

3 Around the Mediterranean – Italy's Rocky Roads

'A WONDERFUL DRIVE BY A GIRL MOTORIST'
'FOG, FROST & SNOW: SPLENDID SPORTING SPIRIT SHOWN BY MRS BRUCE'
'DASH TO RIVIERA'
'HOW THE HON. MRS VICTOR BRUCE CLOCKED IN ON TIME'

News of Mary's victory was splashed all over newspapers in Britain and on the continent. AC's governing director Selwyn Edge could be justifiably proud of the performance of the AC saloon he had entrusted to Mary for the Monte Carlo Rally, and the publicity was a boost for AC sales. But neither Mary nor Edge was content to stop there. Edge wanted even more proof of the durability of his vehicle, and he had found in Mary a dedicated driver ready for that challenge. An endurance run of several thousand miles following the Monte Carlo would generate even more publicity; he knew this adventure was sure to appeal to the Bruces. They had, in fact, already hatched a plan that suited his desires perfectly.

"I've been thinking," Victor had mused one winter evening in 1926 as they sat by the fire, "how about a trip in Africa a little later on?"

"But there's the Monte Carlo Rally in January," Mary reminded him. "Could we get back in time, or do you mean after that?"

"Immediately after," Victor said; "We'll carry on from Monaco when the Rally's over."

"That would be lovely," she said, "let's have a look at the map." They sketched out a route that circled the western Mediterranean. Several factors had to be considered. They did not want to be away from home longer than eight weeks, including the Monte Carlo and the trip to Africa. Mary's son Anthony was away at boarding school but he would be home for the Easter holiday in April, and the racing season at Brooklands would be in full swing by May. As much as possible they would avoid sea crossings, with their expense and the possibility of damage to the car.

There were wonderful places to visit: Rome, Pompeii, the Sahara, Marrakech, Madrid. They added Portugal to the itinerary, in spite of the fact that a revolution had just broken out; perhaps, they hoped, it would be settled before they arrived.

At first they estimated they would cover 100 miles a day, and reserve Sundays for resting and sightseeing. A quick computation, however, told them such an itinerary would take more than three months to complete. Reluctant to miss any adventures or fascinating sights, they increased their anticipated daily driving mileage.

The clerk at the Automobile Club was incredulous when Mary and Victor asked for maps to plan the tour.

"You contemplate taking a car through Italy?" he exclaimed. The roads were quite impracticable in southern Italy, he told them, and "Sicily is absolutely dangerous!" The clerk warned of "huge rocks continually falling all over the roads from the mountainsides" adding that even if the car survived the road trip it would be "smashed to pieces in being shipped to Africa."

"And what about Spain?" Mary inquired, unruffled.

"All I can say about Spain is that if is possible to find worse roads than those of Italy, Spain is the place to look for them!"

It was precisely the kind of challenge that delighted Mary. Undeterred, she and Victor collected their maps and left. "Nothing ventured, nothing gained," they agreed; they went on with their plans.

By 1927, driving had become a regular part of daily life in northern Europe. Use of the automobile for both commerce and recreation increased, opening new territory for travel. Thousands of miles of paved highways were traveled daily, and road building was a constant activity. In southern Europe, however, conditions were more primitive, and would provide a test of the AC even more grueling than the Monte Carlo.

Mary planned to undertake the Mediterranean endurance run in late January at the conclusion of the Rally. An observer from the Royal Automobile Club would go along to verify the details of the journey, sanctioning it as an 'official distance trial'. According to a *Daily Sketch* column by Bobby Beare, who had been a passenger on the Monte Carlo portion of the trip, there was a three-fold object to the Mediterranean circuit: first, demonstrate that a British car was as sturdy and roadworthy under the adverse conditions in southern Europe as one of continental make; second, provide a   firsthand report on the feasibility of tourism for the general public in Italy, Spain, and North Africa; and third, show that a woman could indeed exhibit the stamina necessary to undertake a gruelling motor tour of several weeks' duration.

This last goal was, again, arrived at nearly by default. Victor was a professional driver, and enjoyed it as much as Mary did. They had agreed, in view of the expectations of the press, that she would drive the Monte Carlo portion solo. The Africa journey, however, was conceived more as a test of the automobile than of feminine skill and strength, and they planned to share the driving. Their passengers would be the RAC observer and W. Harold Johnson, Motoring Editor of *Country Life* magazine, who would accompany them as far as Algiers. Beare needed to return to London, but he would rejoin them for the conclusion of the tour in France.

In the few days between the conclusion of the Rally and the beginning of the Mediterranean tour, Mary and her companions enjoyed the sunshine and sights of the Riviera. A favorite spot was a little hotel called Vistaëro, 1,000 feet above Monte Carlo on the seaward side of the Grand Corniche, where the view of the sea below enchanted them all. Another favorite place was the charming medieval village of Peira Cava, high in the Col de Braus, known to geologists for its unusual rock formations.

Waiting at the Monte Carlo railroad station for his train back to London, Beare asked Mary if she planned to drive the entire Mediterranean circuit, as she had the Monte Carlo portion. "I don't think so," she replied. "Why?"

"My paper and the public generally would be much more interested in the affair if you did, but that doesn't matter much to you I suppose," he said.

"But it looks so selfish, doesn't it, especially as my husband is a well-known driver himself?"

"No, scarcely, and he didn't seem to mind being a passenger on the Monte Carlo Rally, did he?"

"I thought he was awfully good, he just let me keep on going as long as I wanted to, but I felt rather guilty at hanging onto the wheel right through."

"I don't think you need to mind what people will say or how Victor will feel; any kudos you may get out of it will be ample compensation for him, while the public will see only a wonderful feat of endurance by a woman driver—a good thing for the motoring members of your sex and for the English car as well, I should say."

Mary agreed. If she could show how easy it was to handle a car under the adverse conditions they were likely to encounter, it would emphasize the excellence of the English automobile. If she was the least bit apprehensive about such an undertaking, it was not apparent to anyone who knew her.

They began the Mediterranean trek in Italy at the end of January, and almost immediately encountered appalling conditions. Loose rock covered the roads, and huge potholes slowed them to a tedious three miles an hour in many spots. Their first night's destination was Genoa, birthplace of another famous adventurer, Christopher Columbus.

The next day's route took them south along the azure waters of the Ligurian Sea, past the great Carrara marble quarries in the mountains to the east. It was slow going; the roads, still in very poor condition, limited their pace to a virtual crawl. Even so, they managed to cover 117 miles that second day, finally passing through the city gates of Pisa long after darkness had fallen. Mary had always longed to see the famous tower and her first view of it that night, by moonlight, was thrilling. 'Unlike some far-famed attractions which are disappointing when at last one actually beholds them, the tower quite came up to my expectations,' she wrote.

A mild earthquake shook Pisa that night; it was Mary's first experience of such a tremor, and she was anxious to know, she said, whether 'the leaning tower had succumbed at last to its age-old fatigue'. Morning revealed no collapse of the landmark and, reassured, they suspended their 'no driving on Sunday' rule to travel as far as Florence, in order to spend the afternoon sightseeing there. The 40 miles between Pisa and Florence proved another ordeal. Pouring rain compounded the difficulty of the extremely rough road through the Tuscan farmland and orange groves, but Florence was worth the effort.

Mary was impressed by its magnificent architecture, particularly the bridges spanning the River Arno. The Ponte Vecchio, the symbol of the city, was built in the mid-fourteenth century to replace an earlier Roman bridge; goldsmith shops crowded both sides of it. Mary was reminded of what London Bridge must have looked like in medieval times, when it was likewise lined with shops and houses.

In Florence they were unable to find a locked garage to secure their car for the night. In an official RAC trial, the observer was not allowed to leave the car unless he could be assured that it would not be altered or damaged in any way. This usually meant that the vehicle was locked in a garage to which the observer held the key. Knowing that this requirement might be difficult to meet in some of the underdeveloped areas along their route, the Bruces had come up with an alternative—perhaps the earliest example of today's car covers. It was a bag made of balloon fabric that completely enveloped the car, which could be locked securely by the observer. It was a bother, but quite necessary, the RAC insisted, to ensure the validity of the trial.

An early start was in order the next day, since Rome was more than 200 miles away. They were grateful to find the roads improved somewhat as they drove south, particularly in the hilly area of Tuscany, climbing over the 2200 foot Somma Pass before descending to the shores of Lake Trasimeno. Celebrated in literature by Goethe and Byron (who called it the 'Silver Veil'), this picturesque lake was known in ancient times as the site of the bloody three-day battle in which Hannibal's army defeated the Romans in 217 B.C. Mary and her passengers skirted the lake as they crossed into Italy's Umbrian heartland.

After lunch in the ancient Etruscan town of Chiusi, they stopped at Orvieto to admire and photograph the spectacular multicolored mosaic façade of its cathedral. It was raining and darkness had fallen before they reached Rome, but they felt that the fatigue of the strenuous day of travel was worth their reward: an extra day of sightseeing in the Eternal City.

They managed to see a great deal of Rome in their two-day stay, visiting the Coliseum and the Forum, but they were soon driving south once more. The road between Rome and Naples was the worst yet, with huge holes in the pavement and piles of refuse everywhere. It was jammed with horses and carts, and progress was slow. They reached Naples at 9 p.m., and the squalor and stench of the city left no question of lingering or sightseeing.

A visit to the post office the following morning provided the only bright spot of the visit to Naples. A wire from newspaperman Bobby Beare informed Mary that the Editor of the *Daily Sketch* had appointed Mary 'Special Correspondent'. She was to wire home news of their tour, a task which Mary greeted with enthusiasm. A series of feature stories would keep the public informed of their progress, fulfilling the dual goal of publicity for the AC and for herself.

The ancient city of Pompeii had fascinated Mary since she first learned of it, and they were eager to exchange the fresh dirt of Naples for the ancient dust of Pompeii. They made their way out of the city, impeded by traffic but also by crowds of street urchins who slowed their progress by jumping on the running boards, begging for money and refusing to get off "until," Mary said, "letting in the clutch with a bang, I spilled them back into the mud from which they sprang."

Not surprisingly, the road to Pompeii was dreadful; it took a full three hours to cover the 15 miles from Naples, but they toured the ancient site, marveling at the excavated city buried by Vesuvius's eruption in 79 A.D. Salerno was their destination that night, and the next day they began the second week of their Mediterranean tour with an ambitious goal: Cosenza, 170 miles to the south over increasingly rough and mountainous roads.

The scenery was beautiful in Calabria, the heel of Italy's boot, and high in the mountains near the village of Castrovillari they found a dazzling sight. On either side was a distant view of the sea—the Gulf of Taranto and the Ionian Sea on the left, and the Tyrrhenian Sea on the right—'a romantic landscape, except for a telegraph wire!'

After seven days of travelling together, Mary wrote, the four had all developed vices. She reflected that such an arduous tour tends to bring out the qualities—good and bad—of the members of the party. The RAC observer insisted on stopping at every post office, however unlikely the chance that there would be mail there—a foible that was a source of annoyance to her. The *Country Life* Motoring Editor had a perpetual passion for coffee and photographs. Mary's vice was baths, and proper bathing facilities were a requirement when choosing a stopping place for the night. She wrote, 'My husband, long-suffering as usual, bore the brunt of my jaded nerves in very sporting and understanding fashion, so I will let him down lightly.'

Autostrada 1927

In Cosenza they found Spartan accommodations for the night, which included beds made of tin, painted to resemble wood. They gladly made an early start the next day, planning to drive to the toe of Italy's boot and catch the ferry to Sicily. Passing through granite mountains near the village of Tiriolo, they found their way blocked by a huge boulder in the middle of the road. Manoeuvering carefully around it, Mary drove on—and found still more boulders in the road. Rounding a corner, the reason suddenly became apparent: the boulders had been set in the road deliberately, to warn of a broken-down bridge that appeared to have collapsed in a dozen places.

Labourers lounged beside the bridge; the language barrier between them and the AC's occupants seemed insurmountable—until Victor brought out some money. The universal language of palm-greasing prevailed, and the labourers quickly began placing planks over the broken decking of the rickety bridge. When it appeared sturdy enough to be trusted, Mary started across—but two of her three passengers found excuses to walk instead of ride. The RAC observer claimed that his absence would lighten the load, while the *Country Life* editor announced he simply could not pass up the opportunity to record the crossing on film. Halfway across the bridge the toolbox, mounted on the rear bumper, jammed into a plank. Full of energy, their palms well greased again, the labourers freed the car and the bridge was crossed.

The travellers continued south to San Giovanni, where they caught the ferry to Sicily for an uneventful crossing. In the entire journey from Naples to the toe of the boot, they had encountered only four other automobiles—three of which were broken down at the side of the road with axle or tyre damage.

Messina, on the east coast of Sicily, held little charm for Mary and her companions. Overcharged at the hotel and besieged by beggars in the streets, they continued west to Palermo. Mary considered Sicily a separate country from Italy, declaring that culturally and historically it was so distinct from Italy as to justify its own sovereignty. 'I've had lots of arguments on this point,' she wrote, 'but I maintain that, whatever the facts of the case, I ought to be allowed to call it a country as it was equal to a dozen for sheer hard work. That is the beauty of writing a book. You can say whatever you like without being corrected at every turn by people who will be so painfully precise.' When Mary counted the number of countries they had traversed, Sicily always held its own place.

Mary and Victor intended to run their AC over Targa Florio, the automobile racecourse that had made Sicily a destination for auto enthusiasts since the early 1900s. Drivers had to cover a grueling circuit of 67 miles with hundreds of hair-raising turns on the steep and rough mountain roads. Earlier in its history, racers had also contended with bandits, wolves, and occasional earthquakes.

It was a Tuesday morning when the travelers arose, intending to spend the day exploring the famed course. Before setting out from their Palermo hotel Mary casually asked the hall porter "What time does the Tunis boat leave on Thursday?" "No boat on Thursday!" was his answer. "One goes at midday today, and after that, no other that can take motorcars for two weeks!"

It was ten o'clock, and they were miles from the ferry port at Trapani; they hastily scrapped their Targa Florio plans. They raced back to their rooms, frantically tossed everything into their bags, paid the hotel bill and ran for the car. A top-speed run brought them to the Trapani ferry port, where another problem arose: the supervisor informed them, in fluent English, "I am very, very sorry but I am afraid it is quite impossible. There is no room on the boat, which has accommodation for one car only, and that is already occupied."

Mary's flair for drama came to the fore. She explained, close to tears, what a disaster a delay of two weeks would mean for their plans, and indeed for the entire motoring world following the odyssey in newsprint. The supervisor was a fan of English automobiles and susceptible to the pleas of a pretty woman. He telephoned the captain of the ship, whose official sanction was required—but first the captain would need to see the car to determine how many cattle would have to be unloaded to make room.

Permission was granted. A space was cleared for the AC and Mary accelerated up the gangplank. To her horror, the same toolbox that had almost caused disaster on the bridge near Tiriolo jammed again just as the ship's whistle gave one final blast. She shrieked in terror as the car, trapped on the gangplank, bobbed between quay and boat. Freed by the deckhands, the AC was successfully loaded, and Mary and her passengers breathed a sigh of relief and bade Italy a heartfelt 'Arrivederci'.

4 Across North Africa and Home

From Sicily, it was a miserable 20-hour voyage across the Mediterranean to North Africa. Uncomfortable accommodations and rough seas made the foursome long for solid ground—even if more boulder-strewn roads and collapsing bridges were to be part of the package.

Approaching Tunis, they sailed past the peninsula on which stood the ruins of the ancient fortified city of Carthage. Johnson, of *Country Life*, had been eagerly anticipating a visit there. Since the boat had sailed from Sicily sooner than they'd expected, they were two days ahead of schedule, allowing some extra time for sightseeing. Shopping was also on the agenda: they had shipped all their warm clothing back to England, assuming that the climate in North Africa would be mild, perhaps even tropical; instead it was cold! Johnson made a beeline for Carthage while Mary and the others wandered in the *soûk* for hours, spellbound by the strange and exotic sights of the native market.

The road west from Tunis was a smooth tarmac delight after the bone-jarring roads of Italy, and by late afternoon they crossed into Algeria. Mary described the ancient city of Constantine, built on a rocky point overlooking a fertile valley, as 'the most extraordinary of all the natural fortresses of North Africa'. Alexander Dumas, describing his first view of Constantine, wrote: 'A shout of admiration, almost astonishment. At the far end of a dark canyon, on the top of a mountain lit by the last red reflections of a setting sun, appeared a fantastic city, something like the flying island of Gulliver.' The narrow streets and overhanging houses in the old city, spilling down the precipitous sides of a gorge, provided two full days of sightseeing pleasure.

Farther west, at Algiers, they turned south, climbing into the Sahara range of the Atlas Mountains. Although altitudes reach 13,550 feet in Morocco's Grand Atlas range, Mary and her passengers faced roads no higher than 7,500 feet—hardly a challenge to the AC saloon, which had already breezed through the Alpine test portion of the Monte Carlo Rally. Threading their way through mountain passes and crossing a fertile high plateau dotted with vineyards, they descended to Laghouat, an oasis town at the northern edge of the vast Sahara desert. At 2,500 feet, Laghouat was a lonely and otherworldly outpost—as intriguing to Mary and her passengers as they and their automobile were to the Arabs who gathered around them at every stop. The oasis settlement was, they were told, as far into the desert as motorcars could hope to penetrate; given their fondness for pushing the limits of possibility, that was just the sort of description that appealed to Mary and Victor.

The loneliness and emptiness at the very edge of the Sahara made a vivid impression on Mary, and she confessed to a creepy feeling from the isolation, even in an oasis. As they retraced their wheel tracks north the next day, she wrote, they 'didn't see anything for hours and then suddenly on the horizon appeared a number of black specks which resolved themselves into a miniature army of humans and camels and herds—a tribe on the march to the mountains, I imagine, since it is the annual custom at about this time of year. A remarkable sight—whole families piled up on the camels complete with baggage, quantities of baby camels trotting alongside.'

They spent the night at Bou Saâda, a busy crossroads oasis midway between Algiers and the Sahara. They watched a performance by dancing girls, and a guide suggested morning camel rides for even more desert flavor. Victor preferred the role of movie cameraman and declined the offer. Mary, always enthusiastic about a new mode of transportation, asked "Can they jump?" The guide said no, but added: "They're easy; once they get started they don't stop for three days; if you want to go to Timbuktu, give him his head." In just two minutes the novelty of riding a camel wore off, and Mary was quite willing to dismount and get back behind the wheel of the AC for their return journey north.

Algiers was a striking contrast to the simple desert towns they had just left. After a century of French colonial rule, it had an air of sophistication that made it seem quite European. For Mary, the elegant charm of Algiers was diminished a bit by a confrontation with a gendarme. The evening traffic was heavy when he whistled her to a stop.

It was the first disapproving response Mary had encountered on this long journey, begun weeks earlier at the northern tip of Scotland. She'd become accustomed to the surprised approval of spectators and officials along the way; traffic stops were not what a Monte Carlo winner expected. The gendarme, Mary said, "accused me of doing everything that was wrong, nothing that was right". Never given to meek submission, she countered with feigned innocence. "I find the best policy on such occasions is to assume an air of absolute stupidity and a complete lack of understanding of the French language. One is then waved on impatiently to save further delay of the traffic."

From Algiers, Mary and her companions drove west. The appearance of the country changed and became, to Mary's eyes, remarkably like England. Only the sight of an occasional native reminded her that they were not crossing the Salisbury Plain. At Mascara, on a mountain slope in a region of wine and olive oil production, they stopped for tea. As was their habit, they lingered until after the sun had set, to avoid driving into its glare.

They pushed on toward their evening goal, the seaport of Oran. The roads in North Africa were a vast improvement over those in Italy, but Mary had been cautioned that rough patches lay ahead. In spite of the warning, the sudden appearance of a railroad line cutting across the pavement before them was a shock. The rails were elevated a foot above the grade of the road; there was no time to slow to a safe speed. At 40 miles an hour they slammed into—and fortunately over—the raised track. Bouncing high off their seats, the driver's and passengers' heads hit the roof of the car. Shaken, everyone piled out to recover their composure and inspect the AC for damage. Fortunately, it appeared minimal; nothing was obvious in the failing light.

As they continued, sobered, Mary gripped the steering wheel firmly, peering into the gathering darkness at the badly deteriorated road surface ahead. Uncertain about the damage to the car, Mary held the AC to a snail's pace. They crept slowly into Oran late that night.

Mary had looked forward to visiting the city. Like Constantine, Oran is built on two sides of a ravine and, like Algiers, it was marked by the contrast of European colonial sophistication, medieval history, and colourful native quarters. After a hundred years of French occupation, Oran's architecture and culture presented a charming synthesis of North African and European influence. But the bone-shaking encounter with the railroad tracks and the dreadful road that followed had put Mary and her passengers behind schedule and there was no time for sightseeing.

By morning's light they determined that the AC's damage was not major. Two leaves were broken on one of the front springs; repairs could be postponed until a replacement was sent from England. Aside from the nearly routine tyre changes—a total of 77 tyres were used on the entire journey—the AC had proven an exceptionally reliable vehicle. The reports that Mary wired to the *Daily Sketch* affirmed its road-worthiness.

After a quick visit to the post office they were off again. But they left Oran at the same glacial speed they had arrived: the road was so poorly maintained that, even with undamaged springs, they could not have covered more than three or four miles an hour.

They crossed into Morocco, overnighting in the ancient mud-walled town of Taza before their much-anticipated approach to Fez. Mary described their first view: 'Winding up and up and suddenly and almost without warning a complete panorama of the city presented itself to our eager gaze. We pulled the car up and looked our fill. It was indeed the most wonderful sight that our tour of Northern Africa, crowded with interest though it had been, had yet produced. The city presented the appearance of a gigantic patchwork of delicate colours: the green roofs of the holy places and the blue of the minarets blending imperceptibly with the green tints of palms and cypresses, with here and there a contrasting gleam of white terrace and palace. Fez in the distance is like a beautiful jewel in a glorious setting.'

At the Palais Jamai, Fez

One of the holy cities of Islam, Fez lived up to Mary's high expectations. The travellers admired the view of the minaret-studded skyline from its ramparts on the way to their accommodations. The luxurious Hotel Palais Jamai had formerly been a sultan's palace.[1] The manager, intrigued when he heard about their journey, offered them the former chamber of the Sultana for the night. The room captivated Mary with its splendid opulence; the jewel-studded walls and doors inlaid with gold were dazzling.

The wealth and glamour of their hotel was a sharp contrast to the abject poverty they encountered in the *soûk*. With a guide they explored the bazaar, admiring the handcrafted leatherwork for which the craftsmen of Fez were renowned. But the guide also led them through the squalid streets surrounding the *soûk*, past hovels where they saw children labouring to produce those splendid goods. It changed Mary's attitude about bargaining in the markets; she had a new understanding of the real value of the work, and vowed to give up inconsiderate bargaining.

The route west from Fez was a great improvement over the abysmally rough roads they had endured. By midmorning they reached Meknes, called 'the Moroccan Versailles' for its opulent palace built by an early sultan. Mary admired the delicate tracery of myriad towers and minarets, and marveled at the unexpected cleanliness and charm of this historic Moorish town. As they crept through the labyrinthine streets, the ultramodern automobile was largely ignored by the crowds watching snake charmers and listening to storytellers in the marketplace—until someone noticed that a woman was at the wheel. Suddenly swarms of children and adults jumped on the running boards and peered through the windows curiously. It was a pattern repeated throughout the tour: nonchalance, for the most part, at the sight of the automobile—but frank amazement at the sight of a female driving it! Crowds routinely gathered as they drove away from their hotel each morning, curiously watching the unfamiliar spectacle of a woman piloting a motor vehicle.

As they left Meknes a horrible grinding sound suddenly emanated from the back axle; investigation revealed that it was totally empty of oil. They concluded that a rock, probably from a rough road in southern Italy, had pierced the axle casing; they must have been losing oil slowly for weeks. The leakage had gone undetected because the vibration of those same rough roads had rendered the oil gauge inoperative. A can of thin oil was found, which served as a stopgap until Victor could replace the gear oil in Casablanca. Together with the damaged front springs, this setback was a reminder that the AC needed watchful awareness.

Their tour of Morocco continued with a visit to Marrakech, in the foothills of the Grand Atlas range. Mary called it 'Marrakech the red', for the way that the setting sun bathed the great walls surrounding the city in a blood-red glow. It was, for her, the most marvelous sight of the whole tour. 'Marrakech in its encircling loop-holed wall is beautiful and ominous,' she wrote. 'The solidity of this great wall emphasizes the grace of the slender minarets soaring high above the domes and flat roofs of palace and hovel. Around and amidst it are thousands of graceful palms, and a fugitive glimmer of the water of the oasis, blood-red also in the rapidly failing light, gave the final touch of glory to this wonderful picture.'

Turning north again, they arrived in their last African city, the seaport of Tangier, on 24 February. They stayed at the Hotel Cecil; Mary remarked that she would not have been at all sorry if it had been the establishment of the same name in London, where they were scheduled to be fêted at a luncheon to celebrate the conclusion of their tour. A mid-morning departure the next day meant there would be no time for exploring Tangier; they were on the quay with the AC before 8 a.m. to arrange for shipping to Gibraltar.

A lifelong animal lover, Mary was horrified by the sight of cattle being loaded onto the ship. A crane lifted the struggling animals by the horns—in groups of three or four—then set them down with a thud on the deck. Reassured that the cattle felt no more pain than does a kitten lifted by the scruff of its neck, the image still stuck in her mind. Warily she watched as the AC was prepared for loading. She was relieved to see it cradled carefully and transferred gently to the ship.

An agent of the Royal Automobile Club met them upon their arrival in Gibraltar, handing them the replacement front spring for the AC. Victor and the RAC observer installed it while Mary used her free time for one of her favorite pastimes, shopping. On the road again, they continued at a more leisurely pace, enjoying the fertile landscape—a distinct contrast to the relatively barren North Africa. The roads were fairly good as far as Jerez de la Frontera, the center of sherry production, but deteriorated dramatically as they drove farther north. Potholes and washboard surfaces rivaling those of Italy became the rule.

Arriving in Seville, they searched among the narrow streets for their hotel. Their directions led them at last to a magnificent building; Mary approached what she took to be the reception area, mentally rehearsing her best Spanish phrases. "Can you put us up for the night?" she enquired politely.

The look of amazement on the clerk's face puzzled Mary. He seemed to have understood her Spanish; why would he be surprised at a request for accommodations? Perhaps her Spanish was not as clear as she thought. She looked around, hoping to find someone who spoke English or French, and with dismay she suddenly grasped the problem. The walls were lined with stuffed fish and lizards—not the usual furnishings for a first-class hotel. She had inadvertently wandered into a museum instead of a hotel. Embarrassed, she retreated, covering her confusion as best she could.

Seville, with its abundance of magnificent Moorish and Gothic architecture, held them spellbound for two days. On the banks of the River Guadalquivir, the city boasted an impressive fifteenth century cathedral with a graceful bell tower, known as La Giralda, once an Arab minaret. Mary's party visited the cathedral, comparing it favorably to St Peter's in Rome, and stopped at the tomb of Christopher Columbus. Although no bullfight was scheduled during their stay (not a disappointment to the animal-loving Bruces) they toured Seville's great bullring. Mary wrote of the evidence of the growing popularity of football and mused that it almost seemed that the authorities were encouraging the youth of the country to take up the pastime in the hope that the public liking for bullfighting would gradually die out.

Portugal was next on their itinerary, and they set out for the border under gray and cloudy skies. Their route took them through several small towns, and by early afternoon they were despairing of finding a place for a meal. Mary was not fond of the Spanish cooking she had sampled, finding it too rich and oily, and had not eaten much. She wrote: 'I have quite made up my mind that I will not stir, in the future, on a long tour at any rate, without proper provisions and a proper place in which to carry them. A good luncheon basket and especially a kettle and spirit stove with a supply of English tea would have been a godsend many a time on this tour of ours.'

Map showing part of the route
(from Mary's book Nine Thousand Miles in Eight Weeks*)*

After an overnight stop in Badajoz, Spain, they departed for the nearby border. Without a hint of the comedy of errors about to unfold, they were checked out of the Spanish customs house and crossed the bridge over the River Caia. They drove on to the advance post of Portuguese customs. Victor went into the border station to attend to the paperwork; Mary fidgeted as 20 minutes went by. He returned shaking his head.

"What's the matter?" Mary asked. "Aren't our papers in order?"

"We've come to the wrong country," Victor replied. "We ought to have gone to Poland."

"Don't be stupid; this is Portugal, isn't it?"

"No—it's No-Man's Land; Portugal is down the road there."

"Well, why don't you get the papers stamped and let's get on with it? I don't want to stay here all day!"

"But didn't I tell you we ought to have gone to Poland? Look here," said Victor, thrusting the papers into her hand. The word on their travel permit was "Pologne"—Poland, not Portugal!

"Well, go and explain the mistake; they'll let us through all right."

"I have, and they won't. There's nothing for it but to turn around and go back to Spain, try and get to Madrid tonight."

"How far is it?"

"A few hundred miles; we'll have the maps out when we get through Spanish customs again."

Cheered to know that Madrid was within reach, Mary turned the car around, and pushed its 'nice but shiny nose' over the river into Spain again. They were not worried, since the Spanish had been so pleasant and helpful when they crossed the border a half hour before—but the friendly staff had gone for the day and the officials now on duty were anything but accommodating. According to them, the AC and its occupants had not been anywhere; they may have left Spain, but—having come from nowhere—they could not be readmitted.

The Spanish officials suggested they return to Portugal, get checked out of that country, and return to Spain. Back over the bridge they went, but Portugal would still not admit them without a visa. Caught in the no-man's land between the two countries, they returned to the Spanish post, where Mary demanded to see 'El Comandante'. Told that he couldn't be disturbed for so trivial an affair, she marched up the stairs before anyone could stop her, dragging Victor and the RAC observer along, and knocked briskly at the door of the Chief Customs Official. She walked boldly in, mustering all her bravery, and faced 'El Comandante'. To her relief, he not only understood the situation, he could even speak English. By this time they were able to appreciate the humour of their dilemma and amid much head shaking and merriment, the documents showing their exit from Spain were canceled and they were back in 'dearly beloved muddy España', as though they had left it only in their dreams. Happily, they bumped their way over muddy washboard roads to Madrid.

They spent a night in Madrid and made time for a little sightseeing. Mary lingered as long as she could in the Museo del Prado, entranced by the works of Goya, Velásquez, and Murillo. The seaport city of San Sebastian, on the Bay of Biscay, was their last stop in Spain; they crossed the border and spent the night in Bergerac, in the heart of France's Dordogne region.

The rear axle oil leak continued to plague them, and stopgap efforts to maintain lubrication were less and less effective. They had intended to conclude the trial with a 1,000-mile run on the racetrack at Montlhéry, near Paris. The goal was to establish that, in spite of the gruelling trial it had just completed, the AC's engine was still capable of running for hour after hour at high speed; 20 hours at 50 mph would be a sufficient test for any touring engine. Their plans were in jeopardy if an effective repair could not be made.

Their luck finally ran out as they reached the medieval walled town of Thiviers. The grinding noise from the rear axle had made Mary and Victor increasingly uncomfortable; they stopped, hoping to ease the problem by adding a bit more oil. When Victor checked, however, there was not a single drop of lubrication remaining. Worse, small nuts, bolts and washers had broken loose and accumulated in the drain plug. The entire axle would have to be replaced; they could go no further. It was midday on Saturday; on Monday morning they were due at Montlhéry to begin their time trial; could the repairs possibly be made in time?

At a run, Mary headed up the hill to the Thiviers post office to send a wire for help. A.W. Pitt, the AC mechanic who had accompanied them on the Monte Carlo portion of their tour, was planning to meet them at Montlhéry for the conclusion of the trial. Could he bring a spare axle with him? And could he, please, deliver it to them in Thiviers?

That Saturday afternoon and evening passed slowly; they wrapped themselves in rugs against the unpleasant chill of the hotel, playing cards to pass the time and hoping that the telegram had reached Pitt before he left England. Shortly after 10 p.m. they had their answer—a return wire from Pitt reading 'Do you want front or rear axle? Reply Dieppe boat. Pitt.'

In her haste, Mary had neglected to specify which axle was to be replaced! To cover any eventuality, Pitt had hurriedly gotten one of each from the AC Service Depot at Thames Ditton and dashed to Victoria Station to catch the boat train for France.

By mid-afternoon Sunday the new axle was installed and the AC was ready for the road again. The 200 miles from Thiviers to Orleans were covered with a welcome absence of worry and mechanical woes. With the end of their 9,000-mile odyssey in sight, Mary's customary optimism returned. Only 100 miles lay between them and Montlhéry, a few miles southwest of Paris.

Montlhéry was a magnet for auto racing enthusiasts. England's Brooklands circuit had been built in 1907 and the United States' first major racetrack, at Indianapolis, in 1909. Although road racing was popular in France, it had no purpose-built, high-speed track for many years. By the early 1920s it had become obvious that one was needed. Industrialist Alexandre Lamblin, hoping to promote the French automobile industry, built the Montlhéry track in 1924. His plan succeeded admirably; the track was an instant success.

In England, complaints from Brooklands' neighbours about the roar of open mufflers and the resulting loss of sleep had brought about noise restrictions and a ban on nighttime racing. The track lost the loyalty of many drivers, who flocked to the new French track. In its first two months of operation, over 100 racing records were set at Montlhéry.

Mary drove straight from Orleans to the track at Montlhéry; she barely paused before beginning the thousand mile trial. Bobby Beare of the *Daily Sketch* had come from England for the finale of the trial, and he and Pitt watched with a crowd of well-wishers as Mary circled the Montlhéry track. Sheets of cold rain fell; the monotonous miles ticked by at a steady 50 mph. She took some ribbing for the slow pace—at one point Victor, Pitt, and Beare dragged out a blackboard with a drawing of a snail.

Over the course of three days, Mary drove the AC for 1,000 miles around the oval track at Montlhéry; it performed admirably. With her penchant for speed, she found the boredom of the slow pace frustrating, but the point of the exercise was to demonstrate the durability of the AC's engine. The steady speed of 50 mph for 20 hours would be ample proof of that. In lieu of the challenge of fast driving, Mary contended with sleet and fierce blasts of wind.

'I don't think it is possible to convey in words,' wrote Beare in the *Daily Sketch*, 'the frightful monotony of driving around that little course at 50 miles an hour for 20 hours. And yet Mrs. Bruce, who would be the last to claim patience as one of her virtues in ordinary affairs, accomplished her task without one solitary word of complaint, although she was ready to drop when each day's portion of the mileage was complete.'

When the last lap was concluded Victor was waiting with a glass of steaming Ovaltine and milk, a beverage which Mary had found so refreshing that she had

WONDERFUL
Endurance
of
Lady Motorist

9,000
miles in
8 weeks

For real grit, nerve power and endurance the feat of the Hon. Mrs. V. A. Bruce is unique. This thrilling adventure commenced on a bleak January morning at John o' Groats. Roads sheeted with ice, blizzards and fog were encountered, but nothing daunted this plucky little woman, whose motto seemed to be: " Onwards, ever Onwards."

Although having been without rest or solid food for 30 hours, she embarked for France immediately on arrival at Folkestone. After 70 hours' driving from the far North of Scotland, 1,600 miles away, the car arrived at Monte Carlo dead on time.

Thrilling experiences in Morocco, 20 hours' lapping of the famous Montlhery track were all negotiated with equal vigour and success.

READ MRS. BRUCE'S TESTIMONY

"If it had not been for " Ovaltine " in the flask I should never have been able to keep my strength and nerves together."

Again it is proved that for maintaining nerves, strength and vigour in perfect condition, delicious "Ovaltine" stands supreme. Make "Ovaltine" the daily food-beverage in your home for health.

OVALTINE
TONIC FOOD BEVERAGE

Builds-up Brain. Nerve and Body

Sold in tins at 1/6, 2/6 and 4/6.

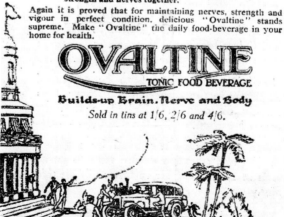

P.425

begun to demand it on any and every occasion—'to such an extent,' she wrote, 'that I had earned the nickname of "The Ovaltine Baby".'

They crossed the English Channel by night, arriving back in England on 10 March. Mary found the last part of the journey incredibly wearisome because of the need to keep within England's strict 20 mph speed limit, as well as remembering to drive on the left side of the road. But she had accomplished a feat that would make her name known throughout the motoring world. Her impressive showing in the Monte Carlo was mere prologue. The thousands of miles that had followed, which she described in colourful detail for eager *Daily Sketch* readers, elevated her standing and ensured her fame.

Selwyn Edge had arranged a welcoming luncheon and reception at London's Hotel Cecil; Mary succeeded in driving into the hotel courtyard at precisely the appointed hour—but the dramatic effect of her arrival was diminished when the long-established habit of driving on the right on the continent momentarily got the better of her and she began to circle the courtyard counter-clockwise, to the surprise of the press and photographers with cameras at the ready. Recovering quickly, Mary brought the AC to a smooth stop at the hotel's entry. The travellers joined the welcoming committee on the steps as cameras recorded their return. Edge was effusive in his praise of driver and car, declaring in his speech, "She's earned that little car; I've given it to her."

11 March 1927 – Mary is greeted by her son Tony at Hotel Cecil

5 On Top of the World: Lapland

Less than four months after the conclusion of the Mediterranean tour, the itch to be on the road again was too strong for Mary to ignore. With the memory of the 1,000 miles of laps at Montlhéry still fresh in her mind, she wanted to 'go somewhere' this time. During those monotonous circuits Mary had complained to Victor, "This is lap-land!" "No," he replied, "but our next trip will be! Lapland! We'll see how far north we can go in a car!" Mary approached Selwyn Edge, who was predictably enthusiastic about the idea of an AC being driven farther north than any other car had ever gone. He had the Bruces' six-cylinder AC freshly painted and supplied with spare parts that might prove necessary on the trek.

In an interview before the trip, Mary told the writer, "We don't know a word of the Lapp language. We shall use sign language as we have done in other countries and I don't suppose things will be any worse in that respect in Lapland than in Spain. I got into a museum instead of a hotel in Spain!"

They packed a portable wireless set and a small movie camera for the trip; Victor would film their progress. Emergency equipment included only a small axe; they decided against taking any weapons. "I am told the wolves are not hungry at this time of the year. We'll have to rough it a bit but it would be no fun if we did not," Mary declared. 'Roughing it' did not extend to giving up afternoon tea; they carried a small spirit stove and a kettle, along with a well-stocked picnic basket and generous provisions.

With their friend and travelling companion, Bobby Beare of the *Daily Sketch*, they set off toward the Arctic Circle on 9 July 1927. After crossing the English Channel to France, they turned north through the Low Countries. Travelling in Holland they came across an 80-year-old woman towing a barge along a canal while her husband and four big strong brothers lay asleep on the barge. When the woman was not working, the dogs were—but never the men. 'It gave Victor the idea that we should drop the whole thing and remain in Holland,' Mary observed.

They had planned to pick up mail in Hamburg, but fog put them behind schedule and they omitted the stop. They missed a letter waiting for them there

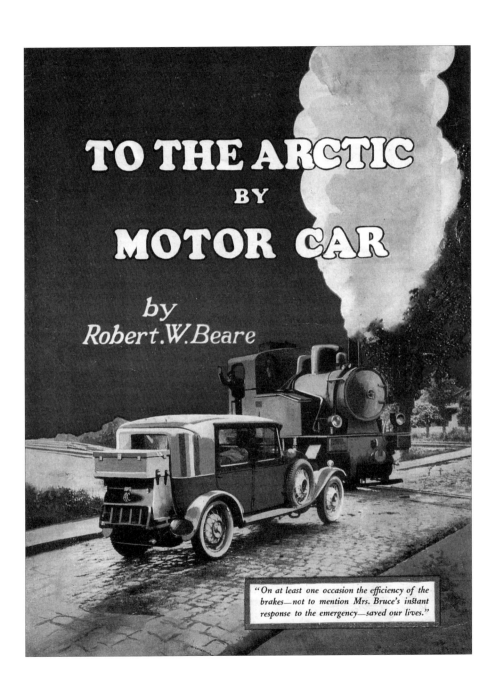

TO THE ARCTIC
BY
MOTOR CAR

by
Robert. W. Beare

"On at least one occasion the efficiency of the brakes—not to mention Mrs. Bruce's instant response to the emergency—saved our lives."

from the King of Denmark who, intrigued by their journey, wanted them to visit the palace in Copenhagen and tell him about it. As they approached the Danish capital they noticed mechanics at every village garage attempting to flag them down. Victor declared, "They're only trying to sell us a fog lamp!" They sped on, unaware that the Palace, realizing that the invitation had not been received in Hamburg, had sent messages to every garage along their route.

Once at their hotel in Copenhagen, the British Ambassador called them and arranged an audience with King Christian. The King listened with interest to the tales of their Monte Carlo triumphs as well as the current journey to Lapland. Prince Harald, the King's brother, and his wife, Princess Helene, attended a dinner and ball held in the travellers' honour that night. In a gesture that Mary found particularly moving, *God Save the King* was played as they entered the ballroom, followed by the Danish national anthem.

Sweden welcomed them next, as they prepared for the last stages of the trek to the Far North. Information about roads in Lapland was sketchy at best, but Mary and her passengers set out again in high spirits. They followed a coastal route north from Stockholm along the Gulf of Bothnia, which lies between Sweden and Finland. At the border town of Haparanda they sped past a large sign in Swedish and crossed a narrow wooden bridge over the River Tornio into Finland. At the customs station their car was immediately surrounded by Finnish guards who eyed them with suspicion and escorted them to an inner chamber. None of the three travellers could understand a word of the guards' language; their English was met with uncomprehending looks. They were searched carefully and the car got a comprehensive inspection as well. At last, understanding dawned: they were suspected of carrying firearms, which was strictly forbidden in Finland. Some English newspapers had printed a rumour that they intended to carry revolvers as protection against wild animals, and apparently the rumour had preceded them.

Cleared of suspicion, they pushed on northward, approaching the Arctic Circle. It was mid-July, and the weather became a problem—but it was not ice and cold, as a first-time visitor to northern Finland might expect. They encountered a polar heat wave—instead of frostbite, they contended with oppressive heat. Car windows were all rolled down; the men removed their coats, collars and ties. Mary purchased light cotton frocks in a village, setting aside her cold-weather wardrobe. They were plagued by mosquito bites.

A summer polar storm caused real difficulties: just south of the Arctic Circle, some 40 miles inland from the Gulf of Bothnia, a lightning strike had ignited the forest. They watched with growing concern as panicked reindeer galloped down the narrow track ahead of them. They realized that the animals were instinctively heading for safety. The map showed a large lake a few miles away, and they followed the reindeer to its edge. Fortunately an earlier fire had cleared the brush and timber along the shore, providing a natural firebreak that protected the travellers, their automobile, and the hundreds of reindeer taking shelter there.

After several hours the fire died down and they continued north, through the smouldering forests. They crossed the Arctic Circle and pressed on toward the Arctic Ocean, following a road of steadily declining quality. Mary described it as 'feet deep in loose rubble, with a top dressing of granite boulders that frequently took the united strength of the three of us to move to allow the passage of the car'. It eventually came to an abrupt end, and only a narrow track continued through the woods. They cleared brush and struggled forward for several hundred feet across the tundra until suddenly they realized the back of the car was beginning to sink into the spongy ground. The top layer of the permafrost, frozen solid for so much of the year, had softened in the unseasonable heat. They had driven into an Arctic swamp.

It required hours of labour to drag the car inch by inch back onto firm ground. They turned south, pausing long enough to continue the tradition of so many pioneering British explorers before them, ceremoniously planting the Union Jack before heading for home.

They chose a more westerly return route, taking them south over smooth, well-kept roads in the largely unpopulated north of Sweden. Mary drove well into the nighttime hours, marvelling at the midnight sun. The smooth pavement beneath the wheels was a treat; Mary pushed the speedometer up to 40 mph. She'd had her fill of rough roads on the Mediterranean circuit and in the forests of Lapland; at last she could go flat-out.

The roads were so good, Mary decided, that Sweden would be her starting point for next year's Monte Carlo. Her admiration for Sweden was returned. A week after she returned to London, the Royal Swedish Automobile Club presented her a silver plaque in memory of her journey through their country.

Mary Bruce was making a name for herself and for the integrity of Selwyn Edge's AC motorcars. Edge considered her exploits a valuable asset for his company, whose sales had begun to lag. But the AC's journey around the Mediterranean, followed by the Arctic adventure, helped boost sales. They boosted Mary's reputation, too. That summer saw the publication of her first book, *Nine Thousand Miles in Eight Weeks – Being an Account of an Epic Journey by Motor-Car through Eleven Countries and Two Continents*. Press reviews were complimentary: 'Brightly written narrative accounts' and 'distinct literary charm'. Mary drank in all the praise.

6 Montlhéry Endurance Record

The 1920s were exciting years in the automotive world. Speed and endurance records were set and broken monthly; drivers were eager to test their own abilities and the limits of their machines. How fast could the automobile go? How far? How high? For how long? Speed and distance trials, hill climbs, endurance runs, the men and women behind the wheels: all captured the interest of the public.

Like a child in a candy store, Mary's most difficult decision was which prize to pursue next. By October of 1927 she had made her choice. In a newspaper she read about a team of American drivers who had set an endurance record, driving on a track at an average of over 60 mph for just under one week, covering 10,000 miles. Then she read that a team from England's Sunbeam Company was planning to challenge that record the following spring. She and Victor decided the prize would be theirs instead.

Once again she went to AC's Selwyn Edge. His appetite for competition had not diminished since his own years as a racer, and he agreed to furnish a car for the attempt. His assistance was limited, however, by an economic downturn in the automotive industry. He could 'hot up' the car, he said, and provide a crew for support, but Mary and Victor would have to pay the rest. Once again, since nighttime racing was forbidden at Brooklands, they chose the track at Montlhéry. There would be the expense of shipping the car across the Channel as well as fees for the use of the track, salaries for the official timekeepers, accommodations, and fuel.

The record attempt would be made in December, Mary decided, so that Edge would have the time necessary to 'hot up' the engine. In addition, the fees at Montlhéry would be lower in the winter months because driving conditions could be hazardous. Mary and Victor scrambled to come up with the money they needed for the trial; both had trusts and both attempted to gain access to their funds. Victor's trustees flatly refused him any money when they heard how he proposed to spend it, on the grounds that the entire proposition was much too risky. Mary then met with the administrator of the trust fund that her Aunt Maud[1] had set up for her. She painted a rosy picture for him of her intention to bring glory to the British automotive industry, not to mention to her family and the entire nation as well. Having inherited more than a little of her mother's penchant for the dramatic, she must have made a memorable plea. The trustee was unmoved, however, maintaining that her aunt had stipulated that the money be spent wisely; this venture, he felt, did not meet that criterion.

For an entire hour Mary pleaded, argued, and cajoled. The trustee was not swayed. Eventually he announced that he was going home for tea; Mary declared that she would wait for him. When he returned an hour later he exclaimed "Good gracious! Don't tell me you're still here! And sitting in the same position too!" She sat motionless and determined, and eventually he sighed and capitulated, and £250 for the rental of the track was secured.

The mechanics at the AC factory began the preparation procedure. The body was streamlined by the removal of the fenders, giving the car the appearance, Mary said, of a wasp without wings. Gearing was improved with a new axle, and the engine was finely tuned.

On 8 December 1927, Mary, Victor, Selwyn Edge, Chief Designer Sydney Smith, and a six-man AC support crew drove from Thames Ditton to the Channel ferry port and sailed with the car to France. Their home base during the attempt was the Château Montlhéry. Just a mile from the racetrack, the hotel was the favourite of racers from all over the world when they came to the French track, and Madame Patrice, the proprietress, loved them all. She welcomed Mary and Victor and their party, who arrived late after being lost for over an hour in dense fog.

Wintry weather was a handicap they had anticipated, and sure enough, the next morning was cold and thick with fog. They presented themselves at the track to register with the timekeepers from the Automobile Club of France, who were bemused when they learned only Mary and Victor intended to drive, instead of a team of four. Mary overheard one official murmur to another, "*Mon Dieu*, we'll be out of here by tomorrow." She realized that the combination of the bitter cold and dense fog would present a serious challenge for a team of four drivers—and one that might be insurmountable for just the two of them. But they were there to drive, she announced, and drive they would.

They each took a trial lap around the track, noting again how different it was from Brooklands. They had driven at Montlhéry just months earlier, at the end of their journey around the western Mediterranean, but the conditions in the dark of December seemed much more difficult. The track was just a mile and a quarter around, less than half the length of Brooklands. With tighter turns and higher banking, it had a much different feel to the drivers; Mary felt dizzy and almost ill after her test laps. She said nothing to Victor but noticed that he too was uncharacteristically quiet after his laps.

They agreed they would each drive for three hours at a time, while the other rested or slept at the Château. With the toss of a coin Mary won the starting assignment. At seven o'clock that evening she began. The fog was dense, right down on the track. Headlights had been removed from the automobile; with the track so steeply banked, the beams they cast would not reach the top or the bottom of the track, and would be useless. The track was lighted by kerosene lamps set out at four-yard intervals.

The fog was so heavy that Mary could see only about five lamps ahead, but she averaged 80 miles an hour for her first three-hour stint. At ten o'clock she pulled into the pits; the car was refuelled and Victor took the wheel for his turn. The AC was back on the track in less than three minutes. Mary returned to the Château for her three-hour break. Too exhausted for the plate of scrambled eggs Madame Patrice prepared for her, she fell into bed and was asleep immediately. Only minutes later, it seemed, Madame Patrice was shaking her shoulder to wake her, and she took the wheel again at one in the morning.

At the end of the first 24 hours they had covered 1,848 miles; after 48 hours the total was 3,820. Their average speed increased from 77 mph to 82 as they hurtled around the steep track, and, as the fog gradually lightened, they reached speeds as high as 95 mph. After three days they concluded that three hours' sleep at a stretch was not enough, and lengthened the shifts to six hours.

The fog receded but a new danger arose: black ice coated the track, making handling on the steeply banked turns even more difficult. The bitter cold presented another problem for Mary and Victor. The open car offered little protection from the elements, and frostbitten fingers were a risk. The support crew took on another duty during pit stops: massaging the drivers' fingers with warm oil to soothe and protect them.

The speeding car created a microclimate of its own on the icy track; a swirl of crystallized droplets surrounded it in a cloud and sleet fell at intervals, further decreasing visibility. As ice accumulated and blocked the view, the driver was forced to peer over the top of the windscreen to see the track ahead. The wiper had been removed, because it would have been whipped off anyway at the high speeds they were clocking. The remedy occurred to Mary over a meal at the Château. As her scrambled eggs got cold, she fashioned a piece of celluloid into a visor. Affixed to the windscreen, it deflected enough ice to allow a clearer view of the track.

Icicles formed on the car, and one of them may have saved them from calamity. On the third day Mary pulled into the pits to refuel, and AC's Sydney Smith spotted a huge icicle hanging from the radiator. He exclaimed, "Thank God for the blizzard! There's a leak in the radiator and the ice is sealing it in. If it starts to thaw, we're beaten!" Mary found it harder to resent the freezing conditions after that.

The hypnotic effect of hurtling around the oval track for hours at a time, staring at the icy track as the lanterns flashed by endlessly, must have contributed to the inattention which caused Mary several uncomfortable minutes. Pulling in for a pit stop one night, she left the car as Victor took his turn. In the darkness she grabbed a bottle of what she thought was water; two big gulps were down before she realized she was swallowing petrol, a mistake that left her feeling quite ill. She claimed later that she never again drank directly from any bottle, under any circumstances![2]

Five days into the marathon the Paris and London newspapers began to speculate about the new record in the making at Montlhéry. The next day an audience of racing fans braved the cold and watched as the Bruces broke the 10,000-mile record set a few months earlier in America. But the sixth day also brought a different drama. Mary was deep in sleep at Château Montlhéry when Madame Patrice apologetically woke her, saying that she feared there was trouble. Mary dressed quickly. Downstairs in the lobby she found four men in a heated conversation with AC's Sydney Smith, who fortunately was fluent in French. He explained to Mary that the men were demanding another £250 for the use of the track; she had paid her fee to the previous owner, who had gone bankrupt and kept the money. These men represented the new management, and proposed to barricade the track and end the record attempt if they were not also paid. Furious, Mary refused their demands. "Tell them," she told Sydney, "that nothing is going to stop me now. I'll drive through their barriers!"

More conversation followed, and eventually the angry tones softened and the tide appeared to be turning in their favour. At last the men began to smile. Shaking hands with Mary, Smith, and Madame Patrice, the visitors wished them luck and departed. Smith explained that the men had decided to drop their demands when it was pointed out that Mary and Victor had already broken over a dozen records, and that interfering at this point would be a tragic mistake. Furthermore, Smith said, he had made it clear that he believed Mary's promise to drive through any barriers they put up—and when the men heard of her victory in the Monte Carlo *Coupe des Dames* less than a year earlier, they believed him. With new respect for this petite, determined Englishwoman, they had dropped their demands for money and left, offering their congratulations and best wishes.

The Bruces' luck faltered on the seventh night. Driving at speeds in excess of 90 mph on a surface which would cause ordinary drivers to creep, it is only surprising that they racked up so many miles before an accident occurred. As Mary pulled in for a pit stop and jumped from the car she shouted to Victor "Solid black ice!" and then nearly fell on the glassy surface. The pit crew scurrying to fill the fuel tank were having trouble with their footing too. Victor took the wheel and Mary retreated to the Château to sleep.

At midnight Victor wakened her. She knew at once there was a major problem, because ordinarily they saw each other only in the pit between driving stints. Seeing that he was unhurt but covered in oil, her next concern was for the car's engine: had it blown up? "The engine's fine," he assured her, "I've been underneath the car, that's all."

'Underneath the car' was a mild phrase to describe what had just happened. At full speed Victor had hit a bump on the icy surface, which caused the car to skid and spin several times before it slid off the track and turned upside down in the mud. The steering wheel had remained intact, and kept Victor from being crushed under the weight of the car. The crew and spectators had lifted the car off him and set it back on its wheels, but they were forbidden to do more. The rules of the French Automobile Club, which governed their record attempt, specified that any work done on a competing vehicle had to be carried out in the pit area, and that no one except the drivers were allowed to move the car on the track.

Mary was up and dressed quickly, and they assessed the job ahead of them. The car had to be pushed back onto the track, then a half-mile to the pit area. It took Mary and Victor a full two hours to maneuver the car out of the mud and back onto the track, just six yards away. At last they reached the pits and the AC mechanics swarmed over the machine. The steering needed major work, they found, and the windscreen had been destroyed when the car rolled over. Repairs were made to the steering but they had brought no spare windscreen. Sydney Smith wired the licence plate in its place as a partial barrier against the freezing wind. Mary and Victor had to peer over the top of it, but it was better than nothing. It took an agonizing 12 hours before they could once again begin driving—12 hours during which Mary fretted endlessly. Could they make up such a significant loss of time? Would their record gains be wiped out?

Back on the track, they found their average speed had dropped to 65 mph; they knew they would have to drive flat-out. With Sydney Smith now down with pneumonia and confined to bed, the attempt on the record seemed in jeopardy

Congratulations!

"IT affords the Acedes Company and myself the greatest pleasure to congratulate the Hon. Victor and Mrs. Bruce on their remarkable drive.

To average 68·01 miles an hour for 15,000 miles in snow and sleet is a wonderful achievement. It becomes amazing when the extremely difficult driving conditions and time lost (through overturning on an icy track) are taken into account. Had it not been for this, the average would have been nearer the lapping speed of 85 m.p.h.

It is a source of great satisfaction that this achievement was carried out on a British Normal Sports Acedes." *S. F. Edge*

THE 15,000 MILES
and
12 OTHER WORLD'S RECORDS SMASHED!

Any model Acedes Car will be gladly driven to your address for inspection and test at leisure. No obligation is implied.

Applications should be addressed to

DEMONSTRATION DEPT.:

A-C (ACEDES) CARS, LTD.,
THAMES DITTON, SURREY, ENGLAND.
Telephone: Kingston 3340 (6 lines)

We are open to appoint Agents in the London Area.

EVERY MODEL GUARANTEED 3 YEARS.

ACEDES
AC
BRITISH AND BEST

ACEDES
AC
BRITISH AND BEST

WE FIT DUNLOP TYRES: THEY ARE THE BEST.

65

unless they took drastic measures. For Mary—the epitome of an independent spirit—asking for help must have been a blow. But swallowing her pride, she and Victor shared the driving duties for the last, all-important 48 hours with relief driver A.J. Joyce from the AC factory team.

They had survived cold, ice, sleet, and a devastating accident but now another threat loomed: snow was forecast. Watching the skies, they pushed the limits of the AC ever harder, praying that the predicted storm would hold off just a little longer. The snow began falling on the final day, just two hours before their final lap. Mary was driving the last shift as the snow began piling up in drifts beside the track. At last she saw the chief engineer hold up a board with a big number 10 on it. Elated, she accelerated through the next nine circuits of the track, snow whipping her face and collecting in the open car.

On the final lap, she heard the cheers of the crowd and her crew, and as she pulled into the pit and climbed out of the car, spectators and mechanics surrounded her and Victor. Draped in garlands of flowers, they learned they had broken seven world records in their ten-day run—15,000 miles, at an average speed of 68 mph.[3]

Their timing was impeccable: within two hours the track was buried under three feet of snow. They were back at the Château by then, still receiving the congratulations of well-wishers, including the proud Madame Patrice. As the December storm raged outside they fell into bed, thoroughly exhausted but triumphant and warm at last.

Too warm, they realized shortly. About two o'clock in the morning Victor leaped out of bed and shouted, "We're on fire!" He opened the door to the corridor and smoke filled their room. At his instruction, Mary began tying sheets together while he wrapped a wet towel around his head and rushed out to see what could be done.

Racing down the corridor, Victor followed the billowing smoke to its source in an adjoining room. One of the AC mechanics had fallen asleep in his bed, cigarette still burning. His hair mattress was smouldering, producing clouds of thick smoke but very little flame. Victor pulled the man out of bed and threw him into a cold bath, then extinguished the fire and opened a window.

A panic-stricken Madame Patrice was shouting from her top floor window that she was going to jump. Mary, meanwhile, found that the four sheets still lacked 20 feet of touching the ground; she struggled to add two thick eiderdown comforters to the makeshift 'rope'. Victor raced back into their room just in time to shout to Madame not to jump—and to reassure her and Mary that the fire was out and all was well.

7 The Legend Grows

In less than a year, Mary had soared to prominence in the automotive world. Her stunning performance in the 1927 Monte Carlo Rally was only the beginning: the ambitious circuit of the Mediterranean, followed by the dash to the frozen north and the record-smashing ten day endurance record at Montlhéry had made her name a household word. Not a week went by without press reports of her exploits, alone or with Victor.

Mary had certainly not gone unnoticed by the Alvis Company, which approached her with an offer of a spot on its racing team; she jumped at the chance. Alvis, one of the best known English car manufacturers of the 1920s, had a reputation for sporty, innovative equipment and speed—characteristics that doubtless persuaded Mary to work for them.

Alvis automobiles were perennial competitors on the racing circuit from the beginning of their production, and joining their team put Mary in competition with the most prominent racers of the day. She raced against Malcolm Campbell, recently returned from America after setting a world's land speed record at Daytona, Florida, with a sizzling 206.9 mph. Born in Kent in 1885, Campbell had, like Mary, developed a passion for speed at an early age. He raced bicycles on the continent in his teen years and motorcycles in Britain in his early twenties. Campbell was briefly interested in airplanes in 1909, around the time Bleriot flew the English Channel and A.V. Roe was developing his first airplane, but in 1910 he began racing automobiles at Brooklands, and made that his career. In a long series of racing cars and speedboats, all named *Bluebird*,[1] Campbell became one of Britain's best-known sportsmen. He was knighted in 1931.[2]

Another of Mary's competitors was the legendary Sir Henry Segrave, who in 1927 became the first man in the world to exceed 200 mph. Segrave and Campbell took turns setting speed records until Segrave died in a boating accident on Lake Windermere in June 1930, in pursuit of a water speed record.[3]

Like Campbell and Segrave, Mary's interest in methods of transportation was wide-ranging. Speeding on water also appealed to Mary. The summer of 1928 found her competing regularly in motorboat races around London. The Welsh Harp, a large reservoir in northwest London's Hendon area, was a frequent venue. She had several boats—*Bob*, *Tiny*, and *Mosquito* among them. Indulging her passion for speed and her habit of 110% effort, she was quickly at home in this new milieu. That is not to say, however, that she didn't have any rough patches or bumpy rides. During a practice run before a Saturday of racing, a newspaper photographer snapped a picture of her being tossed out of *Bob* at a turn in the Welsh Harp course—arms waving and skirt flying. Once back in the boat, she finished the day of racing with no further mishaps—but with no prizes, either.

Mary's specific goal as she honed her boating skills that summer was the establishment of a record time for crossing the English Channel. She determined that no one had claimed a record for this feat; it was a perfect opportunity for her. In July she announced her plans for this headline-capturing venture, then waited impatiently for favourable conditions on the Channel. Her attempt would be under the observation of the Royal Cinque Ports Yacht Club in Dover, from whose site she would begin her run. A powerful Seacar pilot boat was to follow her 12-foot *Mosquito* and verify the completion of the crossing. In mid-September, the time was right.

The official observation by the yacht club's representative did not go exactly as planned. The pilot boat was first out of Dover harbour but Mary, bent on clocking the fastest time possible, soon left it in her wake. She was completely out of sight within minutes. She steered by the sun since, as she pointed out, the bone-jarring vibration from her small but powerful outboard engine would have rendered a compass useless. Hazy conditions prevailed, and she was forced to make several detours to avoid larger ships in the Channel as well as floating masses of seaweed and jettisoned cargo and detritus in the shipping lanes. Once she caught sight of the French coast, navigation to Calais was easy. She slowed to enter the harbour, where she spotted the official timekeeper waiting for her on the pier.

Mary's goal, as announced to the press before the venture, was simply to establish the record for the fastest crossing of the Channel by an outboard motorboat. Nothing was said of the return trip, but as she related the story, she found the impulse to continue the high-speed run too strong to resist. Steering close enough so that the official could identify her clearly and hear her, she waved at him, shouted "*Vive la France!*" and turned and sped out of the harbour, intent on setting a two-way record.

On the return journey, Mary mistook a trail of smoke from an unseen steamer for the first smudgy sight of the English coast. Realizing the error, she was disoriented until she encountered and recognized a particular patch of seaweed which she had avoided on her way out. A close encounter with a school of porpoises in her path presented another challenge; she cut her speed and carefully manoeuvred around the playful mammals.

As she approached the English coast the water became rough. Still moving at top speed, *Mosquito* pounded over the waves, vibrating fiercely. Mary watched apprehensively as the engine bolts worked loose; would they hold until they reached the shore? Would the fuel supply last? Mary tightened the bolts repeatedly with one hand, gripping the steering control with the other. Through the mist she saw, at last, the welcome sight of Dover's white cliffs, and in moments she and *Mosquito* had run up on the sand.

Mary in the Mosquito

Mary had established a record time for the two-way crossing of the Channel: one hour and 47 minutes. It was an immediate challenge, capturing headlines[4] and inspiring others to attempt to beat her mark. An added incentive was Mary's offer of a cash prize for anyone who could surpass her time on the same trip before the end of 1929. That challenge produced a flurry of preparation among would-be record-breakers as they readied engines and boats for the 1929 racing season.

Victor did not share his wife's interest in speedboats; he was busy with speed trials at a variety of venues in England, as well as racing at Brooklands and LeMans. They did, however, share an interest in writing motoring advice columns. Victor had been writing newspaper articles on motoring topics, and there was a ready market for the feminine viewpoint as well. In 1928, encouraged by the reception given to *Nine Thousand Miles in Eight Weeks*, Mary began writing for newspapers, too. Some columns were written under their joint byline; both also wrote individual columns. They were published in newspapers across Britain and syndicated throughout the empire. Readers in such diverse locales as Rhodesia and India could enjoy the valuable information and advice the Bruces dispensed. Mary's column was variously titled 'The Woman Owner Driver', 'Motoring Chat', or 'Motoring for the Millions', although in Rhodesia, where cars were far fewer in number, it appeared as 'Motoring for the Million'. Mary wrote as an advocate for women's automobile ownership and competence in motoring fields. She worked tirelessly to demystify automobiles and driving for women, insisting that feminine skills were equal to those of men.

Victor's themes were usually more technical ('What the New Gear Box Means to the Motorist', 'Watch Your Oil!'), while Mary's articles were technical enough to be of interest to male readers ('Mud and the Motorist—Best Methods for Getting Out of a Bog'), but she frequently ventured into the area of advice for women— both as drivers ('Comfort and Efficiency in Motoring Clothes') and as passengers ('The Art of Being a Front Seat Car Passenger').

Together Mary and Victor competed in a summer Alpine trial, the *Coupe des Alpes*, a road race from Milan to Munich. In the six-cylinder AC that Selwyn Edge had given Mary after the Mediterranean tour, they covered the 1,200-mile route crisscrossing the Alps through many of Europe's highest passes. It was a timed trial over a specified course, and they calculated that their minimum average speed over the narrow mountain roads had to be 30 mph. Mary again did all the driving; Victor was a superb navigator, and together they were a formidable team.

The first day's course took them from Milan to Lugano, set between the Italian lakes of Como and Maggiore, through rolling hills and over comparatively easy grades. On the second day the mountain climbing began in earnest, as they followed a twisting route over the Simplon Pass into Switzerland. In order to maintain their 30 mph average speed, Mary drove flat out whenever she could. They were moving fast when, at a narrow spot on the road, another car attempted to pass theirs and they collided. Mary spotted a wheel bouncing down the road behind them and exclaimed, "We've lost our spare wheel!" "Spare be blowed!" replied Victor, "it's our front wheel!" They were towed to the next village, where repairs were quickly made.

They followed the Rhône River northeast, in the shadow of the towering peaks of the Jungfrau and Aletschhorn, then climbed again to cross the St. Gotthard Pass and the 7,976-foot Furka Pass, ending the day at Merano.

The next day took them farther east, over a series of passes and through hidden Alpine valleys in the mountainous north of Italy. Their goal that day was Belluno, on the banks of the Piave River north of Venice. Turning north the next day, Mary still at the wheel, they rolled past even more spectacular Alpine scenery, into the

Austrian town of Villach. Near the border of Slovenia, Villach had been a tourist destination at least since Celt and Roman conquerors discovered the six thermal springs nearby. If Mary and Victor found time to ease their road-weary muscles in the pools they did not record it. The fifth and final day of the Alpine trial brought a demanding drive north from Villach over the imposing mile-high Tauern Pass and through pristine Austrian valleys.

Victor and Mary finished the rally in Munich by evening, with an overall average speed of 32½ mph. To their disappointment, they were disqualified from competition for the Alpine Cup because they had not done their own repair work after the collision on the second day, but the sponsors recognized their excellent showing with a special plaque instead.

In view of Mary's reputation as the premier woman driver in Britain—her showing in the Monte Carlo Rallies, her tours to the Arctic Circle and the western Mediterranean, the ten-day run at Montlhéry, all were well publicized—it is not surprising that she was in demand for publicity purposes. She endorsed a variety of automobile-related products in newspaper and magazine advertisements, and was frequently invited to participate in public relations events. Loving the spotlight as she did, she rarely turned down the chance to see her name and face in print.

In November 1928 a luxurious Manchester-to-London motorbus service was inaugurated. Following christening ceremonies in London and Manchester, two coaches departed simultaneously, one from each city. The 20-passenger coaches featured armchairs, writing tables, a library, individual lighting controls, a toilet, a cigarette machine, and call bells for attendants. When the company added a London-to-Plymouth route the following week, Mary drove the first coach out of London; the journey was well reported by the press. "The Honourable Mrs Victor Bruce, the 'woman racing motorist,' drove a 31-seater, six-wheeled motor coach through London, while traffic was at its greatest yesterday. It was the first of a new fleet of motor coaches to run to Plymouth. 'Driving a motor coach certainly means muscle,' said Mrs Bruce, 'and there is a great deal of nerve strain, especially on long journeys, but really I think that a woman can stand up to that side of it as well as a man!' "

Similar public relations and advertising opportunities presented themselves regularly, including an ongoing relationship with the manufacturers of her beloved Ovaltine. A caricature of Mary, looking bright-eyed and pert while sipping a cup of the steaming beverage, became a familiar advertisement for the company. 'If it had not been for Ovaltine in the flask I should never have been able to keep my strength and nerves together,' read her testimony. This advertisement first appeared after her 1927 Monte Carlo and Mediterranean trip, was used again after her 24-hour record at Montlhéry, and would appear yet again after her world flight.

8 The Little Lady and the Big Bentley

The year in which Mary set her most astonishing automotive record, 1929, did not begin auspiciously. It was traditional by now for the Bruces to start each new year with the Monte Carlo Rally, and 1929 was no exception. Her 1927 *Coupe des Dames* triumph, followed by a respectable fourth-place showing in 1928, made Mary a formidable entrant; the press was predictably attentive, closely following what turned out to be a near fiasco.

Mary and Victor chose a new starting point: the Baltic seaport of Riga, Latvia. Slightly farther south than their 1928 choice, Stockholm, Riga would still give them extra points for distance. There would be no necessity for a water crossing; the route would be straight southwest through Latvia, Lithuania, Poland, and Germany.

Mary had anticipated driving her six-cylinder AC again, but just before she and Victor left for Riga it was damaged in a car park. Repairs could not be carried out before their departure time, so they arranged to borrow an Arrol-Aster from the manufacturer in Dumfries, Scotland. Arrol-Aster had been the company chosen by Malcolm Campbell in 1928 to restore his record-setting racer, Bluebird, a factor that may have influenced Mary's decision to drive one of their automobiles.

From the outset, the 1929 Monte Carlo was a series of mishaps for Mary and Victor. Travelling north to Riga, they encountered blizzard and sub-zero conditions, which worsened as they made their way through Germany. Just short of the Polish border a snowdrift stopped them; the Arrol-Aster slid into a ditch. Unhurt, they climbed up to the road and began to walk, mindful of the danger of giving in to their inclination to burrow down in the car and go to sleep. The nearest village, some three miles down the road, finally was within sight; they knocked at the door of the first cottage they came to. The farmer's initial suspicion was softened somewhat as they explained—Mary using bits of German she remembered from school—what had happened to them, but his hospitality was assured when he caught side of Victor's fingers, nearly frostbitten. He welcomed them into his tiny home, lit a fire, and shared his supper with them. Gratefully they spent the night sleeping on the cottage floor. In the morning their host arranged for them to hire two horses, and eventually the car (now buried nearly completely under the snow) was pulled from the ditch.

They knew that they would be unable to reach Riga by road in time to start the Monte Carlo from there, so they turned south to Berlin. The Monte Carlo regulations stipulated that if competitors could not reach their chosen starting point because of road closures, they could start from the nearest town where there would be a club official to see them off.

An electrical problem gave them intermittent concern on the way to Berlin: one of the lights appeared to flicker, but they could not take the time to investigate and make repairs. The slide into the snowy ditch had cost them hours of time. Hoping for the best, they checked in with the Monte Carlo official in Berlin and set out for Monaco immediately. They made good time once they got started, and by Paris they had caught up with most of the other competitors. South through France they sped, but one final calamity befell them as they approached the ancient city of Avignon. Just before dawn all of the lights went out, and smoke began to pour from under the hood. Their fire extinguisher saved the car, but the night in the snowy ditch had caused a short-circuit in the wiring, and the engine was a total loss. Their 1929 Monte Carlo attempt was history and they took a train home. Victor wrote, with classic understatement, 'Our luck was out in 1929 unfortunately, and the less said about the terrible journey up towards Riga, which snowdrifts prevented us from reaching, and down towards Monte Carlo against heavy odds all the time, the better.'

Back in England again, they turned their attention to different ventures. Following Mary's lead, Victor expanded his racing to include boats as well as cars, and the spring of 1929 found him competing in speedboat races for the first time. In the three years of their marriage they had undertaken many joint ventures centered around the automobile. When Mary began racing speedboats, Victor initially stuck to dry land. Perhaps in an effort to strengthen their relationship through more shared interests, he followed her into the new field. It was a pattern that would be repeated: she taking on a new challenge, he following.

Mary, meantime, was planning a solo venture that would be her most daring record attempt yet. Selwyn Edge, her good friend and mentor, was a true automotive pioneer; he had created the world record for single-handed driving for 24 hours in June of 1907 on the brand-new Brooklands track. He drove a 60 hp Napier a total of 1,581 miles in 24 hours, for an average speed of just under 66 mph. With 352 red lanterns spaced around the track for night lighting, Edge stopped only for tyre changes, fuel, and brief rest stops, nourishing himself with cocoa, beef tea, and fruit.

His record stood until 1925 when Thomas Gillett[1] managed 1,980 miles at an average of 82.5 mph to set a new 24-hour single-handed mark at Montlhéry. Characteristically, the generous Edge had loaned Gillett an AC car for the run. Mary knew Edge as a sportsman who was always interested in testing the limits, and she approached him in May of 1929 with a request for his assistance in setting a new 24-hour solo record.

The automotive industry in general was having financial problems. Arrol-Aster was in its last year of full production. Several manufacturers, including AC, were considering reducing or eliminating their racing teams and curtailing their busy schedules of speed trials, endurance runs, and hill climbs. In addition, Edge, at 61, was in poor health. He could offer Mary only moral support. Her faithful AC saloon, which had carried her for thousands of record-setting miles, could not be modified sufficiently to make a new record-breaking run.

She turned the problem over in her mind: where could she find a car fast enough and strong enough to run at record-breaking speeds for 24 hours? At breakfast one morning, the answer suddenly occurred to her: she needed a big Bentley! Bentleys were perennial winners in Grand Prix racing during the 1920s; they were heavy, powerful machines that were well suited to high-speed endurance racing. Mary did not hesitate; breakfast abandoned, she telephoned for an appointment with W.O. Bentley himself.

The next morning she met with Bentley and Captain Woolf Barnato, one of the popular 'Bentley Boys'. Regarded by W.O. Bentley as 'the best driver we ever had,' Barnato was achieving spectacular success on the racetracks of Europe. His family had amassed a fortune in South African diamond mines; he was providing needed financial support to Bentley, and took over that year as chairman of the company.

Mary explained her intention to set a new 24-hour single-handed record, and asked for the use of a Bentley for the attempt. W.O. Bentley replied that only one of their cars would be suitable for the run, but it would be needed by Bentley racing team member Earl Howe later in June for a 24-hour race at Le Mans and by Henry 'Tim' Birkin for more international races later in the year. It was a 4.5-litre Bentley, then the most powerful automobile in their line; Barnato, driving with teammate Bernard Rubin, had won the 1928 Le Mans with a similar Bentley. Mary knew that he was concerned that she might damage the powerful automobile, possibly rendering it inoperative for Howe and Birkin's races.

The two men listened as Mary made her pitch: a 24-hour run at Montlhéry would provide a great warm-up for the car before its appearance at Le Mans. She watched their faces; it was Bentley who first mused, "You know, I believe she might do it." Barnato nodded, and Mary had her vehicle. She quickly added that the Bentley would have to be capable of speeds over 100 mph if she were to have a chance of breaking Gillett's record. Bentley and Barnato agreed to provide the engineering preparation, a support team, and transport of the automobile to and from the French track.

Mary in the Bentley

Obstacles remained, not the least of which was the necessity of coming up with rental fee for the track at Montlhéry. The trust fund established by her Aunt Maud could not be tapped again; she and Victor were not well enough off to pay for the facilities themselves. They were, however, well known to the public for their newspaper automotive columns, as well as their ten-day record-breaking run at Montlhéry and their Arctic and Mediterranean trips. Already they were in demand for publicity and advertising campaigns: motor oils, spark plugs, and windshield wipers were only a few of the products they had endorsed in print—for a fee, of course.

Mary paid a call on Sir George Beharrell, the Chairman of the Dunlop Tyre Company, telling him that W.O. Bentley was lending her a car so that she could set a new 24-hour record. She would, naturally, run on Dunlop tyres; would he be interested in sponsoring her? Hearing that she proposed to make the run single-handedly, he declined. "Little lady, you can't do it without a co-driver. Don't try." Never one to share the limelight unnecessarily, she insisted that she would break Gillett's solo record. She had no interest in a team effort for this undertaking, she told him; she would drive the distance herself. He smiled and shook his head, "I still think you'd be ill-advised to try; but if you do and if you succeed, come and see me."

That was all Mary needed to hear; with the Bentley works behind her, she was fully confident that she would break the record—and now, she knew, she would also have Dunlop's financial assistance! To celebrate, she treated herself to a trip to the smart shops of Bond Street, where she chose a pale blue leather jacket for the record-breaking run.

Mary loved shopping for clothes, and was known as one of the best-dressed sportswomen of her time. She was thoroughly feminine, in spite of her adrenaline-fueled racing hobbies, and chose feminine attire for all occasions—including races. A July 1928 photograph, showing her at the wheel of a hydroplane she was racing on the Thames, reveals a string of pearls beneath the heavy plastic face-shield of the racing helmet she wore. In 1929 a London newspaper columnist wrote of Mary: 'She is always beautifully dressed and the last time I saw her at Brooklands she introduced an interesting novelty for women motorists in the form of a tiny mica face screen that fitted round her helmet and protected her skin from the dust of the track while racing.' With her new blue leather jacket, Mary's 24-hour attempt at Montlhéry would find her equally well turned out.

It was early June when Mary went to Montlhéry, but the weather was anything but spring-like. Under leaden skies she and the Bentley support team met in the pits to discuss the driving and maintenance schedule. She would make a pit stop every three hours for no longer than three minutes, giving the mechanics time to fill the gas tank and check the tyres, water, and oil.

Stepping into the Bentley for a trial lap, she encountered a problem immediately: compared with her beloved AC, the Bentley was a behemoth! The petite Mary—she was barely five feet tall—could neither reach the pedals nor see well over the dashboard. A Bentley mechanic borrowed three cushions from the Montlhéry timekeepers; she sat on one and put two behind her back, which solved that problem. The next obstacle was the realization that the hand brake was inaccessible: for that model Bentley, the brake was a huge lever mounted on the outside of the car. Mary dismissed that problem, saying, "I don't expect I'll need that—but if I do, I'll have to stand up to reach it!"

She drove her test lap on the track, already so slick from the rain that no one could walk up the steep banking. She and Victor had driven the same track on black ice just 18 months earlier, however, and she was confident that the rain would prove no more treacherous. She quickly reached 105 mph, the fastest she had ever driven, and got reacquainted with the uneven surface of the track. Having driven her AC over the track for ten days and nights, the bumps were all too familiar to her, but they felt far worse in the Bentley. The mechanics had tightened down the suspension as far as possible, to prevent the heavy Bentley from becoming airborne when it encountered a bump at high speed. Consequently, the ride was incredibly firm, shaking Mary and throwing her around in the seat.

She checked in with the Montlhéry timekeepers, and recognized the chief timekeeper from the record-setting ten-day run she and Victor had made in 1927. He greeted her with a smile, with no suggestion this time that he and his fellow timekeepers might be on their way home soon. Not only did he not enquire as to whether she had brought a relief driver with her, but he confided to her that they had scheduled relief timekeepers for themselves—an indication to Mary that they fully expected her to drive the entire 24 hours.

Rain was falling steadily when she took to the track at noon. She soon settled into a steady rhythm, holding the big engine's revs constant to minimize strain and maximize efficiency. At the Bentley's top speed of 107 mph, she lapped the track every 57 seconds, never varying by more than a second or two. At that speed, she travelled high on the bankings, and felt the massive and powerful Bentley poised to sail over the top; she could not afford to lose concentration for a moment.

Refuelling the Bentley

Hours passed steadily; the every-three-hourly pit stops were Mary's only relief from the relentless concentration and effort. Night fell, and the hurricane lamps marking the track edges blinked past in a blur. To the monotony of the laps was added the challenge of staying awake as the hours went by. Near dawn, sleep nearly brought a tragic end to the run. It was the change in the sound of the engine that woke her, Mary wrote, as she drifted off to sleep while the Bentley was screaming around so high on the bankings that it was nearly brushing the wooden fencing at the top of the track.

It was a scare that completely chased away the remotest possibility of sleep. Refuelled by adrenaline, she renewed her concentration and as morning broke she knew the record was within reach. As noon approached she saw the pit crew scurrying around, and on her next lap the men held up a board with the number 10 on it. Elated, she watched as each lap was counted down for her 3, 2, 1, and it was over! Twenty-four hours after she began, she climbed from the Bentley at last, having covered 2,149.68 miles at an average speed of 89.57 mph.[2]

Earl Howe, who was soon to drive the same Bentley in the 24-hour race at Le Mans, treated her to an elegant lunch in Paris after the run. Over coffee he announced that, in his capacity as President of the British Racing Drivers' Club, he was proposing her for Honorary Life Membership. It was a tribute that no woman had previously received, and—once the club's committee approved her nomination—was a lifelong source of great pride.

9   On the Water

Summer was Mary's favourite season; the possibilities for speed and adventure seemed nearly limitless, and never brighter than in the summer of 1929. Once the excitement of the 24-hour run at Montlhéry began to fade, Mary turned to other challenges. Looking to the water, she watched as a dozen competitors tried to win the cash prize she had offered for anyone who could beat her 107-minute record for the double crossing of the English Channel before year's end.

Mary waited for a successful challenge to her Channel record, no doubt anxious for an excuse to reset the mark. She was impatient, too, to see more substantial financial rewards than the modest income from her newspaper columns or the occasional cheque for publicity appearances and product endorsements. Sir George Beharrell of the Dunlop Tyre Company had cheerfully kept his word, giving her an envelope containing a cheque for £1,000, which she always referred to as 'manna from heaven'. But Mary sought a steadier, more reliable source of income.

Capitalizing on her motorboating reputation, she started Southern Speed Boats, an excursion company offering outings on the Channel waters. In the seaside resort village of Bognor Regis, some 70 miles south of London, Mary cashed in on a wave of interest in boating that summer, which was fuelled partly by the publicity given to her own Channel speed record established the previous fall and by the continuing attempts on that record. Weekend afternoons found her company doing a brisk business, giving rides to thrill-seeking vacationers.

Most of her customers were well satisfied, judging from her financial records (one afternoon in June yielded a £27 profit after salaries and expenses, equivalent to more than £1000 in purchasing power today). One unhappy rider, however, complained that one of Mary's boat pilots had driven so recklessly and carelessly that he and his companions had been drenched to the skin by a huge wave. 'We were able to dry out,' the man wrote, 'by sitting about in bathing costumes until six-thirty in the evening whilst our underclothes were drying in the sun.' He demanded compensation for the expense of dry-cleaning his wife's dress, as well as the suits that he and a male friend had been wearing. The total requested was £1 and 16 shillings—a request which was at first ignored and then denied by Mary. Eventually she paid the claim while steadfastly refusing to admit any liability. Whether or not such an attitude was a factor, the business seems to have existed for only a few months during the summer of 1929.

Mary's speed record for the Channel crossing finally fell that August when automobile racer and sportsman Kaye Don, after several abortive attempts, made the roundtrip in a 200 hp 14-seater Hoylecraft speedboat in 83 minutes, breaking Mary's record by 24 minutes. His powerful inboard dwarfed the 12-foot Mosquito with which Mary had set the record the year before.

Don held the record for less than three weeks before Mary took it back, driving an outboard ChrisCraft with a time of 79 minutes and 24 seconds. Upon her return to Dover, she was quoted by the London *Daily Mail*: 'It was one of the most thrilling dashes I've ever made. I took a compass with me but did not refer to it once, as I was able to steer by landmarks on both sides. I am told that I did not deviate a mile from the straight line.'

Her new mark stood for only two weeks before adventurer J.P. Turner shaved nine minutes off her time, making the circuit in 70 minutes. It was the culmination of a long and frustrating effort for Turner, who had made dozens of attempts on Mary's record over the course of several months. Disregarding sailors' advice to the contrary, he had repeatedly set out under less than ideal circumstances, so anxious was he to capture the record. On more than one occasion that summer, search efforts were launched when Turner was reported lost at sea while attempting to best Mary's record.

By the time Turner finally succeeded, Mary had moved on to a different quest. Months earlier she had established the endurance record at Montlhéry. Perpetually on the lookout for new records to set and new thrills to embrace, Mary had been considering other ventures. Next on her agenda, she decided, would be the same sort of 24-hour mark—but this time on water. In mid-September, just days after she recaptured the Dover–Calais roundtrip speedboat record, Mary started her attempt on the Solent, between the south coast and the Isle of Wight. Her intention was to race around a six-mile course, racking up as many miles as possible and establishing a motorboating endurance record.

Her goal was to break the existing record of 691 nautical miles covered in 24 hours, a mark established, according to Mary, by the liner *Berengaria*.[1] It would be safer, she reckoned, than the cross-Channel dash; she would follow a defined course well out of the shipping lanes, making one circuit every six minutes between a lightship and the timekeeper's yacht. Furthermore, she would be driving a powerful, 23-foot inboard motorboat for this attempt; a second powerboat would stand by, in case any mishap befell the first.

The attempt began on a Friday afternoon—a choice Mary soon regretted, when she realized that the steamship traffic from nearby Southampton was at its weekly peak. She found the lights of the ships confusing, and the monotonous circuit around the lightship quickly became tiresome. Mary began to feel like an automaton, she said, and looked forward to her refuelling stops every four hours.

Several hours into the run, well after dark, the propeller of her boat struck a piece of driftwood just as she was turning to cross the path of a large oncoming Channel steamer. Her engine stopped abruptly; she tried frantically to restart it, without success, drifting powerless in the steamer's path. Mary turned on her searchlight, flashing it in hopes that the crew on the big ship would see her. Fortunately, the passing yacht *Kiwi* did see her plight; a speedboat tore out and towed her to safety.

Back at the timekeeper's yacht, Mary changed boats and was out on the course again within ten minutes. The close call with the steamer had sent a surge of adrenaline through her, and with her characteristic determination, she turned back to the task at hand. The 24 hours passed at last, and she pulled up beside the timekeeper's yacht to hear the news. She had broken the existing record by three nautical miles—by an eyelash—but a new record it was, and that was enough to satisfy her.

In later years Mary fiercely denied that she was a feminist, perhaps equating that term with the strident demands of some early voices of the movement. However, she was invariably eager to promote opportunities for women, particularly in motor sports. She still loved motorcycles, her first wheeled challenge, and she held the office of Vice President of the London Ladies Motor Cycle Club.

She was also chief motor advisor to the Women's Automobile and Sports Association. Her newest scheme that summer of 1929 was launched under the auspices of the Association. As reported by London's *Daily Herald* in September, 'Smart uniformed girls will soon be seen on our main roads, mounted on motorcycles and equipped for dealing with motor breakdowns and roadside accidents.' Mary's ambitious vision was a corps of women patrolling the roads in search of motorists in need of assistance.

She had some difficulty in recruiting just the type of young woman she was looking for. "I've been trying to launch this historic innovation," she told an interviewer, "but I have not been able to get the ideal blending of smart appearance, mechanical knowledge and a slight acquaintance with first aid. I am trying now to choose three girls. They must be slim and intelligent and able to stand a life on the open road. They are to be the forerunners of an army of women road patrols."

By the end of September the scheme had become reality, as the press duly reported—although Mary's plan to provide movable trailers equipped with tea baskets apparently never was realised. However, the attire the young women would wear got far more news coverage than what services they would provide to motorists. 'England's first girl road scout, Miss Grace New, is obviously proud of the smart new black uniform which she was wearing when a *Daily News* representative had tea with her yesterday. "It's designed by Mrs. Victor Bruce," she said. "The gold braid zip fastener is particularly useful. I have had to see about getting some red facings put on, as the plain black does not show up very well." With the uniform, she was wearing Wellington boots and an attractive black, white and red tie. Miss New, who began her patrol duties on Saturday, is disappointed at having had no breakdowns to deal with yet.'[2]

The absence of breakdowns to deal with did, however, allow plenty of time for Miss New to pose for the newspaper photographers and to give interviews to the press. One writer reported, apparently tongue in cheek, 'The 23-year-old blonde's equipment consists of a striking uniform: black coat with white and red facing, tight red striped breeches, Wellington boots, a black and white pillbox hat, also an eight horsepower motorcycle equipped with repair tools and first aid kit, and a supply of powder puffs.' The rookie road patroller told reporters she'd had no special training; the job would be second nature to her. She had always loved tinkering with automobile engines, she said, and her favourite hobby was decarbonising her friends' engines. "That's how I usually spend my Sundays," she said.

The records Mary set in 1929—her 24-hour run at Montlhéry, a new roundtrip Channel crossing, and the 24-hour motorboat endurance mark—were only a part of what one London newspaper summed up as 'Britain's Fastest Year'. For the first time, it was noted, Britain held the world's speed records for land, sea, and air. Women set their share of records, and public recognition was given. In November, Mary was invited, along with fellow record-setters Lady Catherine Bailey and Molly Gourlay, to be a guest of honour at the British Sportsmen's Club dinner at London's Savoy Hotel—the first time in club history that women had been invited.

Lady Bailey had flown her Gipsy Moth solo to Capetown, South Africa and back, the first woman to do so, while Molly Gourlay was honoured for winning both English and French golf championships. It was the 24-hour solo record at

Montlhéry that prompted Mary's invitation. The gentlemen of the Sportsmen's Club need not have worried that the women would linger too long in their domain. Newspapers reported that the evening was 'distinguished by very short speeches' by the honourees, including the 'dark and vivacious Mrs Victor Bruce'.

Accolades were fine, but Mary's craving for new challenges continued unabated. The automotive and boating endurance records were hers; she was regularly published in newspapers and magazines; what could she do next?

10   Taking Flight

Mary was restless in the spring of 1930. After four Rallies, the challenge of the Monte Carlo had faded a bit. She had stunned the motoring world with her 24-hour solo record at Montlhéry, won trophies at the Bournemouth Motor Rally, and set and reset cross-Channel speedboat records. The British land and water endurance records were hers. She was regularly published in newspapers and magazines. What could she do next? She was keeping her eyes open for a new challenge.

Along with the rest of England, Mary was enthralled by the adventure undertaken by Amy Johnson. In early May, the 26-year-old novice pilot from Hull set out on a solo flight to Australia in her two-year-old Gipsy Moth *Jason*. Her goal was to break the record of 15 days for the flight, set in 1928 by Australian Bert Hinkler. But a series of mishaps and delays cost Amy any chance at the record. Exhausted and disheartened, she arrived in Australia after 19 days.

As the first woman to make the flight, however, Amy was met with a heroine's reception. And, as the first British flyer to do so, she enjoyed an outpouring of adulation upon her return—by ship and commercial airline—to England. Also awaiting her were gifts of two new airplanes and an automobile, as well as a £10,000 award from the *Daily Mail*, in recognition of her accomplishment. She began a 40-town publicity tour set up by that newspaper, but the gruelling schedule proved too difficult and she was unable to maintain the pace; the tour was cancelled.

The press had been full of aviation news for months. The previous June, American pilot Evelyn 'Bobbi' Trout had set a new altitude record for light aircraft when she climbed to 15,200 feet in a 90 hp Golden Eagle Chief. Two months later the Women's Air Derby—dubbed the 'Powder Puff Derby' by American humorist Will Rogers—was inaugurated.[1] Fifteen of the 20 entrants who began the race completed it; the winner was Louise Thaden, a record-holding pilot who in 1928 had become the first pilot to hold the women's altitude, endurance, and speed records in light planes simultaneously. Amelia Earhart, who finished in third place, credited the Derby as 'the event that started concerted activity among women flyers.'[2]

Airports were being built and expanded at an unprecedented rate, both to accommodate existing traffic and to attract new passengers. Regular passenger air routes were being established and records fell regularly. In April 1930 Charles and Anne Morrow Lindbergh had flown from Los Angeles to New York in 14 hours and 45 minutes, setting an American transcontinental speed record. The following month Amy Johnson had made her celebrated solo flight to Australia—a feat which clearly galvanized Mary to action. Johnson's daring achievement—and the flood of publicity which accompanied it—reinforced Mary's growing fascination with flying.

The oft-told tale of how Mary entered the world of aviation is romantic and somewhat fanciful, a whimsy that probably even Mary herself came to believe. She had inherited her mother's flair for the dramatic, and the account she loved to relate has all the earmarks of great theatre. It was June 1930, she wrote, a rather 'wintry summer day' in London. Mary had a luncheon date at one o'clock, but she left her Esher cottage earlier than she had intended when her housekeeper announced that the water heater had sprung a leak. Arriving in the centre of London at noon, she parked her car and strolled down Burlington Gardens, just off Regent Street, near Piccadilly. With an hour to spare before lunch, window-shopping seemed the perfect solution. She was surprised to spot, in the window of Auto-Auctions, Ltd., a pretty little blue and silver airplane, a Blackburn Bluebird, with a sign on it declaring 'Ready to go anywhere'.

She had never seen an airplane offered for sale so casually, and thought, 'What are we coming to now, when we can buy aeroplanes out of shop windows?' But she said to herself, "No, flying is not for you!" She had never cared for it, she claimed, and in fact wrote that she had always been afraid of flying, and had only once been up in the air.

A little farther down Burlington Gardens she came to another shop, this one with a more conventional window display: a very attractive frock. 'It was,' she wrote, 'easily the best I had seen for years', and she went inside to try it on. It did not suit her, and soon she was back on the street, still with most of an hour to while away. She retraced her steps for another look at the airplane. The salesman may have noticed her interest earlier, for now there was another sign on the airplane with the words 'Honeymoon Model', indicating that the seats were side by side, and not one behind the other, as was customary in light airplanes of that period. On a whim, she went inside and asked the price.

"Five hundred and fifty pounds, Madam," the salesman replied smoothly, "and chromium plating on the handles will be only five pounds extra."

She was struck by how ordinary it all sounded; the idea of buying an airplane out of a shop, the same way one would buy a packet of tea or a frock, was intriguing.

"Could one fly round the world in this?" she asked.

"Of course, Madam, easily; look, it folds."

As the salesman began to fold the wings on the small plane, Mary suddenly wondered if he was going to say, "Will you take it with you or shall I send it?"

She would think about it, she told him, and left to keep her luncheon date. She thought of little else that afternoon, wondering if her reluctance to fly marked her as old-fashioned. If aviation were indeed the wave of the future, she had to be on the crest of it; she could not be left behind.

Back home in Esher, she learned that Victor would be late coming home for supper. With a little more time on her hands, she took down an atlas and looked at a map of the world. 'From that moment,' she wrote, 'I felt I must take up flying, and see all the countries of the world.' With a pencil she drew a route on the map: across the English Channel to Belgium, Germany, Austria, and southeast to Turkey; across Turkey to Syria, then along the Euphrates River to Baghdad, and south via the Persian Gulf to India; east across the great Indian subcontinent to Rangoon. Here her pencil paused while she considered her options. Just weeks earlier, Amy Johnson had become the first woman to fly solo from England to Australia; Mary turned her pencil northeast, choosing, as always, to break new ground. On the map she traced a route over the jungles of Burma and Siam[3] and up the China coast to Hong Kong and Shanghai. At the edge of the Yellow Sea her pencil paused again. 'It looked so easy on the map,' she wrote later, 'just about an inch. "That's nothing!" I thought, and so finished the line across to Tokyo.'

Knowing that the Bluebird was much too small to fly the Pacific, she decided that she would fold its wings and transport it to North America by ship; she pencilled a line across the Pacific to British Columbia. Flying across America would give her the opportunity to visit her mother's birthplace, New Albany, Indiana. In the 42 years since she had left America, Jennie had never returned to her hometown. Mary drew a line down the west coast to Los Angeles, then east across the American southwest to the Mississippi River, and north to Indiana. She counted on the visit to New Albany to help soften her mother's almost certain objections to the scheme. Always apprehensive about Mary's thrill-seeking activities, Jennie would surely be horrified at the thought of her only daughter flying alone around the world in a tiny plane. From New Albany, Mary drew a line to New York, where she would once again put the airplane aboard a ship for the crossing to France; then she could fly the last lap home to England.

The world had been circled by air years earlier. The first successful round-the-world flight came in 1924, as the result of an informal international competition for bragging rights and aeronautical supremacy. Billy Mitchell, hero of America's World War I Army Air Corps, envisioned the feat in the years immediately following that conflict, the first in which air power played a significant role. At his urging, the Army Air Corps commissioned the construction of amphibious aircraft capable of long flights under difficult conditions. In April 1924 four Douglas World Cruisers, each with an Army Air Corps pilot and mechanic, began the circuit with a flight from Seattle, Washington to Prince Rupert, British Columbia. The 400 hp single engine, open cockpit biplanes—fitted with pontoons as well as wheels—were named the *Chicago*, the *Seattle*, the *Boston*, and the *New Orleans*. Not everyone shared the optimism of Billy Mitchell and the crews who flew them. Lt. Leigh Wade, pilot of the *Boston*, wrote in his log that a friend considered the mission akin to suicide: "You might as well crook your toe in a trigger and get it over with," Wade was told.[4]

By late September the historic mission was finished. Two of the original airplanes had completed the journey. One was forced down by engine failure and a replacement for it finished the course. One crashed; no lives were lost. These pioneers of the air had accomplished in just weeks what it had taken Magellan's crew three years to do in an earlier age. The American flyers had proven that circumnavigation was feasible; now it remained for others to refine the record. Mary—always ready for a challenge—wanted to go it alone.

Two days after she first saw the Bluebird, Mary visited her mother and announced her intention to fly to Indiana to visit New Albany and find her mother's childhood home. "You will do nothing of the kind!" Jennie exclaimed. "Go up in one of those Instruments of Torture? You'll never come back! You'll never come back!"

It took a lot of talking before Jennie accepted the idea but she had, after all, watched for over thirty years as her headstrong daughter threw herself into one adrenaline-fuelled venture after another. Eventually swallowing her objections, Jennie gave Mary an American flag, saying, "If you do find the house—and I doubt whether you will, because it was always flooded when I lived in it, and probably by now it has been washed away by the River Ohio—but if you do, drop this American flag on it from the air."

Once her mother had accepted the idea Mary proceeded with her plan. The next day she returned to Auto-Auctions, Ltd. in Burlington Gardens and bought the airplane. The enormity of the undertaking quickly became apparent as Mary began making arrangements. Both the machine and its pilot would need extensive preparation.

Mary began with a visit to the Air Ministry, to enquire about the best time of the year to make the flight. Early autumn was the only time to begin, she was told, so as to be ahead of the monsoon season in Southeast Asia. She immediately rejected the thought of putting off the attempt until the following year. Armed with 69 pages of weather information from the Ministry, and with only weeks in which to prepare, she flew into action.

The first order of business was to plot a route. Mary went to the Automobile Association for maps. The clerks in the Map Department were very interested when they learned of her plans.

"When did you take up flying?" they asked her. "We had not heard that you had learnt to fly!"

"Oh, to tell the truth," Mary replied, "I haven't learnt yet, but I will before I go." She remembered looks of astonishment on their faces, she wrote, but since it would take some time to have the maps prepared and time was short, ordering them before she started flying lessons seemed the prudent thing to do. They asked her to pay for the maps—in advance—and that, she claimed, completely sealed her fate. "When I returned home and told my husband, who is a Scotsman, he said: 'Well, that has done it! Now you've jolly well got to go!'"

In addition to maps, Mary began planning other supplies. She pared her packing list to the bare essentials, in order to minimize weight in the Bluebird's two small luggage compartments and thus maximize her fuel capacity. In a small shoulder bag she packed her passport and logbook, along with a supply of make-up which the newspapers of the day reported in detail: six powder puffs, two boxes of powder and four pieces of lip salve. With her route taking her through the arid reaches of the Middle East, she included a water bottle and sun helmet. In addition to her flying clothes—skirts, blouses, leather jacket, goggles—she packed her ever-present string of pearls. For foul weather, she had a Burberry[5] coat for warmth. She included two light cotton dresses and, doubtless anticipating formal receptions along the way, an evening gown.

Arranging for fuel supplies in distant places was accomplished with the help of two major oil companies, Anglo-Persian and Rising Sun. Mary contracted with both companies for fuel supplies, and accepted their sponsorship. Supplies of fuel earmarked for the Bluebird would be delivered to her intended destinations in remote locations.

As Mary related the story, it was two weeks before she found time to arrange flying lessons. She went to Brooklands, not only Britain's centre of automobile racing but also home to the Brooklands School of Flying. She asked for a lesson at

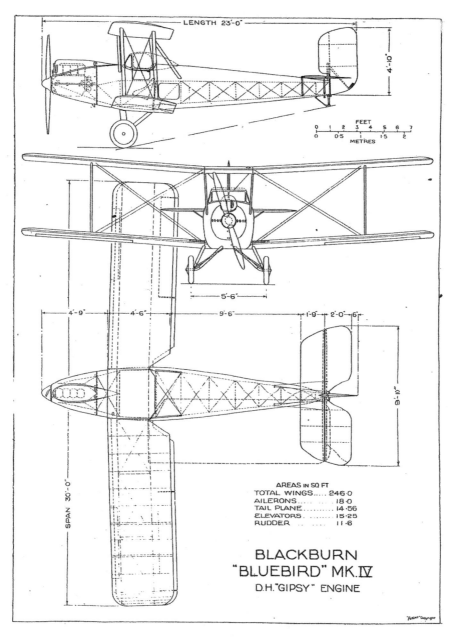

LENGTH 23'-0"

4'-10"

FEET
0 1 2 3 4 5 6 7
0   0·5   1   1·5   2
METRES

5'-6"

4'-9"   4'-6"   9'-6"   1'-9" 2'-0" 6"

9'-10"

SPAN 30'-0"

AREAS in SQ FT
TOTAL WINGS..... 246·0
AILERONS........... 18·0
TAIL PLANE.......... 14·56
ELEVATORS......... 15·25
RUDDER ...... 11·6

BLACKBURN
"BLUEBIRD" MK.IV
D.H."GIPSY" ENGINE

THE BLACKBURN "BLUEBIRD," MARK IV : General Arrangement Drawings. The machine is shown fitted with a " Gipsy " engine, but can also be supplied with either " Cirrus III " or " Genet." When the latter engine is used, the main planes are slightly swept back.

(Courtesy of Brough Heritage Centre)

once, and was told that the teaching staff was too busy to fit her in for another two weeks. "That's absolutely useless," she said, "because I'm flying around the world in little more than a fortnight, and I simply must have a lesson today." Whether it was due to her characteristic persistence or her reputation as one of Britain's best known auto and motorboat racers, she claimed she got her first flying lesson that very day.

Mary later attributed the ease with which she learned to fly to the side-by-side seating arrangement in the Bluebird, which made instruction and demonstration by the instructor far easier than the traditional front seat/back seat arrangement common in other small airplanes of the era. An article in a 1929 issue of *Flight* magazine pointed out that it was originally thought that the effect of side-by-side seating would be a decrease in performance—a misconception that was quickly disproved by the Blackburn Bluebird. Side-by-side seating was a tremendous boon to aviation in general, encouraging as it did easier instruction and far more enjoyable flying for two people together.

After a week of daily lessons, Mary wrote, she soloed. She later noted, ruefully, that an ambulance had been standing by during that flight, and that all the other planes on the landing field had been moved out of her way when she returned. 'Every machine had disappeared,' she wrote, 'their owners having pushed them under cover for safety!'

Private pilot's licence #2855 was issued on 26 July 1930. Mary's four-by-six inch pilot's log book gives her name as 'Hon. Mrs. Victor Bruce', and her residence as 'The Woodbines, Esher, Surrey'. The date of her last physical exam was June 1930, with no problems noted. The printed entry for 'Past experience as a pilot: Military' is blank; under 'Civil' is the notation 'First logbook'.

Forty hours of flying time is recorded: the first 32 were in a Blackburn Bluebird, and under the heading 'Number of accidents' is one—a 'forced landing owing to weather', with a resulting 'broken undercarriage'. The remaining eight hours required for a licence were flown in a Gipsy Moth. Turning the page after the 40 hours of solo time reveals the simple heading: 'World Flight'.

Mary's pilot training had been short but intense, with long hours of practise. Besides learning and practising the mechanical skills of operating the aircraft, she plunged into the intricacies of navigation, rising at 4 o'clock each morning to study. A master mariner was engaged to teach her this complicated but necessary component of flying in just six lessons. She wrote: 'He was naturally a little dubious about it and I shall never forget the politeness with which he concealed his despondency when leading me to a blackboard in his office he drew a series of chalk lines on it and remarked, "Now, you see those meridians?" "Meridians?" I said, "What are they?" They might have been a range of mountains for all I knew, and my instructor realized that he had to start right from the very beginning. Almost every post brought me diagrams, picturesque drawings of lightships, and similar matters which I had to swot up before the next lesson. They say that prominent men such as Mr. Joseph Chamberlain and Mr. Lloyd George experience a distinct enlargement of the forehead as a result of their concentrated brainwork. I can believe it, for without exaggeration after this condensed instruction, my head became a good quarter of an inch larger and I actually had to change my previously quite comfortable flying helmet for a larger size. My friends, as one might expect, said that I had just had an ordinary attack of swollen head, but whatever the cause, there is no doubt about the effect."[6]

The Blackburn Bluebird was available with a variety of equipment; Mary had selected a 120 hp DeHavilland Gipsy engine, as well as an assortment of options including screw pickets, mooring cables, and a shoulder safety strap. Modifications were made to Mary's Bluebird at the Blackburn factory in Brough, near Hull. The passenger seat was removed and an auxiliary fuel tank was installed in its place, increasing the Bluebird's fuel capacity from 22 to 90 gallons and giving Mary a range in excess of one thousand miles. A hand pump was utilised to transfer fuel from the auxiliary tank to the main tank, which then fed fuel to the engine by gravity. The auxiliary tank was covered over with decking, making her Bluebird a single-seater.

Mary's diminutive stature presented the same difficulty in the Bluebird as it had in the big Bentley. The pilot's seat was raised so that she could see out the windows without sitting on pillows.

She had quickly learned the skill of flying, and had diligently studied the art of navigation. But she steadfastly refused to learn Morse code, rejecting that cumbersome form of radio communication. As an alternative, the Blackburn mechanics fitted the Bluebird with a long-range wireless transmitter that was capable of automatically sending a clockwork-driven Morse signal at 15-minute intervals. The device was patterned on transmitters developed during World War I for use on small steamers that carried no radio operators. There was no capacity for receiving any radio calls, but Mary could initiate any one of five possible signals by putting a plug into the appropriate socket on a control panel in the cockpit. The signals were: 'OK—normal flight'; 'LG—making normal landing'; 'MP—flying, but engine or aircraft unsatisfactory'; 'FA—making forced landing ashore'; and 'SOS—making dangerous descent, possibly in water, require immediate assistance'. She was warned not to use the 'SOS' except in the direst emergency, since it would probably cost the British Government several thousand pounds to send out a rescue team for her.

The broadcast signals could be received by wireless operators on the ground. The Radio Society of Great Britain organised hundreds of amateur wireless enthusiasts all over the world who would listen for Mary's transmissions from the Bluebird. Any operator receiving the signal would re-transmit it immediately to a station near London[7] where it would be interpreted. If needed, a message could then be sent to the nearest ground station equipped to offer whatever assistance she required.

The automatic radio transmitter came at a significant price. Adding its weight to the Bluebird necessitated cutting the fuel capacity by ten gallons—an hour's flying, Mary calculated. Still, the ability to send a message when needed seemed worth it, and she was glad to make the concession.

This was not the only decision that was affected by the capacity of the Bluebird. Mary was determined to record her impressions along the way, and settled on a Dictaphone as the perfect solution. She could talk as she flew, without removing her hands from the plane's controls, and when one record was full she could mail it home to Victor. It was an innovative use for a piece of equipment that previously had been used primarily in business offices, where letters were dictated for later transcription by typists. Common sense decreed that she should take a parachute as well, but the weight of the Bluebird was already at its maximum capacity, and a choice had to be made between the Dictaphone and a parachute. The Blackburn mechanics looked to her for a decision, but it was Victor who settled the matter by saying "For Heaven's sake, let her take the Dictaphone! She'll never be happy unless she's talking!"

The crew at Blackburn's Brough facility spent more than two weeks making modifications to Mary's Bluebird, working long hours to ensure that it would be airworthy and properly equipped for a very long flight. The Air Ministry assigned registration letters for the Bluebird: G-ABDS. This identifier was to be painted on the airplane, and used in all official references to name the craft. A visitor to Brough noticed the letters being painted on the Bluebird's wings and asked Blackburn's head engineer what they stood for. "A Bloody Daft Stunt," he replied.

On Sunday, 21 September, Mary's new Bluebird was flown from Brough to Heston Aerodrome. Mary and Victor stored more supplies in the small luggage compartments: a bottle of water, a few packets of crackers, her clothing and personal items, an alarm clock. On Tuesday Mary filed her flight plan with the Air Ministry, giving a destination of Nuremberg, Vienna, or Budapest. No further destination was required.

The press had been speculating all summer about her plans. Well-known as a racing car driver and motorboating speedster, Mary's venture into the skies came as little surprise to anyone, despite her previous protestations that she had always hated the thought of flying. But she was the epitome of the adventurous woman of that era; she had announced that she intended to make a long flight, leaving in September. That answered the 'Who?' and 'When?' Her reputation as a daredevil answered the 'Why?' although she later elaborated for one interviewer that she had set out to prove that 'a pilot of little experience could, in an all-British light aeroplane, undertake really long distance flights with comparative safety.'

The burning question in the newspapers was 'Where?'. Every reporter had a guess, but Mary refused to give a specific answer. She later claimed that her evasiveness was deliberate; if she did not announce her intention to fly around the world, she could not then be embarrassed by negative publicity if she failed to reach that goal. But her avowed aim of visiting her mother's birthplace and her desire to eclipse at least the first part of Amy Johnson's record (from England to India) had clearly shaped her goal of a solo circumnavigation. She would not merely try to shorten Johnson's time; she would go for her own glory, as the first person to fly from England to Japan.

As take-off neared, there were still conflicting reports in the press. Speculation abounded; she was variously rumoured to be heading for Tokyo, Alexandria, Cape Town, Australia, and around the world. One interviewer quoted Mary as saying that she was undecided whether to attempt an around-the-world flight or to join the expedition to fly to the South Pole. "Two things are certain," she said, "I am determined to embark on a lone flight no woman has yet attempted, and I will start the end of next month."

~

That is the way Mary always told the story, but it is clear that her keen appreciation for drama coloured the way she related the events leading up to her world flight. The picture of a woman buying an airplane on a whim, taking six days of flying lessons, and setting off around the world in a few weeks' time was captivating. Most—but not all—of the elements of Mary's story are accurate.

It was hardly a spur of the moment inspiration that propelled her into the air. As early as the fall of 1928, Mary had taken note of the mounting popularity of aviation; the combination of speed and adventure that flying promised undoubtedly attracted her. The British government was subsidizing 13 private flying clubs; London's Mayfair Flying Club reported ten letters from interested women for every one from a man. At that time the Air Ministry was offering scholarships for women who could not afford the fees for instruction, but many women taking lessons had no need for scholarships. Wealthy and socially prominent women—among them Lady Heath, Lady Bailey, and the Duchess of Bedford—took to the air with enthusiasm. One of the members of the Mayfair Flying Club was Mary Bruce.[8]

In January 1930, Mary competed in her fourth and last Monte Carlo Rally, driving a Hillman Segrave Straight 8 saloon from Sundsvaal, Sweden. Even as her attention was focused on the road before her, her growing interest in the skies was being noted by a newspaper columnist called Jehu who wrote: 'The Hon. Mrs. Victor Bruce's name must have, in some previous incarnation, been Alexander or else Columbus, for there are no elements which she seems not to desire to conquer. At the present time Monte Carlo via Lapland is her latest objective and, that being accomplished, it would appear that she is anxious to get off the earth altogether, and appear in the light of a pilot of her own Moth aeroplane. She will do it, and do it well of course, but I am told she will find it very dull and certainly all her innumerable friends will miss her very much if she refuses to come back to her native element. Not that I am afraid. Cars have her heart, and I have an idea that the aeroplane will share with the motorboat a mere also-ran in her affections.'[9] Days later, newspapers carried a photograph of Mary at Heston Aerodrome, standing before the Hillman saloon—and her Gipsy Moth aeroplane—long before that 'wintry summer day' when she was struck by the sight of the Blackburn Bluebird in Burlington Gardens. There is, however, no indication that she actually flew any airplane until months later.

It can hardly be a coincidence that Mary had her first flying lesson on 25 May 1930—the very day after Amy Johnson landed in Darwin, Australia.[10] Along with adrenaline, fame was Mary's drug of choice. She was, after all, England's reigning queen of speed and endurance in race cars and speedboats; could she allow Amy Johnson to retain that title in the air? Unthinkable!

It was 22 June before Mary first flew solo, Victor recorded in his diary; her pilot's licence was issued five weeks later, on 26 July. The following day Victor was her first passenger, for a short flight from Brooklands to Heston.

All during August the Bruces made flights around southern England, often to the Isle of Wight. It was 12 September before Victor and Mary drove from their home in Esher to the Blackburn factory at Brough to see what Victor called "her new Bluebird." Mechanics and engineers at Blackburn's factory had been working for weeks on the necessary modifications and preparation.

The charming story Mary related of the startling sight of the Bluebird in the shop window in Burlington Gardens is probably true. But the question that was answered that June day was not 'Shall I take up flying?' It was 'Is this the airplane that can take me on a journey that will outshine Amy Johnson?' The matter was settled when the salesman answered "Of course, Madam!" to Mary's query "Could one fly round the world in this?"

Mary freely admitted that she adored the limelight.[11] Given the adulation and gifts heaped upon Amy Johnson after her flight to Australia, what kind of lavish reward could Mary expect if she circled the globe alone?

11   Up and Away

It was long before dawn on the morning of 25 September 1930 when Mary and Victor arose in their Esher cottage; by 4 a.m. they were on their way to Heston Aerodrome.

On a last-minute shopping trip to nearby Kingston-on-Thames the night before, Mary had purchased a small leather bag to hold her passport and logbook. Its shoulder strap, she noted, would make it easier to carry if she had a forced landing and had to walk for help. She slipped one final item into the bag: Victor had given her his cherished pocket compass. Lighter in weight and sturdier than a standard navigating compass, it would prove useful if she got lost—something, Victor teased, she was frequently liable to do.

An hour before departure, Mary still had not chosen a name for her airplane. Friends had suggested many names and she struggled to make her choice. It struck her, she said, like choosing wallpaper; she always seemed to like the last one best. But the decision could be put off no longer, and eventually she decided 'It has a name already and I will not change it. It is a Blackburn Bluebird, and *Bluebird* it shall remain!' A Heston mechanic fetched a jar of paint and a brush, and Mary—flying coat, helmet, goggles and gloves already in place—hastily painted 'Bluebird' on the fuselage.

She was seated in the cockpit by 7 a.m., and the final pre-flight checks were made. She mentally reviewed the provisions stowed aboard: several small tins of biscuits, chocolates, and a flask of brandy. 'So little of it, yet enough, if all goes well,' she wrote. 'Anyway, I shall not have time to eat much. It will be like watching the map of the world unroll beneath my feet, flying into the rising sun.' She hastily wrote more last-minute thoughts: 'Sitting in this cramped cockpit and scribbling my last notes before setting out on the greatest venture of my life, I am conscious of a great peace. Away in front, fingers of mist wreathe the trees, making them appear ghostlike, and there is a subdued murmur of talk from the mechanics who are putting the finishing touches to the Bluebird. For weeks I have lived in a whirl. Plans, maps, distances, figures that dance like motes in a sunbeam. Oh, and the advice I have received! Words, arguments pouring over me like a cascade: discussions of weight, load, petrol capacity, and a hundred and one details. The Bluebird carries 80 gallons of petrol, sufficient for a hop of a little more than a thousand miles. Will that prove enough if I meet with headwinds over the Burma jungles?'

"It is a Blackburn Bluebird, and 'Bluebird' it shall remain!"

She looked out again at the small crowd of onlookers, among them her father and her ten-year-old son, Tony. Victor stood by the right wing of the Bluebird as the mechanic shouted, "Contact!"

"Yes, contact!" she replied.

"Switch off, suck in!"

"Switch off!" she repeated.

The mechanic slowly pulled the propeller over and she heard another "Contact!" followed by the sputter and cough of the engine. It caught and idled, ticking like a giant watch. She sat tensely while the engine warmed up, feeling cold in spite of her leather jacket and helmet. The signal came at last, and she opened the throttle and heard the engine rev up. She called "All set!" and the mechanic pulled the chocks from the wheels and the Bluebird began to roll. She saw the waving hands of her friends, she wrote, 'and hats being slowly raised, and somehow I was reminded of a passing funeral'.

Victor, still holding the right wing, walked beside the little plane as she taxied across the field and then turned into the wind. Mary leaned out of the cockpit to share a farewell kiss with Victor, thinking how much worse it is to be the one left behind. With a final 'Goodbye' and 'Don't forget to put the milk out for the cat!' she pushed the stick forward. The Bluebird gathered speed slowly under the heavy weight and she felt the wheels leave the ground. 'Don't be in a hurry to get her up' had been her instructor's last words of warning. She rose slowly, but comfortably cleared the hangars and clubhouse. She circled the aerodrome, leaned out to wave to the little group below, and struck out in the direction of Lympne and the English Channel.

Leaving Heston Aerodrome at dawn on 25 September 1930
(Courtesy of Wiltshire Swindon Archives)

Mary's confidence grew as the sun rose over the English Channel; she sent her first wireless message: 'Flying OK'. She spotted Cap Griz Nez on the French coast, and continued on past Calais. She saw boats below, and must have reflected on the fact that she had now crossed the Channel by two very different modes of travel. Farther up the coast she flew over Dunkirk, and turned east toward Brussels. Beyond the Belgian capital, ground mist made navigation more difficult. Ninety minutes later she spotted the mighty Rhine River at Cologne; she followed it south to Frankfurt.

Four hours had elapsed since departure, and she had covered 420 miles. She was pleased to note that she was making better time than she had figured, but dark clouds were visible to the southeast and she took careful note of the location of the large airport at Frankfurt as she flew over it, in case she needed to turn back and land.

Less than half an hour later the rain began. With more mountainous country ahead—several ranges of hills and mountains lay between her and Vienna, her goal for the day—she turned back and landed at Frankfurt to get a weather report.

The news was not good. The Meteorology Office at the airport told her that even the airmail plane had not been able to get through because of bad weather. She was advised to try for Munich instead; she would encounter marginally better weather and would fly over significantly smoother terrain. Aloft again, she skirted several storms on the way south; it was nearly dark by the time she landed at Munich. At her hotel, she put in a call to Victor at once. She announced proudly, "I'm here!"

"Where?" he enquired; "In Kent?"

'He was overjoyed,' she wrote, 'on learning that I had made so good a journey, and told me that none of my friends had expected that I should succeed in getting out of England. They thought I should probably come down before reaching the Channel'.

Budapest was her second day's goal, but the smell of fuel altered her plan. She was still one hundred miles west of Vienna; could a tank be leaking? Uneasy, she was relieved to land at Vienna at last. An inspection revealed that a crack had developed in the smaller of the Bluebird's two fuel tanks. Two mechanics worked through the night to make repairs.

The third morning of her journey brought better weather, greatly easing the task of navigation. Good visibility from the cockpit was crucial: not only did stormy weather threaten the Bluebird's stability, it also obscured landmarks below. Mary had two primary navigational aids: one was her stack of maps from the Automobile Association, showing roads, rivers, and mountains. The other was the network of railway lines connecting cities and towns, which enabled pilots to follow the tracks, in a practice they called 'flying by Bradshaw'.[1]

Grateful for a clear sky, Mary was easily able to follow the Danube from Vienna all the way to Budapest. Landing long enough for lunch and a weather report, she continued along the Danube to Belgrade. She found the Yugoslavian capital unexpectedly festive: a holiday celebration was in progress, and there were throngs of peasants dressed in colourful costumes. Strolling the brightly lit boulevards that evening, she realised that the weather had warmed over the course of her journey. She wrote, 'I was thoroughly enjoying my adventure. It seemed marvellous to have flown so quickly out of cold weather into this lovely warm sunshine, and I was longing for tomorrow and the still warmer climate of Constantinople.'

Mary was at the aerodrome at dawn; the Bluebird had been refuelled, and she took off into cloudless skies. She followed a railroad and the Morava River southeast across the northern plains of the Balkan Peninsula toward Sofia, but soon was over hills of increasing altitude. Flying low over the winding railroad tracks, Mary was threading her way through the Dragoman Pass, with high mountains on either side—when she got the fright of her life: 'Suddenly the railroad took a sharp turn,' she wrote, 'and before being able to see what lay beyond, I found myself confronted with a barrier of mountain. The sides of the gorge had closed together and the railway had disappeared into a tunnel. Travelling at a hundred miles an hour, there was not time for me to turn or climb. Not knowing what to do, I threw the machine over on its side and somehow found myself facing the other way. I made up my mind to climb higher before turning back to clear the gorge, but this was easier said than done, for I found myself in a valley of still air. As soon as I got a little height I dropped again into a downward current. It took me nearly an hour circling this enclosed valley before I managed to get sufficient height to clear the side of the gorge. I had learned my lesson: never again would I fly low over railways running through gorges which left me nothing but a railway tunnel for an exit. Later it struck me how funny I should have looked if I had flown into the tunnel and come out the other end all covered with soot.'

She was more than a little relieved to leave the pass behind and sight Bulgaria's capital city, Sofia, with majestic Mt. Vitos towering 15,000 feet in the background. From Sofia, Mary's guide was the Marica River, flowing east past the ancient city of Philippopolis. The river turned south to the Aegean Sea, while Mary continued east to Constantinople. Founded by Greeks as Byzantium around 660 B.C., this great city occupied a strategically vital position for trade and warfare in the ancient world. It was renamed for Constantine in the fourth century A.D., who

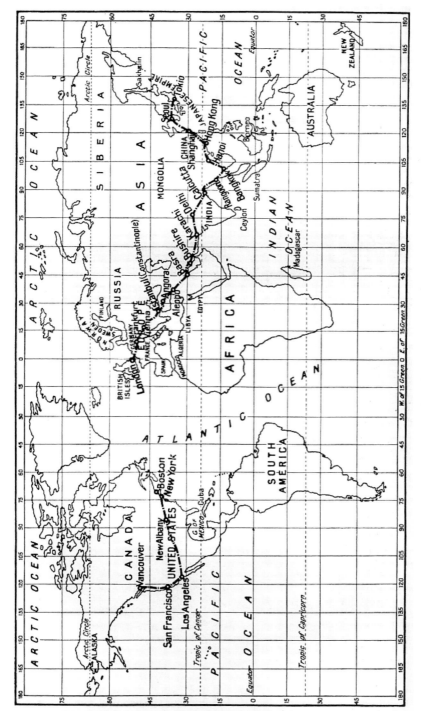

The Bluebird's flight

101

chose it as the capital of his new Eastern Roman—or Byzantine—Empire. In 1930 the name was changed again, to Istanbul, although Westerners continued to call it Constantinople for decades; that was undoubtedly the name by which Mary thought of it.

It was nearly dark when she landed at Stamboul Aerodrome on the outskirts of the city. The ancient cities of Turkey held special interest for Mary, but she had been warned before leaving England that the entire Turkish Republic might be off limits to her. The government of the new Republic of Turkey was suspicious of foreign visitors, and Mary's welcome was not cordial. She was forbidden to take off from Constantinople until she obtained an exit visa, and the officials claimed that her wireless set was 'not in order for Turkey'.

She had planned to fly next to Aleppo, in Syria. The distance was about seven hundred miles, beyond the Taurus Mountains, and Mary was concerned that, with headwinds, she would not have enough fuel for the flight. Could she land and refuel halfway, she enquired? The Turkish officials were adamant. "We can't possibly allow you to land in Asia Minor! If you do, you will probably be held up for some weeks; all our aerodromes are secret!" One official suggested that she try to obtain permission to land from the Governor at Angora. He was a very vain man, the official confided, and gullible too; if Mary were to tell him that she had flown all the way from England because she wanted to shake his hand, he would believe her. She would leave a visit to the Governor as a last resort, she decided, and head directly to Aleppo. With luck, loading an additional ten gallons of fuel should give her the range she needed.

It did not. She had flown less than one hundred and fifty miles when she realized that her fuel would never hold out for the entire hop to Aleppo. Near Eski-shehr, one of Turkey's 'secret military aerodromes', she turned north toward Angora, intending to seek out the Governor for permission to land and refuel.

Approaching Angora, Mary scanned the terrain for the aerodrome. She circled for nearly twenty minutes, searching without success. With the fuel gauge dipping dangerously close to 'empty' she decided on an emergency alternative. She spotted a level green field right in the middle of town, big enough for an easy landing. Unfortunately, it turned out to be a stadium, filled with football fans watching a match. She swooped low, hoping to clear the field, but the surprised throng below only looked up and waved in delight. She circled, then swooped in again, even lower; there were more waves of delight.

Inspiration struck. Mary was carrying smoke bombs for use in finding the direction of the wind. On the third pass she dropped one. Her aim was perfect; the bomb burst with a cloud of dust and smoke, right in the middle of the players. As the crowd scattered, she landed. 'They immediately rushed back to the aeroplane,' she wrote, 'and I was a trifle nervous that they might think I was actually bombing them, so I snatched off my flying helmet and started to comb my hair, to show that I was a woman and that they mustn't dare to hurt me.'

Not knowing a word of the Turkish language, Mary tried her schoolgirl French to explain that she had come to see the Governor. Someone in the crowd understood, and a car was brought alongside; and she was escorted to the his official residence. Surrounded by guards, she was taken to the severe-looking Governor. Mary explained that she had flown all the way from England for the express purpose of shaking his hand. Fortunately the Governor was also fluent in French.

"You have come all this way just to see me?" he exclaimed.

"Yes," she replied, hanging her head in her best attempt at sheepishness.

"Ah!" he said, "*Mon petit oiseau bleu!* You have the freedom of Turkey. I will immediately signal to all the aerodromes and tell them to give you every assistance possible!"

He kept his word, even ordering her plane refuelled before she took off from the stadium. She landed that night as Eski-shehr, the largest and finest of Turkey's many military aerodromes, and was greeted by the Commandant and officers. She was their guest at supper, and they provided her lodging for the night.

In the morning, the Commandant told her that less-than-ideal flying weather was predicted for the Taurus Mountains to the south; if it was too severe after she passed Konia, she should return and land there. He sent a military plane to escort her on a shortcut through the mountains. Above Konia, the escort waved goodbye and Mary followed the tracks of a railway crossing the great Salt Desert toward the Taurus Mountains.

As she approached the mountains at midday, the force of the winds mounted. Reluctant to turn back, Mary flew on. By early afternoon, thunder and lightning added to her anxiety. Stubbornly she carried on, ignoring the warning of the Commandant at Eski-shehr. She reminded herself of the advice she'd been given when learning to fly: no matter how bad the bumps from turbulent air may be, or how much they make you feel as though your aeroplane is going to fall to pieces, they never really cause any serious trouble, only minor discomforts to the pilot.

Near disaster was the result of Mary's decision to continue. The turbulence had blown some oil onto the windscreen, partially obscuring her vision. She reached over the top to wipe it away and knocked the rudder just as the plane was falling into an air pocket. Suddenly the Bluebird was in a spin, rushing toward the earth just 500 feet below. Frantically Mary made a grab at the rudder. She managed to regain control and pull out of the spin a mere twenty feet above the ground.

Enormous black clouds filled the sky, threatening more violent weather. Shaken, Mary turned the Bluebird back toward Konia. She was now flying into headwinds that she estimated at 40 to 50 mph; she managed to cover only 50 miles in two hours. Her fuel was running low, and she knew she would have to land soon. Anxiously she scanned the desolate terrain below. A solitary railroad line bisected the bleak landscape. Struggling against the howling winds, Mary managed to land beside the tracks.

12 Unhappy Landings

Mary's first concern was the Bluebird's safety. The fierce gale that had buffeted her so in the air was equally strong on the ground. Fearing that a strong gust would blow the little plane over, she quickly pulled out cables and screw pickets and secured the Bluebird to the ground.

Help soon appeared in the form of a peasant, driving his horse-drawn wagon along the road beside the tracks. No common language was needed as he took in the situation, looked from the Bluebird to the pilot, and gestured for her to climb into the seat beside him. He handed her a bunch of grapes, which she gratefully devoured; she had not eaten since breakfast at Eski-Shehr.

It was a two and a half hour ride to the ancient city of Konia, perched on a plateau at the south-west edge of central Turkey. To Mary's western eyes, Konia was a wonder, filled with strange sights and unfamiliar sounds and smells. Within the high walls of the city, ancient buildings were crowded together along narrow, winding cobblestone streets filled with ragged peasants. Veiled women peeped at her from narrow windows as the driver gestured for Mary to climb down from the wagon and follow him on foot.

Up a steep hill they went, with a growing crowd of curious villagers following. At the summit, they were stopped by a sentry guarding the gate of the imposing home of the Governor of the province of Konia. The peasant spoke to the sentry at length, and Mary was led to the Governor. Fortunately he spoke French and understood as Mary explained her presence. She was careful to let him know of her meeting with the Governor of Angora, and that she had been given the freedom of Turkey. The Governor of Konia, obviously not to be outdone, immediately welcomed her and escorted her to the home of his mother. The elderly woman, bedridden for years, was fascinated by this extraordinary and unexpected visitor. Over tea, she and the Governor listened attentively as Mary explained her goal of circling the world.

After tea the Governor took Mary outside the city walls to a derelict hovel in which lived a local celebrity of sorts. An old man came out to greet them. Mary described him thus: 'His face was a picture, covered with thousands of wrinkles, which reminded me of an elephant's hide. At first I could not imagine why the Governor had brought me to see him, and when he came toward me I edged away from him because he seemed to be encrusted with the dust of centuries.' The Governor reassured her, declaring that this was the oldest man in the world, and to be touched by him would bring good luck. Rather than offend anyone, and probably reflecting that she could use every bit of good luck available, Mary allowed the old fellow to put his hands on her shoulders.

She spent the night at the Governor's house and awoke to continued threatening weather. She was taken—by car this time—to the Bluebird, which had been guarded overnight by a party of soldiers sent out by the Governor. She managed to take off without difficulty, except that the soldier who had gallantly offered to swing the propeller for her suffered some badly bruised knuckles for his trouble, when the engine backfired.

As Mary flew south, thick black clouds still towered over the imposing Taurus Mountains. Reluctantly she changed course to avoid the highest peaks, skirting the mountains and bringing her finally to her first sighting of the Mediterranean.

She flew along the coastline of the Gulf of Iskenderun, crossing into Syria late in the afternoon. Mary kept a worried eye on her fuel gauge; the detour around the Taurus Mountains had added many miles to her route, and her goal of Aleppo seemed more out of reach with every passing minute. The needle on the gauge ticked over to the danger mark when she was still sixty miles from Aleppo. Having heard that the natives in that part of Syria could be unruly and inhospitable, she considered flying on—but concluded that running out of fuel in midair was even a more dangerous option than facing a hostile reception on the ground.

She landed on the hard sand of the desert, and almost immediately several men came running down the hill and surrounded the Bluebird. Another man rode up on horseback. Clearly the chief of the band, he gestured insistently for Mary to climb up on the back of his horse. Refusing did not seem to be an option; she and the Bluebird might be left alone in the middle of the desert without fuel—or worse. She hesitated only a moment, and soon was seated uneasily behind the man. He had the saddle, while she sat on the bare and bony backbone of the horse. He made a point of admiring her wristwatch and, rather than risk annoying him, she took it off and gave it to him.

After a long, uncomfortable ride, they reached a small village of poor huts and hovels. It did not look like the sort of place where fuel would be available, but Mary was delighted to see a disreputable old Ford automobile coming toward them along the camel track—there must be a fuel supply nearby, she reasoned.

Her optimism turned to anxiety, however, after she dismounted from the horse and found that the driver was an aggressive Armenian who immediately began loudly demanding "*Baksheesh! Baksheesh!*" She handed him about £1—equivalent to roughly £50 today— but he demanded still more. Eventually he gestured for Mary to get into his automobile, and he drove her to the village where he led her to a dirty little shop. After more argument and more demands for '*Baksheesh!*' Mary was able to purchase a can of fuel. She climbed back into the Ford, but the chief who had taken her most of the way to the village on his horse also began loudly demanding money, jumping onto the back of the car and shaking his fist. Mary clung to the can of fuel, and finally was returned to her little airplane—minus her wristwatch and nearly £5 cash.

The sun had gone down, and Mary hurried to refuel the Bluebird and get under way again. She had never taken off at night, nor tried to find an unfamiliar aerodrome and land in the dark, but the prospect of spending a night among these disagreeable men was all the incentive she needed to make the attempt.

The sound of jingling bells reached her ears as she was about to start the engine. In amazement she watched as a troop of uniformed soldiers of the French Foreign Legion wearing red fezzes galloped up, led by an officer riding a white Arabian horse. Mary pushed her way through the crowd of Armenians and desert tribesmen to the leader, tapped him on the arm and declared "*C'est moi!*"

She wrote, 'I shall never forget the look and smile that came over his face as he saw me with no hat, covered with oil and grime from the aeroplane, and standing among all these priceless people, gasping "*C'est moi!*" ' The officer detailed some of his soldiers to guard the airplane overnight, offered Mary one of the best of his horses, and she rode with the men to their small military outpost. She was fussed over and given a room for the night. The soldier whose room was commandeered for her use went out and picked a bunch of wildflowers to put by her bed. A phone call was made to the Commandant of the airfield at Aleppo, to arrange for a mechanic to come in the morning to help start the Bluebird.

Needless to say, Mary was having a grand time. 'It had all been just like a fairy story—these horsemen riding up just at the critical moment. It seemed that everything was going right with me on this trip, for when I was met with all kinds of adversities, something always turned up at the eleventh hour—some miraculous aid—to straighten things out.'

As promised, help from Aleppo appeared in the morning. Mary was already out at the Bluebird when a huge monoplane arrived, bearing not only a mechanic but the Commandant of the airfield. The Bluebird was started easily, and Mary flew to Aleppo to refuel. By 9:30 a.m. she was on her way south again, hoping to make Baghdad that day.

Mary followed the Euphrates River eastward, peering down at the picturesque and well-preserved ruins of ancient Mesopotamian villages. Two more hours brought her to the Tigris River and a landing at Baghdad. She took a taxi to her hotel, soaking up the exotic sights of the cosmopolitan city as she passed. She longed to have more time to linger, describing Baghdad as 'ablaze with life and colour and teeming with people of various nationalities'.

Several English journalists interviewed Mary over dinner, anxious for details of her adventures. One reporter elaborated on her account of the rescue by the French Foreign Legion west of Aleppo. The story he filed with his London paper gave Victor a scare when he wrote that Mary had been abducted by a sheik.

At sunrise she was off again, following the Tigris south toward the Persian Gulf. Less than an hour south of Baghdad she passed over the ancient town of Ctesiphon, photographing the well-preserved ruins of its palace's great vaulted audience room. Only about fifty miles away lay the ruins of the legendary city of Babylon, but Mary did not dare stray that far from the Tigris, whose southward course was her main navigational aid. She knew that the dust storms common to the area could make navigation so difficult that the Royal Air Force did not permit its planes to fly alone in the region, but sent them aloft only in pairs. She stayed above the river, and contented herself with looking for signs of the reputed location of the Garden of Eden.

By mid-morning she reached Basra, landing to refuel at the Royal Air Force's Shaiba Aerodrome. The appearance of an English woman was a great event in the lonely and monotonous routine of the RAF officers stationed there; they tried to persuade Mary to stay for a day. She was impatient to leave, though, mindful of the approaching monsoon season in Southeast Asia.

In the air again she followed the Shatt-al-Arab, the great channel formed by the confluence of the Tigris and Euphrates Rivers, past the huge white tanks of the Abadan oil fields. Before noon the sparkling blue water of the Persian Gulf was in sight. Flying down the eastern shore of the Gulf along the coast of Persia, she reached the seaport city of Bushire around 3 p.m.

She was greeted there by mechanics of Imperial Airways, who had received a telegram from Basra to announce the Bluebird's arrival. Mary had been worrying for some days about oil loss from the Gipsy engine. She had fitted new washers at Constantinople, but the oil leakage continued. The mechanics suggested that she should wait there for two or three weeks so that replacement seals could be ordered from England; flying through the desolate stretches before her could be perilous if the Bluebird continued to lose oil. Mary, in her single-minded determination, could think only of the approaching monsoon weather; she rejected the idea of any delay.

She spent the evening as the guest of Colonel Biscoe, the British Resident. They discussed the next day's flight to Jask, a seaport city on the Gulf of Oman. The center of British colonial life in the Gulf area, Jask was an important cable station for the Indo-European Telegraph Department as well as the major Middle East base of operations for Imperial Airways.

Biscoe told Mary that there were two British ships lying at anchor near the island of Hanjam in the Strait of Hormuz. She agreed to swoop down over the ships and signal to them; he would alert them to be watching for her, and to wire him when she had arrived safely at that point. She also agreed to send Biscoe a wire upon her arrival in Jask.

In the morning she checked the Bluebird carefully, mindful of the oil leakage which had been plaguing her and the warnings of the Imperial Airways mechanics at Basra. Everything seemed in order, and her first Dictaphone note of the day was 'The time is 5 a.m. The sun is just coming up over the horizon and I have just left the landing ground at Bushire.'

Mary enjoyed flying low, in spite of her instructor's warning to 'keep high; flying low can be dangerous!' Interviewed years later, she recalled: 'I used to be almost at ground level; by flying low—about a hundred feet—I got the sense of speed. It was just as well the engine didn't cut out because I'd have had no place to land the thing!' Besides providing a closer look at the passing scene below, she found the air less turbulent at lower altitudes.

She was hoping to spot some sharks in the Gulf—it was reputedly infested with them—and was disappointed not to find any. The desolate scenery was monotonous and she longed for a bit of excitement: a shark sighting would have been a welcome diversion!

Mary was delighted to see the Union Jack flying from the masts of the two sloops lying at anchor near Hanjam. Throttling back, she glided down to within 50 feet above them, waving back at the men on the decks. She set her compass to 90 degrees and began the last leg of the day's journey. To her right she sighted the barren point of Ras Massandam, jutting north from the Arabian Peninsula. Passing this last finger of land, she struck out across the Strait of Hormuz; 100 miles of open water lay between her and her destination, Jask.

As she scanned the instrument panel, the last thing she wanted to see was the alarming sight before her: the oil pressure needle was dropping! Oil poured from the thrust race housing, splattering the windscreen. Acutely conscious of the threat of sharks in the water below, Mary strained her eyes for a glimpse of land ahead. Plugging in the wireless transmitter to broadcast 'Flying in trouble,' she reached for her Dictaphone. 'I am losing a great deal of oil from my engine, and am very anxious about it,' she recorded.

She adjusted her course. Jask was to the southeast; she would head due east, making for the closest point on the Persian coast. Minutes passed; she kept a steady gaze on the horizon, willing land to appear. Repeatedly she checked the oil gauge; the needle continued its slow downward movement. 'Oil failing rapidly, grave doubts whether engine will hold out long enough to reach land,' she recorded on the Dictaphone. In the distance a dark smudge of land appeared at last; the sight did little to buoy her spirits. 'This may be my end, as the oil pressure is down to naught. See land in distance, but fear engine will fail before I reach it.'

The Bluebird struggled on. Mary listened closely to the sound of the engine as the minutes ticked by. Approaching the coast, she was distressed to see a sandstorm blowing, severely limiting visibility. There was no chance of climbing above the swirling sand; the engine must be nearly bone dry.

Reaching once more for the Dictaphone she said: "Have reached the coast; am about to make a forced landing on the sand."

She recounts the dramatic story of her landing: "Closing the throttle, I decided to make a landing on the sand near the water, the only place possible, with the intention of filling up with fresh oil, a can of which I was carrying in the fuselage. As I landed I felt the wheels of the undercarriage sink, and the nose of the machine dive downwards. At the same time I was shot violently forward against the windscreen. Amid a deafening sound of splintering wood and a smell of escaping petrol, I found myself hanging by my straps, the tail of the machine bolt upright in the air, and the engine buried out of sight in the soft sand. I had landed on quicksand! Half dazed, I released myself, and realized that I was alone on the Persian Gulf in one of the most desolate stretches of desert on that coast."[1]

13 Life with the Baluchis

Free of her safety harness, Mary carefully climbed from the cockpit and slid to the sand below. The Bluebird stood silent in the fierce noonday sun, nose buried and tail pointing skyward. Mary looked with dismay at the empty landscape in which she found herself. Relief at having made solid ground—not quicksand, as she had feared at first—was tempered by the realization of her isolation, and by her apprehension about the extent of damage to the Bluebird. Mary sought shelter from the blistering heat under the wing of the airplane.

As desolate and empty as this shore of the Gulf of Oman appeared, the approach and crash-landing of the Bluebird had not gone unnoticed. From the shadow beneath the wing Mary saw in the distance a cluster of small black specks that grew as they approached; it was a band of desert tribesmen. They were Baluchis, members of one of the oldest tribes in the Middle East, with branches in what are now Pakistan and Afghanistan as well as Iran.

The men swarmed around Mary and the Bluebird, shouting angrily and flashing their knives. Knowing it could be fatal to show fear, she smiled and strode confidently up to the apparent leader, a fierce-looking old man with a flowing black beard. She shook his hand firmly, and the scowls of the tribesmen turned to smiles. Mary quickly made friends with the children in the group, and soon was playing games and laughing with them. When the tribesmen got restless she reached into the storage compartment and pulled out her alarm clock to amuse them. It was a game that kept them pacified for hours—watching with anticipation as Mary wound the clock, then exclaiming and dancing about when the bell rang.

Once she felt herself out of danger from the desert dwellers, she turned to the problems confronting her. Getting help was the first order of business. The wireless transmitter worked only when the engine was running so there was no way to send out a signal now. She wrote a quick message to the British Consul: 'Please send help. Have crashed. Mrs Bruce.' Using gestures, she indicated that someone should take the message to Jask. One of the tribesmen seemed to understand; he took the message and disappeared to the south.

Another concern was thirst. She had already drunk most of her small supply of water. Using sign language, she asked if she would be able to get more. The Baluchi chief nodded reassuringly.

Mary inspected the Bluebird, relieved to see that the major damage was a broken propeller. She was carrying a spare onboard, but still had some doubts about getting the little plane airborne again. The nose was buried four feet into the soft sand, and there was sure to be some grit in the engine. She dropped to her knees and began to dig the sand away from the nose. The engine cowling was bent, but there did not seem to be any other serious damage. After nearly an hour of digging she had cleared the sand away from the engine, but the winds that had whipped the sand into a storm when she crashed were still blowing, and threatened to blow the Bluebird over onto its back. With a shout, she called the Baluchis for help in righting the plane. She cheered when it fell with a gentle bump back onto its wheels, and the Baluchis happily took up her cries of pleasure. Joining hands they danced around the airplane, insisting that she join them.

As the suffocating heat of the day lessened slightly, she sat under the Bluebird's wing and studied her map. She was able to pinpoint her position exactly, since she had come down near a pinnacle of rock identified as Ras Mubarak. The map showed a village called Kuh-i-Mubarak some five miles distant, but there were no roads or even camel tracks anywhere in the vicinity. She was dismayed to see that Jask was more than 50 miles distant. Knowing that it was only a small settlement, with perhaps no more than a dozen or two Europeans stationed there, she wondered what kind of help her message could possibly produce—and how long it might take for help to reach her.

Mary had never been reluctant to get her hands dirty working on an engine. Since her first experience modifying her brother Louis's Matchless motorcycle, mechanical work had been second nature. She waited until the sun was down, then went to work on the Bluebird's propeller.

Her work was complicated by the fact that she was missing most of the tools she needed, and she surmised that they had been left in Bushire when the engine was last checked. She made do with her knife, scraping her hands as she worked. Once the spare propeller was in place, she turned to cleaning the sand from the engine with the only suitable tool she could find, a toothbrush. By nightfall she had cleaned the carburettor and spark plugs, added oil, and put back the damaged engine cowling so that—if help did arrive in the morning—the Bluebird would be ready to start.

To her relief, the Baluchi tribesmen brought her a sheepskin of brackish water.

Unappetizing as it was, she gratefully drank her fill and replenished her water bottle and thermos flask. As night fell, the tribesmen disappeared into the dark, going back to their home, which she later learned was in a date grove at Kuh-i-Mubarak. The old chief stayed to guard her, for which she was thankful.

It was a restless night for Mary. She slept under the wing of the plane, and constant desert winds continued to blow; she woke frequently, shaking off the sand that was blown over her in drifts. Lying wakeful in the dark, she listened for hours to the sounds of the waves breaking on the nearby shore and the wind whistling through the struts of the Bluebird above her.

At daybreak Mary arose and began tinkering with the Bluebird's engine. She started the engine, and tried without success to taxi to a packed-down area of sand she thought might be a camel track. But revving the engine caused the wheels to dig into the sand, and the nose threatened to dive into the sand again. Frustrated, she abandoned the attempt, realizing that she would need ropes and manpower to move the airplane to firmer ground.

When the Baluchis returned they brought more water, and some dates which, Mary saw with revulsion, were crawling with insects. Nauseated, she declined them, regretting that she had distributed most of her meagre supply of snacks among the Baluchi children the day before. She had been carrying chocolates and biscuits, and a supply of a meat concentrate called Brand's Essence[1], but in an effort to ensure her welcome, she had given nearly everything (including some of her treasured Ovaltine) to the Baluchis.

Around noon Mary spotted smoke on the horizon out to sea. Certain that it was ships coming to rescue her, she turned to the Baluchis and shouted "*Anglais, Anglais!*" 'I am sure I don't know why I should have imagined that they would understand French better than English,' she wrote, 'but they did seem to understand, and ran with me down to the seashore.' On the horizon two ships steamed out of sight as she waved her handkerchief in vain. They were searching for wreckage in the gulf, she surmised, not realizing that she could have made the shore.

Returning to the Bluebird, she saw several of the tribesmen and children seated in a circle with something in their hands which they were trying to eat, without success. It was, she discovered with amused annoyance, one of her Dictaphone records, which they apparently had mistaken for more chocolate. 'Judging from their expression, they were not enjoying their fare, but in the meantime they had spoiled the perfectly good message which I had made for my husband while crossing the Taurus Mountains.'

The blistering sun drove her under the shelter of the Bluebird's wing again, where she turned her attention to the problem of her painful hands. She had cut and scraped them while digging in the sand and working on the engine, and the wounds were festering badly. She began painting them with iodine from her first aid kit, which drew an immediate circle of fascinated Baluchis. They stuck their feet out, pointing at cuts, begging her to paint them as well. She complied, but the Baluchis danced in surprise when they felt the sting of the iodine.

Even after several hours with the Baluchis, Mary discovered that the chieftain still lacked one vital piece of information about her, when he produced a pipe from his pocket, filled and lit it, and passed it to her. She declined with a shake of her head, but he was insistent. Did the chief think she was a man, she wondered? With a short haircut, and bare-legged in shorts, could he have failed to note her gender? She reached for a comb and began combing her hair, and pointed at the female Baluchi children. Amazement showed on the face of the old chieftain as he exclaimed "*Y'ai, y'ai, y'ai!*"

'It did not do me much good letting them know I was a female,' she wrote, 'for from then onwards, anything which had to be done, such as filling up the Thermos flask with water or screwing the machine tighter down to the ground, had to be done by me. Also it seemed to worry the chief on finding I was a woman that I should be gallivanting about in shorts. Taking a big scarf from his head, he insisted that I should wrap it round my legs, with the consequence that I kept tripping over it every time I wanted to get something out of the airplane. Not satisfied with that, he seemed to want me to hang something over my face, which is the custom with the Baluchi women, and taking a piece of cardboard from one of the old Dictaphone boxes he put this up against my nose. Then I went on strike, and shaking my head said, '*N'ai, n'ai, n'ai!*' back to him.'

She napped in the afternoon, and was awakened by a crowd of Baluchi men running toward her from the sea, and shouting with excitement. They carried a large parcel wrapped in brown paper and laid it at her feet ceremoniously. Her heart leapt with joy as she read on the wrapper: 'Mrs. Bruce. Please deliver immediately. For the aeroplane G-ABDS. URGENT.' An airplane must have seen the downed Bluebird and dropped this from the air, she concluded. Eagerly she tore open the package—and out fell a mass of dead fish. Confounded, she turned the paper over, reading the words again. And then she remembered that, just before take-off from Heston, a special messenger had delivered a spare cylinder for the Bluebird. The Baluchis must have found the wrapping paper in the storage compartment and thought it would please her to receive the day's catch of fish in this special fancy packaging.

As evening approached, the Baluchis seemed to be getting restless, looking toward the mountains and gesturing. Mary surmised that something unpleasant was coming; the Baluchis took money from her bag and hid it in the cockpit. She had been told, in Bushire, of brigands in this area who tried to capture people who landed here, demanding ransom and killing the prisoners if they didn't get paid. After two hours she saw horsemen approaching out of the dusk. The Baluchis were huddled in a little group and were chattering among themselves; the chief was upset and tried to hide her. She insisted on walking out toward the approaching riders, intending to shake hands with them. She took the alarm clock with her, thinking that might help to pacify them, as it had the Baluchis.

There were three horsemen, well armed with rifles, revolvers, and bandoliers of cartridges slung around their shoulders. Mary approached the leader with a smile, and held up the ticking alarm clock for his entertainment. He brushed it aside impatiently, shouting "Rupee! Rupee!" She realized that these men were quite a different breed from the Baluchis, and led him back to the Bluebird. She handed him about £5 worth of rupees, which seemed to satisfy him.

The airplane intrigued the brigand leader. Dismounting from his horse, he approached the Bluebird, climbed into the cockpit, and began working the controls. He put on Mary's flying helmet and sat happily working the ailerons up and down and waggling the rudder. A lack of oil caused a squeaking, which added to his glee. His two companions stood by—one watching the leader with amusement, the other staring steadily at Mary, following her every move with a scowl. The brigand in the cockpit opened Mary's satchel and pulled out her evening gown. He tried to put it on, to the vast amusement of the other men. Tiring of the dress and the control panel, he climbed down and sat under the Bluebird, sharing a pipe with his companions. Mary noted with interest that his matches came from a box labelled 'Soviet Russia', and guessed that their up-to-date weapons came from there as well.

As they stood and prepared to leave, an argument arose between the brigand leader and the old Baluchi chieftain. Mary suspected that she was the subject of the argument, and her suspicion was confirmed when the brigand tried to lift her up onto his horse as he exclaimed "Jask! Jask!" She was willing to get on the horse with him if it meant a ride to Jask, but the old Baluchi chief pulled her behind the airplane and hissed at her "Jask? N'ya Jask!" while he motioned toward his own throat with his knife, and pointed to the mountains in the distance.

Mary understood that the chief was saying the brigands meant to take her away into the mountains; a friendly lift to Jask was definitely not on their agenda. She refused to go with them, gesturing at her airplane to indicate that she had to stay with it. Eventually they rode away, and all the Baluchis except the old chief drifted back to their settlement in the Kuh-i-Mubarak date grove. Grateful for his presence, Mary settled down for another restless night. She shivered in the cool desert air, regretting her impulsive generosity in giving her Burberry coat to a Baluchi tribesman who had clearly been taken with it.

At first light she was up, determined that she must get to Jask. She tried to communicate this to the old chieftain, but he adamantly shook his head "Jask! N'ya Jask!" She pointed to her feet, indicating that she would walk. He shook his head. With a stick she drew a picture of a camel in the sand. Another shake of the head. She insisted "Jask! Jask!" and finally the chief gathered her things together in her shoulder bag—the one she and Victor had bought the night before her departure—as she wrote on the wings and fuselage of the Bluebird 'I am walking to Jask.'

The chieftain led the way out across the desert toward the date grove. The heat was already merciless; Mary stumbled and fell more than once. After a couple of miles her shoes began to pinch her feet. She took them off, and left them in the sand. On they went, the chief leading the way and Mary struggling to keep up in the heat. She saw palm trees in the distance, and thought at first that she was seeing a mirage. Soon, though, she could make out dwellings among the trees, and she knew that they were approaching the tribesmen's encampment.

Reaching the trees at last, Mary collapsed, exhausted, in the shelter of the nearest tree. She was surrounded at once by the women of the Baluchi tribe. They were a strange sight, with veiled faces, nose rings, black-stained teeth, and long, dark garments. They reminded Mary of big black penguins, she wrote, as they stood in a semicircle around her, shaking their heads as they noticed her cuts and bruises. But their expressions were very friendly, and one of the women brought Mary a big bowl of goat's milk. She drank it gratefully.

She slept under the date palms until midmorning, when the Baluchis awakened her with great excitement, pointing out into the desert. Even at a distance, Mary could tell from their white sun helmets that the two men approaching were rescuers from Jask. Forgetting her exhaustion, she hurried out to meet them. She was weak with hunger, and crying with joy as they came together on the sand. The men carried her back to the oasis, where they were served breakfast by the Baluchi women—a feast of dates and goat's milk nicely augmented by the tea and tinned goods the rescuers had brought from Jask.

As they sat beneath the trees, Mary heard her rescuers' account. The Baluchi tribesman who carried her written message to Jask had made the trek in two days and two nights, including the crossing of seven shark-infested creeks. On the second evening he collapsed on the steps of the British-operated cable station in

Jask, after handing Mary's note to the British Political Officer, Mr. Murray.

Within two hours Murray had organised a rescue party, including a doctor, a ground engineer from Imperial Airways, two men from the cable station, and the Baluchi messenger. They packed a week's worth of provisions into a small sailing dhow and set off to locate Mary.

They sailed west and north along the coast toward the Bay of Bandar Abbas, arriving about 8 a.m. near the spot where Mary had crash-landed three days earlier. They made for the plane at once, and read the message she had left, 'I am walking to Jask'. The rescue party divided, with Mr Murray and Dr James setting off into the desert, following the footsteps that led toward the date grove at Kuh-i-Mubarak. The others stayed with the Bluebird, assisting George Wilson, the Imperial Airways ground engineer, as he inspected the plane. He was able to start the Bluebird's engine, but the group was unable to pull the plane to firm enough ground to taxi.

The men who followed the footsteps across the sand found Mary's shoes; worried that this was a sign of trouble, they hurried onward and soon met a Baluchi native who told them that she was safe in their village. They sent him to the plane to inform the rest of the rescue party and proceeded to the date grove and a happy meeting with the relieved pilot.

Stories exchanged, Mary and the rescue party went back to the Bluebird. The engine was running smoothly, and all that remained was to move the plane to firmer ground, which was accomplished with the help of a 30-strong gang of the Baluchi tribesmen. Mary bade farewell to the old chieftain, trying to express her gratitude to him for his protection and assistance. The rescue party had brought her money from Jask, and she made it a thank-you gift to the tribe.

Wilson, the engineer, insisted on flying with Mary back to Jask. Since the passenger seat had been removed when the auxiliary fuel tank was installed, there was no room for him in the cockpit. The engineer climbed onto the fuselage and lay face down, tightly gripping the back of the cockpit, for the 45-minute flight to Jask. Just at sunset the Bluebird landed and taxied to the Imperial Airways hangar for repairs. Spare parts had to be ordered from England. Mary knew that, facing several days of delay in this remote outpost, her race against the monsoon season was almost certainly lost.

In a letter to the Blackburn factory Mary wrote, 'We arrived with the oil pressure at zero and engine nearly red-hot. She would not have lasted another five minutes, but all's well that ends well, and the machine is OK.' She blamed the problems on 'the dreadful engine De Havilland supplied,' but said 'the little Bluebird has been wonderful—if only the engine had been as good!'

14 Desert to Jungle

At Jask, Mary waited impatiently. In spite of comfortable accommodations there—she was the houseguest of Mr Murray—Mary fretted over the lost time and the approach of the monsoon season. The heat was stifling, frequently over one hundred degrees. Lingering symptoms of dysentery, a result of the brackish water she had drunk in the desert, contributed to Mary's general malaise.

Jask was a regular refuelling stop for flights between northern Europe and India. There were twice-weekly visits by the Dutch airmail service and the London-based Imperial Airways; visitors and crews brought news from the outside world and provided lively chat in the evenings.

It was the middle of October when at last the replacement parts arrived by air from the Blackburn factory. Mary and George Wilson, the Imperial Airways ground engineer, got to work at once on the Bluebird's repairs. The engine had been thoroughly cleaned and prepared for fitting the new parts, but another three days' work was needed before Mary could test-fly the little airplane. She was tempted to fly back to the date grove at Kuh-i-Mubarak to try to spot some of her Baluchi friends but hesitated to do so, mindful of how dreadful it would be if anything went wrong and she had to land there again. Instead she tested the Bluebird by circling over Jask for two hours.

Later that same afternoon she was delighted to welcome fellow British pilot Oscar Garden to Jask. Garden was another novice, having earned his private pilot's licence the previous July, the same month as Mary. He had set out from England on 16 October, intending to fly to Australia in his second-hand Gipsy Moth to accumulate more air hours in an effort to earn a commercial licence.[1]

With the successful test flight behind her, Mary was eager to resume her trip, and she proposed to Garden that they fly the next leg of the trip together. On 20 October Mary took off from Jask at dawn, with Garden following. For the first two hundred miles they stayed within a few hundred yards of each other, both enjoying the companionship. At the seaport town of Charbar, Garden turned inland, preferring to fly over the hills while Mary—probably remembering her near disaster at the Dragoman Pass—opted for skimming along the water's edge.

They landed that afternoon at the seaport city of Karachi, on the Arabian Sea. The airfield was dominated by the shed that had recently been built to house Britain's giant new airship R101. The huge hangar stood empty and unused at the Karachi airfield, a sobering sight for the two novice flyers. The pioneering dirigible had crashed in France just two weeks earlier, on its maiden voyage to Egypt and India.[2]

Garden, hoping to set a new speed record to Australia, was anxious to push on. He left at dawn the next morning while Mary agreed to a one-day layover. The Karachi representative for the De Havilland Company, which had manufactured the Bluebird's Gipsy II engine, wanted to check it over. Mary occupied herself that day with a visit to the Pool of the Sacred Crocodiles at a Sufi temple in Manghopir, on the outskirts of Karachi. She was fascinated—and repelled—by the mass of huge reptiles in the pond. They lay motionless but menacing until they were stirred to frenetic action as the temple's high priest tossed them large hunks of meat brought to the shrine by worshippers.

The next day Mary was on her way again, flying east toward Allahabad, midway across the great Indian subcontinent. She was 'flying by Bradshaw', following a long straight railroad line. Fierce winds slowed her progress, and while crossing the Sind Desert a sandstorm completely blocked her view of the railroad. She flew nearly blindly for an hour before the tracks could be seen again. She had unexpected and unwelcome company in the air over the desert when several large vultures swooped down at the Bluebird. 'I think they must have objected to my being up in their air,' she wrote, 'for they came side-slipping towards me, missing the machine by inches.' She worried about striking one, guessing that the force of such an encounter would break the propeller and force a landing in the hot and arid emptiness.[3]

The 'disgusting great birds' behind her at last, Mary realized that the headwinds had slowed her progress so much that Allahabad was out of reach for that day, and she would have to find a place to land short of her goal. A quick look at a map told her that would be Jodhpur. She had paid scant attention to the name on the map, assuming any settlement in this area would be merely an outpost of civilization, with little chance of cultural sophistication. Her mood was decidedly irritable as she circled over the town, which looked unattractive from the air, thanks to a blowing dust storm. Colonel Wyndham, the British Resident, had evidently seen the little plane approach and hurried to meet her. She alighted from the Bluebird feeling out of sorts, saying: "Oh bother! I suppose I shall have to stay in this God-forsaken place. Is there any hope of getting a bed or something to eat?"

Colonel Wyndham smiled and allowed that, while food might be a problem, they could probably find her a place to sleep. She had no time to respond before she spotted a smart Rolls-Royce approaching, and began to realize that she had neatly put her foot in her mouth. 'Jodhpur—Jodhpur,' she thought to herself. 'Why, I believe that's one of the most fashionable places in India!' Mortified, she continued to grumble aloud about having landed in a wild native town, hoping that Wyndham would think she had been joking all along.

She spent a very comfortable night as the overnight guest of Colonel and Mrs. Wyndham in their palatial home, arriving at the airfield the next morning to find, written across the Bluebird's wing: 'The best of luck from the Bandits of Jodhpur!'

Mary's course took her northeast that day, as she wanted to see Delhi from the air. Impressed by the golden domes shining in the sunlight, she regretted that she had not allowed time for a visit there. She landed to refuel, and then turned southeast, following the course of the Jumna River to its confluence with the sacred Ganges at Allahabad. There she was the overnight guest of the British Resident Captain Pendlebury and his family. In the course of the evening's conversation he enquired whether she was carrying any firearms for her protection. Mary replied that she had never used a gun, and did not have one with her. Alarmed, he insisted that she take one of his automatic pistols, pointing out that she would soon be travelling over very desolate jungle, and might need to signal for help or frighten away wild animals.

In the morning Mary once again found the Ganges, and began following it south toward Benares. Twenty minutes into the flight the Bluebird's cockpit suddenly filled with smoke. Panicked, Mary waved the smoke away and searched for the cause. The engine sounded smooth; the gauges gave no indication of trouble. Residual wisps of smoke led her to the answer: just before take-off Captain Pendlebury had dropped his pistol into the cockpit pocket in which Mary's smoke bombs were stored. The weight of the pistol had broken the protective glass around one of the bombs, releasing a cloud of smoke. No harm was done, except to Mary's nerves.

Beyond Benares, Mary followed a major railway line to Burdwan, then the River Hooghly led her southeast to Calcutta. Around four in the afternoon Mary landed at Dum Dum[4] Airport, a few miles outside of the city. She was elated to be greeted by Oscar Garden. He should have been well on his way to Australia, she knew, but he had run into trouble after he left Jodhpur when he attempted to land in a field in the dark and his plane turned over. A little damage had been sustained, and some repairs were being made at Calcutta. They agreed to fly together to Rangoon, potentially the most dangerous part of their common route.

Mary spent the night with British friends, impressed by both the European style of the buildings and by the hundreds of people sleeping in the street as she made her way to the airport early the next morning. Having no sense of the profound poverty that characterised that city, she naïvely assumed that they chose to sleep outside because of the stifling heat. In spite of her realization that many were sleeping in the gutters of the squalid streets, she found the sight 'very interesting' rather than disturbing or distressing.

Mary's route eastward from Calcutta would take her over the northernmost part of the Bay of Bengal, then southward over Burma to the capital, Rangoon. She would be flying over swampland and jungle, as well as the formidable Arakan Yoma Mountains, the southeasternmost range of the Himalayas, which forms the spiny backbone of western Burma.

Mary and Oscar Garden left Dum Dum at dawn, passing over the marshy Ganges Delta and the swampy region known as the Sundarbans. The pair had agreed before they took off that if either of them had to land in that wild and dangerous stretch, the other would fly on in search of help, knowing that if they both landed, they might both be lost. It was a 'desolate stretch of country,' Mary wrote, 'with never a human habitation, and endless reaches of inland seas and great, winding, crocodile-infested rivers, a landing among which would have left little chance of escape.'

Four hours in the air brought them to the mouth of the Haringhata River, where they cut across the Bay of Bengal to Chittagong. Turning south they passed over the Karnapuli River and flew down the coast of Burma to Akyab, where they landed to refuel. They did not linger, hoping to get to Rangoon before nightfall.

Crossing the Arakan Yoma Range proved much easier than Mary had feared, and once over the mountains she spotted the great Irrawaddy River, which flows south for more than 1,300 miles from its source in the Himalayas to its miles-wide delta in the Bay of Bengal. She and Garden followed the broad river—the 'road to Mandalay' of Kipling's poem—to Rangoon. Mary drank in the sight of the city's skyline, dominated by the spectacular Schwedagon Pagoda made of 60 tons of pure gold and topped by a spire embellished with a 76-carat diamond. But after nearly twelve hours in the air, broken by only the half-hour stop at Akyab, Mary and Garden were both grateful to set down their planes at last.

Rangoon was the point of separation for the two pilots; Garden was to continue south down the Malay Peninsula, heading for Australia. Mary would turn east toward Japan, crossing over the dense jungles of Siam and French Indo-China. They were both at Rangoon's airfield before dawn the next day. Exchanging goodbyes and wishes for a safe journey, the two climbed into their cockpits and took to the skies again.

Mary's route took her east, across the Gulf of Martaban. As she approached the coast near Moulmein, she saw the great pagoda Kipling wrote of: 'For the temple-bells are callin', and it's there that I would be—by the old Moulmein Pagoda, looking lazy at the sea'. She barely gave it a glance, though, her mind on the daunting Dawna Mountains over which she had to fly. Even higher than the Arakan Yoma the previous day, the Dawna Range, forming the boundary between Burma and Siam, stood swathed in heavy black clouds as she approached. With peaks ranging upwards of 6,800 feet, Mary had a nerve-wracking flight through a blanket of mist. With relief, she cleared the mountains and spotted the Menam River, following it to Bangkok.

Mary had arrived at the point in her journey which she had dreaded from the beginning. In her mind, the following day would bring her most daunting challenge. It had been the jungles that frightened Mary the most, from the earliest days of planning her trip. Now several forced landings had tested her skills as a pilot and her resilience in the face of the unknown. But the thought of the dense green jungles of Southeast Asia still unnerved her—and miles of jungle lay beyond Bangkok.

Mary spent the evening absorbed in maintenance duties; it was necessary preparation for both the Bluebird and herself. Her hands busy with the familiar tasks, she mentally reviewed the next day's route. Engrossed in the satisfying routine of changing the Bluebird's oil and spark plugs, thoughts of the jungle intruded; it would be infinitely preferable to fly above open land, where she would be able to spot a potential landing site in case of engine failure.

Mary checked and rechecked the engine and studied her maps. Satisfied at last that the Bluebird was ready, she retired to spend an uncomfortable night in a room in the soldiers' quarters at the airport.

Mary was up well before dawn, 'anxious to get the agony over'. Her first goal was the village of Korat, deep in the jungle. The ancient walled town had become a railway junction point, and she had arranged, weeks in advance, for supplies of fuel and oil to be shipped there and held for her arrival.

Mary had hoped to be able to follow the railroad tracks to Korat, but the heat of the rising sun caused a dense mist to rise from the jungle below, and she was forced to rely on her compass to navigate. Four tense hours passed as she flew above the thick white cloud of mist. It did not help her peace of mind to picture the impenetrable carpet of jungle hidden below.

Elated, Mary finally spotted the rough airstrip and few buildings of Korat in a clearing. She landed and refuelled, taking time to check over the Bluebird's engine carefully again before departure. Six hundred and eighty more miles of jungle lay between Korat and Hanoi, her final goal for the day.

For the first few hours after Korat Mary flew over solid teak jungle, never seeing any sign of human habitation. The endless sea of trees on the Korat Plateau rolled away beneath her, stretching in every direction as far as she could see. The monotony was broken only once, when she suddenly noticed that the branches of the trees below her wings were waving to and fro.

Thinking at first that a windstorm had sprung up, Mary looked below and spotted hundreds of grey shapes crashing through the forest; she had disturbed a herd of wild elephants. She watched as they dashed madly through the thick jungle, smashing down trees in their stride. Realizing that the sound of the Bluebird's engine was the cause of their fright, Mary hastily climbed out of their hearing and lost sight of the stampeding herd.

It was early afternoon when she reached the northeastern border of Siam at the Mekong River, which rises in the mountains of Tibet and flows 2,700 miles to the South China Sea. Across the river lay Laos, and in the distance towered the great Annam Cordillera Range. Mary's heart sank when she saw huge black clouds obscuring the peaks. She flew on toward the clouds, hoping for a break that would allow her to get through the storm. Her hopes were dashed as the Bluebird was suddenly pounded by torrential rains; the monsoon had caught her after all! The downpour pelted the little airplane with such fury that the sound of the engine was drowned out. The Bluebird steadily lost altitude as the force of the rains bore down, pouring gallons of water into the open cockpit and obscuring Mary's view almost completely. Her face was stung by rain, and she could barely see the tips of the wings in the semi-darkness. There was no hope of remaining airborne for long. Her worst fears had been realized: she would have to make a forced landing in the jungle.

Mary turned back toward the Mekong, remembering advice she had been given that, faced with such a catastrophe, it would be best to come down near a river if possible. There would be a chance, then, of being spotted by someone using the waterway; another consideration was the relative absence of snakes and leeches near a river.

The river appeared at last, and miraculously she saw a tiny clearing at its edge. Surrounded by trees and sharp stumps of cut-back bamboo, it seemed an impossible task to set the Bluebird down without damage, but Mary had no choice but to attempt it. She circled several times, considering the best approach, and spoke into her Dictaphone: "I see a clearing in the trees. I'm about to come down. I shall smash the machine, though." Throttling back the engine, she took a deep breath and cautiously descended over the trees toward the clearing.

15 Siam to China

As the wheels touched the sodden earth Mary felt something catch the tip of the right wing; the plane spun around. A stump of bamboo had ripped loose a strip of fabric, but the Bluebird was safely down.

Mary sat in the plane for an hour, waiting for the downpour to lessen and occasionally bailing out the cockpit, which otherwise would have overflowed. 'In this abomination of desolation one might have expected peace,' she wrote, 'but far away in the jungle I could hear the screeching of a monkey, while all around the deafening chirping of crickets, together with the incessant drumming of the rain, added to the eeriness of the place.'

Mary reviewed her options. It would be dark in an hour; she was determined not to spend the night in that clearing. She had to get into the air as soon as the rains ceased. A look at the map lifted her spirits: only 90 miles up the Mekong was a village called Lakhon. She had a goal now—but could she get the Bluebird off the ground?

The rain stopped as suddenly as it had begun, and Mary sprang into action. She paced off the longest stretch of clear ground, figuring it at 180 yards. The Bluebird needed 150 yards in which to rise, but there were tall trees all around. Could she clear them? Knowing that the weight of the plane would be a critical factor, Mary threw out every non-essential item she carried: food, clothes, even tools. Hoping that she had stripped enough weight, she turned the Bluebird, positioning it for the longest run possible—but the engine was waterlogged. She quickly changed the spark plugs and cleaned the magneto points. Repeatedly she swung the propeller, perspiration pouring off her face in the oppressive heat.

At last the engine burst into life. Mary leapt into the cockpit and manipulated the throttle. For two or three seconds she heard only sputtering and backfiring— and then the smooth even firing that her ears were so accustomed to. With a final glance at the distant trees, she revved up the engine and pushed the stick forward. The Bluebird gained speed slowly over the rough surface, and began to climb just thirty yards from the trees.

Mary dared not pull the stick up another inch, knowing she would lose flying speed and drop to the ground. Instead, she pushed the stick forward, diving to increase speed. Then, at the last moment, she pulled the stick back again, hoping to be able to jump the trees. She heard a crash and thought the propeller had fouled the branches, but it was only the wheels of the undercarriage. Surprised and relieved, Mary found herself quickly rising clear of the interminable jungle and flying up the river. She followed the Mekong north for an hour and landed at Lakhon just as the sun was setting.

Mary set the Bluebird down in a clearing next to the local Governor's house. He welcomed her to the village, but he was pessimistic about the prospects for crossing the mountains by air. Only recently, he told Mary, two French aviators had died when they hit the cloud-swathed peaks while attempting to cross from Hanoi. A steamer came up the Mekong from Saigon every month, the Governor informed her. Why didn't she disassemble the Bluebird and ship it to Hanoi by steamer? Mary rejected that proposal immediately; she was determined to reach Japan by air—not by sea!

Mary was charmed by the Governor's house, which seemed to her to be a perfect Victorian English cottage. White picket fences in the garden completed the picture, although she noted with amusement that they surrounded banana trees instead of rose bushes. She was served tea with cream and sugar, and relaxed in comfort after her eventful day. After tea the Governor drove her around in his car (the only one in the village) and she found the shops and sights fascinating. When it came time to settle in for the night, however, she was taken aback to be shown to a depressing and sparsely furnished room in a separate building. She spent a restless and uncomfortable night under mosquito netting, and was up and out at first light.

The Governor had mentioned that there was a French colony, Takhek, just across the Mekong. Officials there were in close contact by radio with Hanoi, he told her, and would have up-to-the-minute weather information crucial to any attempt to fly over the mountains.

Mary crossed the Mekong in the Governor's launch and met the French Commissaire, Monsieur Loupy. Over a breakfast of French coffee and rolls, he told her that crossing the Annamitic Range would be difficult but possible—if she had good weather. He promised to keep her informed daily.

The Siamese Governor in Lakhon had a dinner party that evening, with special musical entertainment. Mary found the orchestra of little girls and their unfamiliar music captivating. One girl was struggling to play an accordion, and at the conclusion of the program Mary asked to borrow it, and delighted the French Commissaire by playing *La Marseillaise*.

Another restless night in the cheerless little guesthouse followed, and Mary awoke early, feeling ill. She felt her temperature climbing, and by early afternoon she realized that she was seriously ill. Knowing that medical care would be available in the French village, she made her way across the river. Exhausted by fever and weakness, she struggled to the Commissaire's house, where she was immediately put to bed. A doctor appeared shortly and diagnosed malaria, prescribing quinine and bed rest.

An enforced delay due to health was an added frustration, but at least she was being cared for in what Mary considered a much more civilised setting than the miserable accommodations the Governor had provided at Lakhon.

Within three days she was much better, and when the Commissaire asked if she felt up to joining him and some friends on a tiger hunt, she jumped at the chance. The party drove two hours into the jungle to a small village where they picked up a dozen native guides and a new mode of transportation: elephants. As they proceeded farther into the dense jungle, Mary marvelled at the thick, overhanging vegetation. She was far happier moving through the jungle on the back of an elephant than she had been flying over it.

A frantic peasant appeared in the path ahead of the party, gesturing to the body of one of his oxen which, he said, had just been killed by a tiger. There was no sign of the tiger, but Mary was told that it was probably nearby, waiting for a quieter moment to return to its kill for a meal.

The hunting party divided, Mary and a few others staying near the carcass of the ox. The natives beat the jungle, tossing stones into the tall grass, and after a few minutes Mary heard a series of gunshots in the distance. One of the hunters returned to fetch them, and Mary and the others hurried to see the prize. She was photographed, unloaded gun in hand and one foot set jauntily on the dead tiger. In telling the story of the hunt later, she sometimes claimed she had shot the tiger—a story that went down particularly well in America.

Besides the excitement of the tiger hunt, the day's excursion into the jungle provided Mary with a glimpse of a life totally foreign to her. She was delighted by the sight of a herd of elephants drinking at a watering hole. She admired trays of yellow silkworm cocoons drying in the sun beside native huts, and laughed at monkeys screeching as they swung through the dense canopy of trees above her.

Mary waited impatiently for a promising weather forecast, anxious to get on with her journey. To add to her frustration, the weather appeared fine in the riverside village; it was hard to believe that, just miles away, conditions were too treacherous to attempt a flight. She had wheeled 25 gallons of fuel from the Governor—half of his monthly allotment from Saigon. On Sunday, Mary attended Roman Catholic Mass at a church in the little French colony. That afternoon she visited another Catholic church, this one in the Siamese village of Lakhon. There the priest listened with fascination to the story of her flight. Promising to pray for her while she flew over the mountains, he gave her a St. Christopher medal to fasten in the cockpit of the Bluebird.

Mary on a tiger hunt

On the morning of the seventh day, the long-awaited telegram arrived from Hanoi: the wind was from the north, and the weather on the far side of the Annamitic Range was good. Within an hour, she was ready to leave. Bidding goodbye to the Governor and the small crowd assembled to watch her departure, Mary took off toward the towering mountains to the east.

The Governor had cautioned her that she would have to fly well above the mountain peaks, and not try to go through any mountain passes. She dared not descend through the clouds until at least two hours had passed, he warned. "Then you will be able to see the coast beyond the mountains. But wait until you can actually see the sea, for otherwise you will probably hit the top of the mountains."

After climbing steadily for more than an hour, the Bluebird was flying at

11,000 feet—higher than Mary had ever flown. A seemingly endless carpet of billowy white clouds lay beneath her as she flew eastward. 'Soon I began to feel terribly lonely,' she wrote. 'The vast emptiness of it all and the utter insignificance of my little machine alone in that great expanse of the heavens stressed my sense of solitariness.'

Two hours passed, and then three. At last Mary saw in the distance a patch of a darker colour, and she flew toward what she assumed was the sea at last. After another hour, though, the patch had come no nearer; she had been chasing a cloud mirage.

Four hours had passed; she should have spotted the sea long since. Mary had only enough fuel for one more hour of flying, but where was the ocean? Remembering the Governor's warning, she was afraid to descend through the clouds. Their humpbacked shapes suggested to her that jagged peaks might lie just below them, hidden from view.

Nearly frantic, Mary turned back toward Lakhon, but then realized that she could not return. There was not nearly enough fuel left in the Bluebird's tanks, and daylight would soon fade. She circled above the clouds, crying aloud "Four hours! Four hours!" In all her life, she had never felt so desperate. Was she about to run out of luck?

Mustering her courage, she quickly decided on her course of action. She reached for her Dictaphone and spoke: "The time is 3 p.m. and I am lost above the clouds. This may be the end. I've done the best I can and if I come through it, it will only be by the grace of God. Goodbye!"

She closed the throttle, and began to dive. The altimeter dropped, showing 10,000 . . . 8,000 . . . 6,000 feet. The descent seemed endless. She peered into the clouds, expecting to see a rocky hillside before her at any moment. The steady sound of the Bluebird's engine and the whistling of the wind were the only sounds she heard; her heart was pounding as the needle showed 4,000 feet, then 2,000. As the gauge neared 1,000 feet a new terror arose: had she flown so far that she was now above the sea, diving toward a watery grave instead of a mountainside?

At an altitude of little more than 1,000 feet, the Bluebird burst through the last wispy layers of cloud cover and Mary saw below her neither a mountain peak nor the sea, but miles and miles of swamp—and sparkling in the light of the setting sun was a ribbon of steel: railroad tracks. She was elated; a railway meant civilization, and she needed only to follow it to safety.

In less than five minutes she knew she was saved: ahead lay the towers of a telegraph transmitting station and the skyline of a city. Was it possible, she wondered, that she had found Hanoi after all? It seemed too good to be true.

Minutes later, she spotted an airfield; she circled and gratefully touched down at last. Much to her surprise, there was a welcoming committee waiting for her, bouquets in hand. Still unwilling to trust her good fortune she hesitantly asked, "Is this Hanoi?" "*Mais oui!*" came the response—and only then was she really able to breathe a sigh of relief. She wrote that, ever after that day, she regarded her safe arrival in Hanoi as 'a miracle wrought in answer to the prayers of the priest at Lakhon and the St. Christopher medal.'

Hanoi was the bustling centre of French Indo-China, and the combination of French sophistication and native charm was very appealing to Mary. She was the guest of the French Air Force commander, whose hospitality included arranging a welcoming banquet that evening for about two hundred guests. His wife took Mary on a sightseeing and shopping excursion the next day. Riding through crowded streets in a rickshaw, Mary wrote, 'was the nearest thing to a thrill that I had experienced since my last race at Brooklands'. The streets teemed with hundreds of horse-drawn carts, speeding motorcycles, automobiles, and rickshaws all jostling together. Enchanted by the architecture, gardens, and especially the shops, Mary wandered for an hour, choosing small curios and souvenirs.

A large crowd gathered at the airfield on the morning of Mary's departure and watched as she was presented with the Order of the Million Elephants and the White Umbrella, a magnificent gold and enamel medal which was pinned ceremoniously to her flying jacket. It was a very highly esteemed decoration, she was told, which entitled her to own a million elephants and to have a white umbrella held over her head. The Governor had ordered it conferred upon her, as the first woman and the first Briton ever to fly to French Indo-China.

Morning fog delayed her departure from Hanoi. As the minutes went by Mary wondered if she could reach her goal for the day, Hong Kong, nearly 600 miles away. The Air Force officers advised her that Fort Bayard, a small French colony on China's Luichow Peninsula, could be an alternative landing place if she could not make Hong Kong.

A dozen military planes escorted her as she left Hanoi, turning back when they reached the Gulf of Tonkin. Mary was struck by the beauty of the rocky coastline, with purple shadows cast on the brilliant sapphire blue surface of the sea. Her appreciation of the beauty of the rugged scenery below was tempered by concern about the consequences of a possible forced landing in such craggy terrain. Scenery was soon forgotten; her attention was fully on the sky as towering black clouds loomed before her. The wind increased, cutting her speed, and she knew that Hong Kong was out of reach for the day.

Mary reached the narrow Luichow Peninsula but somehow missed Fort

Bayard, flying south beyond it nearly to Hainan Island. As she realized her error and turned to retrace her route, she spied what she thought might be a pirate ship lying in Hainan Strait. Flying a red flag, it struck her as very different from other ships she had seen. She flew low over it, noticing the men aboard. 'They were gaily dressed with bright scarves, which made me more sure than ever that they were pirates,' she wrote. Caution overcame her curiosity, and she quickly climbed to a safer altitude and continued north.

When Mary landed at Fort Bayard she found her welcoming committee much relieved at her safe arrival. Earlier they had seen her flying south, and feared that she might come down near Hainan, where she could be captured and held for ransom by the pirates who headquartered there.

She was a guest that evening at a Chinese wedding celebration, and was greeted upon her entrance by a rousing rendition of *God Save the King* by the French and Chinese residents. The feast that followed was a meal to remember—except, she wrote, she had no idea what she was eating and had been advised not to enquire about the ingredients.

She was up and ready to fly shortly after daybreak, and once again found a crowd of people at the airport to see her off on her 200-mile hop from Fort Bayard to Hong Kong. They swarmed around the Bluebird, adding their signatures to the hundreds already inscribed on the wings and fuselage. An elderly Chinese man caught her eye; she was fascinated by his long pigtail, an unusual sight in 1930.[1]

Mary's keen appreciation for a business opportunity far eclipsed her cultural sensitivity: she immediately offered to trade a piece of the Bluebird's broken propeller for his pigtail, thinking she could sell it as a souvenir when she reached America. He seemed not to mind but his wife was clearly against the scheme. In the end, Mary settled for a photograph of him. She climbed into the cockpit, waved, and shouted a friendly "*Vive la France!*" to the onlookers, and was on her way.

16 The Yellow Sea and Japan

It was early November as Mary flew north along the China coast toward Hong Kong. She was weeks behind her original schedule, thanks to the crash in the desert, her bout of malaria and the difficulty crossing the Annamitic Range. She had been concerned about the monsoon season causing a delay—as indeed it had—but she was revelling in the delight of discovery, and in the strange customs and scenery she was encountering.

In Hong Kong Mary was the guest of the British Governor of the territory, Sir William Peel. She exclaimed over the beauty of the city, particularly the nighttime view from the roof garden of Peel's residence, Government House. 'Although I had heard a great many people speak of the beauty of Hong Kong, I never realized how wonderful it was until that night. Bathed in moonlight, thousands of lights from the ships and the shore throwing shafts and pools of glimmering brilliance on the dark waters, the city seemed transfigured, just like some fairy town you see in dreams.'

She had planned to stay just one night in Hong Kong, but dense ground fog prevented her departure the next morning. Mary accepted an invitation from the Governor to spend the day at Happy Valley, Hong Kong's racetrack. It had been months since she had ridden a horse—or even seen one—but she soon found herself astride a handsome grey. He was hard to hold back, so she decided to give him his head and let him run for a while. At a full gallop, the horse's knees buckled and he went to the ground in a complete somersault; Mary scraped her arm against a fence as she flew off, but neither she nor the horse suffered serious injury. In spite of the spill, her enjoyment of the day at Happy Valley so filled her mind that when she was handed a cable that evening from Victor and Tony, wishing her 'Many happy returns of the day,' she was mystified—until she suddenly remembered the date: 10 November, her thirty-fifth birthday!

The next day's weather was brighter, and Mary was off before ten o'clock. Members of Hong Kong's British colony were preparing for Remembrance Day services, but she could not fall another day behind schedule. After an hour's flight the clock showed 11 a.m.; Mary decided to observe the solemn moment with the traditional two minutes of silence. She was flying fairly high, and reached forward and shut off the Bluebird's engine, intending to glide in silence for two minutes. It was a heartfelt (and typically dramatic) gesture, but unsuccessful; she was losing altitude at too great a rate and had to restart the engine after only 30 seconds.

In striking contrast to the barren landscapes of the Persian Gulf and the dense and frightening jungles of Burma and Siam, the scenery north of Hong Kong was a visual delight. Mary was enchanted by the beauty of Bias Bay, an inlet on the South China Sea that was notorious as the headquarters of pirates.[1] Rocks rose from the azure waters and she admired the odd little Chinese ships sailing on the bay. She also spotted a larger ship, a steamer flying the Norwegian flag. Alongside it, she was surprised to realise, was the ship she had taken for a pirate ship a few days earlier in Hainan Strait.

By afternoon, monsoon headwinds blew up and her average speed dropped to a mere 38 mph. The Bluebird was tossed about violently. Mary fought to control the little plane, feeling a bit ill from the constant pitching. She credited her safety harness with keeping her in the cockpit, writing: 'If it had not been for my straps I should have been thrown out on more than one occasion. Two or three times I dropped so violently that my head hit the roof of the machine and I had to pull my straps tighter to prevent this happening again.'

Locating her destination for the day, Amoy Island, was not a simple matter. Mary found several small islands in the Formosa Strait, any one of which could be Amoy. Consulting her map, she quickly determined that the small airstrip had been marked on the wrong island. The gale winds shaking the Bluebird did not abate as she circled each island, until she located the narrow grass landing strip.

The wind indicator swung violently from one direction to another as she considered her approach. She dictated, "The time is ten minutes past five. I have sighted the aerodrome, but the wind is blowing with hurricane force. I fear very much for what will happen when I land. Here goes, anyway. I shall come down."

With an eye on the wind indicator beside the strip, Mary began her approach. There was a sudden shift in the wind direction and she pulled the Bluebird's nose up and circled again. Crosswinds buffeted her as she descended a second time; one ferocious gust battered the little plane just as the wheels touched the grass. Desperately trying to avoid cartwheeling, Mary gunned the engine and turned into the wind. As the Bluebird spun around, Mary managed to regain control and bring it safely to a stop.

At Amoy, Mary was the guest of the Manager of the Asiatic Petroleum

Company, a part of the Royal Dutch/Shell group, one of the suppliers of fuel for the Bluebird's flight. Her hosts nodded as they heard her description of the pirate ship she had seen as she flew over Bias Bay. The Norwegian ship had indeed been the victim of piracy, and the captain and some of the wealthier passengers were being held for ransom. It was a particularly bad year for piracy, she was told, because of a food shortage. Mary had heard that aviators were especially attractive targets, fetching handsome prices for their release. Flying along the coast of China raised the level of excitement, with the constant possibility, however remote, of capture by pirates.

The port city of Amoy had been a centre of Chinese seafaring life for centuries; beginning in the mid-1600s it was the most important port at which Dutch and English merchant ships traded. By the 1700s tea was the major commodity shipped from Amoy. A direct trade route was established between England and China, but England's trade deficit increased as more Chinese tea flowed in than English exports flowed out.[2]

Amoy gradually declined in importance as a seaport and had a reputation as a somewhat squalid little town by the time of Mary's visit in 1930. She found it in the throes of major redevelopment, with streets being widened and new buildings replacing old. She noted the widespread interest in aviation among the Chinese people, which was vividly demonstrated when she went to the airport to check on preparations for her flight the next day. She found a crowd around the Bluebird and hundreds of new signatures in Chinese characters inscribed on the plane's fabric covering. One old Chinese *amah* was terribly thrilled at the idea of Mary going up in the air, and told her, "You all same big bird!"—an assessment the old woman wrote in Chinese characters on the Bluebird's fabric.

Mary's intended destination the next day was Shanghai, nearly seven hundred miles up the Chinese coast, but just as she was ready to take off, word was received of the outbreak of fighting at Foochow, the midway point where she had planned to refuel. She sent a telegram to the general who was commanding the garrison at Foochow to ask permission to land long enough to refuel; his reply was 'Sorry impossible for you to land; too busy with the war.'

Mary's solution was to take off in the middle of the night, hoping to cover most of the distance to Shanghai before the coastal winds came up, which would slow her progress and surely force her to land short of her goal. She flew the straightest possible course toward Shanghai. Following the coastline, which was always her preference, would have taken too long; with fuel at a premium, she chose an inland route over the coastal mountains. As she reached Foochow, she wrote, 'I could see numbers of Chinese soldiers dashing about in all directions; in fact, I had a perfect view of the war and, with strict impartiality, dropped a smoke bomb.'

At the end of the eight-hour flight, a crowd of several hundred people greeted Mary in Shanghai. She spent three busy days as the guest of the British Consul-General, during which the Bluebird was thoroughly checked in preparation for her crossing of the Yellow Sea. That little one-inch hop she had first contemplated while looking at her atlas months earlier was looming larger as she got closer to it. The problem of leaking engine oil, which had plagued her nearly from the outset, continued. A mechanic of the British Air Force at Shanghai lowered the oil pressure of the engine, which seemed to cure the problem at last.

On her test flight after this adjustment, Mary flew over the Yangtze River, noticing a big white steamer lying at anchor. To her delight, it was the *Empress of Japan*, on which she had booked passage from Yokohama to Victoria, B.C., for the following month.[3] She flew down and made several low circles over the ship, by way of introducing herself.

On 17 November, the last afternoon before Mary left Shanghai, she visited the Ziccawei Observatory, the most important meteorological station in the Far East. She was welcomed by the French Jesuits who operated the site. The chief meteorologist promised to stay up that night and gather data from the reporting stations at sea, so that Mary could have the most up-to-the-minute weather forecast possible before she took off in the morning.

Mary awoke at 3 a.m. Uneasily she contemplated her flight plan for the day. In the weeks since she had left England, her skill as a pilot had grown immensely. She had proven to herself that she could plot a compass course and follow it, handle the vagaries of weather conditions, and maintain her concentration and composure during long hours of solo flying. But today's flight was special. It would set a new world's record: the first solo crossing by air of the Yellow Sea. With the Bluebird's tanks loaded to capacity, there would barely be enough fuel for the 750-mile crossing under good conditions—and a strong headwind would spell certain defeat. She thought about a postcard she had received from a fortune-teller before leaving England, predicting that she would meet her death in the Yellow Sea. If she did come down in the water, chances of survival would be slim. She had bought a tiny inflatable boat in Bangkok, but even if she could inflate it and get into it, she would still be adrift far out of the main shipping channels, in cold November waters. Although not a superstitious person, she wrote, 'On that day I was fully alive to the risk I was taking.'

In the 5 a.m. darkness Mary arrived at the Shanghai aerodrome. She stared again at her maps, memorizing the route. She would cross hundreds of miles of open sea, trying to find tiny Ross Island, the first landfall on her direct route to

Seoul. Had she plotted correctly? She checked and rechecked her supplies and equipment, waiting anxiously for the morning's weather report promised her by the Jesuit meteorologist at the Ziccawei Observatory. At last it was handed to her: 'Visibility at sea: Fine. Best wishes.' Mary climbed into the cockpit and took one more look at the gauges before her. She heard "Contact!" and the engine burst into life. She opened the throttle and the Bluebird, loaded to capacity, slowly rolled down the runway and rose into the air.

Within an hour Mary lost sight of the land behind her; steadily she flew by compass, listening to the engine and occasionally making notes into her Dictaphone. There were no ships on the sea; the weather was clear. Even with nothing to report, she made hourly recordings, partly just to pass the time. Five hours into the flight—at midday—she opened her lunch, only to find that her appetite had deserted her. Her mouth was dry; she drank a little water. And then she went cold with fear as she heard a change in the sound of the engine: it seemed to be missing. She checked her instruments; everything appeared normal. With relief, she saw a tiny stream of smoke escaping the exhaust pipe near the manifold. That was the source of the noise! It would not affect the running of the engine, but the mystery was solved.

Seven hours into the flight, Mary peered forward anxiously: she should be sighting land by now. Alarmed, she thought of turning back—but wisely resisted the impulse. Still, she wondered, what if she had missed Korea altogether, and was heading straight out into the Sea of Japan? Had her navigation been faulty?

Visibility was decreasing and the cold wind was picking up; Mary leaned out for a better view. Suddenly her goggles were blown off, making it nearly impossible to see in the stinging wind. Tensely, she leaned forward, scanning the horizon through the windscreen.

Eight hours had passed before a dark shape appeared on the horizon; not trusting that it was really land, Mary waited until there was no doubt. Triumphantly she grabbed her Dictaphone and crowed: "Definitely can see land! It is Ross Island; I am dead on my course!"

Mary was ecstatic; after flying eight hours with no sight of land, she had not deviated a single degree from her course. Relief and joy flooded her, lifting her spirits as she passed over Ross Island toward the mainland, then followed railway lines through the mountains of southern Korea.

Mary flew a beeline to Seoul and the clamorous reception that awaited her at the airfield. Little girls with bouquets of flowers crowded around the Bluebird, and the British community turned out *en masse* to celebrate this first air crossing of the Yellow Sea. It was Mary's first major air record—the longest solo sea flight since Lindbergh's Atlantic crossing in 1927.

Two days later, an even bigger reception celebrated an even greater accomplishment—Mary's completion of the first flight from England to Japan. Crossing the Korea Strait was a piece of cake; while it was a far greater over-water distance than the English Channel or the Persian Gulf, it was a fraction of the Yellow Sea crossing which had proven Mary's navigational skill and courage just days earlier. The flight barely rated a mention in her Dictaphone record; she reserved her excitement for her approach to Osaka.

Mary crossed the towering Chugoko Mountains of western Honshu and circled low over the airfield at Hiroshima, where a Japanese military plane climbed up to greet her and escort her to Osaka. "I am full of excitement!" she recorded; "The Osaka aeroplane is flying very low and I can see the pilot waving and smiling. This certainly is the best part of the trip. The country and the scenery are magnificent!"

Several thousand people were on hand to greet Mary as she splashed down on the muddy runway. With wild enthusiasm they carried her on their shoulders over the rain-soaked runway to an enthusiastic reception in the hangar. Champagne flowed as one official greeting followed another, setting the tone for the days of extravagant celebration that marked most of Mary's stay in Japan.

In Osaka she saw firsthand the culture she had eagerly read about while preparing for her trip. She was delighted with the woven straw mats and sliding panels in the homes. Mary's first meal was afternoon tea, served as she sat on cushions at a low polished ebony table in a room hung with delicate silk panels painted with branches of cherry blossoms. Her second meal—a banquet in her honour hosted that evening by members of the Japanese press—provided an even more memorable experience. After an array of exotic dishes had appeared, a huge steaming fish was brought in and set before Mary with great ceremony. Her hostess declared, "We are about to pay you a great honour. Tonight we have cooked for you the lucky *tai* fish;[4] now we are going to pay you a still higher honour." Mary waited expectantly. "We are going to present you with the fish's eye to eat."

It was a flash of brilliance that saved her. In spite of the arduous activities of the day—the flight of nearly 700 miles from Seoul, the exuberant greeting by the crowd at the airfield, the champagne reception, the strain of absorbing new cultural traditions and ceremonies, and the dazzling glitter of the banquet—Mary rose to the occasion. She turned to her hostess and smiled graciously: "Madam, I do not know how to thank you for the honour you have conferred upon me. But somehow I feel ashamed, because you have done so much for me and I am able to do so little for you, and therefore I am going to do you the still greater and higher honour of giving it back to you!" The hostess beamed with pleasure and immediately gobbled up the eye, to Mary's profound relief.

As delightful as Mary found Osaka, and as welcoming as the people were, she was itching to get to Tokyo, which she considered the most important public goal of her journey. A visit to her mother's hometown in America, she thought, would be the private emotional highpoint. But the record-setting flight from England to Japan—that pinnacle would truly come to pass with her landing in Tokyo.

It was late November, but the weather cooperated nicely as Mary made the scenic 250-mile flight from Osaka. She and an escort plane flew east along Japan's Inland Sea, sighting the snowcapped peak of Fujiyama around noon. 'It is quite impossible,' she wrote, 'to describe in mere words the simplicity, yet beauty and power, of this most beautiful of all mountains. As I flew by I was almost forgetting to keep my course, so spellbound was I by the glory.' More and more airplanes joined the Bluebird in the air, their pilots and passengers waving handkerchiefs and shouting encouragement; Mary could see one passenger winding the handle of a movie camera. She hastily counted 20 other planes, and reluctantly tore her eyes away from the mesmerizing sight of Fujiyama to concentrate on flying in the crowded airspace.

Preparing to land at the modern Tachikawa airfield, Mary reached for the Dictaphone and spoke: "The time is 2 p.m. The aerodrome is crowded with people. I am sure I shall make a bad landing. I have made two complete circuits of the aerodrome. I am surrounded by airplanes. I am sure I shall bump into one of them in a minute. Here goes. I am about to land. Half of my journey completed!"

A throng of people engulfed Mary and the Bluebird the moment the propeller stopped turning. Mounted police could not begin to hold back the crowd, and Mary feared briefly for the safety of her airplane. She was carried again, shoulder high, to another champagne reception in a hangar, where the formal greetings were delivered and introductions made. Mary was enchanted by the floral displays—dozens of exotic bouquets and fanciful arrangements, some in the form of small airplanes. One small girl was completely enveloped in a floral model of the Bluebird.

Mary was greeted by government officials and civilian celebrities, many from the world of aviation. Among them was Lieutenant General Gaishi Nagaoka who was known as Japan's 'Grandfather of Aviation.' In his seventies, Nagaoka was a charming old man who sported an extraordinary moustache, reputedly the longest in the world. It was, in fact, a source of great pride to him. Mary wrote that he appeared at every function during her stay in Tokyo, and contrived to appear in nearly every photograph, holding out his moustache for the best possible camera angle. [5]

Mary with General Nagaoka at a banquet

At the conclusion of the welcoming reception, Mary was led outside to a Hillman automobile, which was put at her disposal for her stay in Tokyo. She was delighted at the prospect of driving again; she had not been behind the wheel for nearly two months. Leaning out the window to wave before she drove away, she felt something tickle her cheek. Thinking it was a part of a bouquet of flowers, she quickly brushed it away—and then turned her head and saw that it was the trailing moustache of General Nagaoka.

Her destination that night was the Imperial Hotel, the only building in central Tokyo that withstood the devastating great Kanto earthquake of 1923.[6] Mary was kept busy that evening receiving and answering dozens of congratulatory telegrams and telephone calls, and preparing a speech to be broadcast that night, giving a brief account of her record-setting flight. She met with executives from the Rising Sun Petroleum Company who had provided fuel and other support for her trip, but was able to excuse herself and fall into bed, exhausted, well before midnight.

Mary was awakened by the violent shaking of her bed—then realized that the entire room was shaking. A powerful earthquake was rocking the hotel. The electricity had failed; she heard decorative vases and bouquets of flowers crashing to the floor all around her. She staggered to the door and opened it, barely able to keep her footing, and saw her fellow guests streaming by in the corridor, clad in nightclothes, faces white with fear. She turned and looked out the window of her room at a sky turning yellow with the distant flames of raging fires. A bellboy passed by in the corridor shouting assurances to the guests as the shaking subsided and stopped at last. Mary lay awake the rest of the night, longing for the daylight and thinking of the earthquake just seven years earlier, which had levelled Tokyo and caused thousands of deaths.

In the morning she learned that the powerful quake had left hundreds of casualties, and there was an urgent need for relief funds. She volunteered to give a series of lectures about her journey; they were quickly organised and she donated the proceeds to the relief effort.

Earthquake or no, Tokyo was determined to entertain Mary royally in the days that followed. Nearly every moment was scheduled with teas, receptions, dinners and parties. She managed to squeeze in an excursion to Miyanoshita, a resort in the hills famous for hot springs and a stunning view of Fujiyama. Located near the village of Hakone, the epicentre of the earthquake that had jolted Tokyo days earlier, the resort seemed both beautiful and dangerous. Mary wrote that she felt the earth quivering that night, and in spite of the lovely surroundings, she was not anxious to linger long.

The Japanese press commented on the skimpy wardrobe that Mary had brought with her. Of necessity, she had packed very light, but it was apparent that the women of Tokyo—especially those members of the British colony—viewed this as a challenge. Dozens of beautiful kimonos were delivered, along with pearl jewellery, scarves, and shoes. Packing in Tokyo was a great deal more time consuming than it had been in Esher, but at least there was a large ocean liner waiting to convey Mary, the Bluebird, and her rapidly expanding wardrobe to North America. She dared not think about what she would do when she reached America and had to pack up and start flying again.[7]

On 4 December Mary drove to Yokohama and watched as the Bluebird, wings folded, was hoisted aboard the *Empress of Japan*. Looking far larger than it had when Mary flew over it at Shanghai, the sleek Canadian Pacific liner had set a new record for crossing the Pacific just weeks earlier, from Yokohama to Vancouver in eight days and six hours. Any record-setting mode of transportation held great appeal for Mary.

The ship was crowded with the press and well-wishers who had come to see Mary off. In the centre of the crowd was General Nagaoka, and it was with genuine regret that Mary bade the cheerful old man farewell. The warning whistle blew and the visitors departed; Mary stood at the railing with the other passengers and waved and watched as the liner got underway and Yokohama faded into the distance.

What adventures, she wondered, lay before her on the second half of her flight?

17 To the New World

The Pacific crossing was anything but peaceful. Once beyond the shelter of Yokohama harbor the *Empress of Japan* met rough December seas. Mary, who claimed she had always been a poor sailor, was grateful for the ship's up-to-date engineering, which kept the new liner relatively stable. This was her first major ocean crossing, and she was fascinated by the range of activities and amenities available on board: the swimming pool, gymnasium, movie theatre, and ballroom all offered diversion during the eight-day crossing. After ten weeks of flying and one official function after another, Mary found the shipboard interlude a real treat. She wrote to Victor that she had 'flown halfway round the world and was now dancing across the Pacific'. It was, she claimed, the cure for seasickness; as long as she danced, she barely noticed the motion of the ship, even during a gale!

Gales in the north Pacific prevented the *Empress of Japan* from calling at Victoria, British Columbia, to pick up mail. A small lighter that came out from the harbour to attempt to deliver the mail was unable to manoeuvre close enough for the transfer, much to Mary's disappointment; she knew that Victor had been sending all his letters to her there.

On the evening of 12 December they docked at Vancouver. The sight of the city's brilliantly lit skyscrapers, the first she had ever seen, entranced Mary. The press was at the dock to greet Mary, and she smiled as the flashbulbs added to the festive atmosphere.

Vancouver welcomed her with enthusiasm. Crowds appeared at the airport to see the Bluebird, and several new signatures were added to the hundreds already decorating the fuselage and wings. While the Bluebird underwent a thorough maintenance inspection and engine tune-up, Mary enjoyed shopping and exploring the city. One evening she gave a lecture about her adventures to an enthralled audience of several hundred people.

The Standard Oil Company stepped in and solved one of Mary's most vexing dilemmas. She had left England with a minimum of clothing and accessories, acutely conscious of the need to balance fuel weight and gear. But—as is so often the case—possessions had accumulated along the way. She had been the recipient of several proclamations and official welcome gifts, and she had done quite a bit of souvenir shopping too. In addition, of course, the ladies of Seoul and Tokyo had augmented her wardrobe. Even after shipping five trunks home from Japan, the baggage still exceeded the storage space in the Bluebird. To Mary's relief, Standard Oil supplied an airplane to carry her baggage and accompany her on her flight down the west coast of North America, and arranged for the Bluebird to be serviced at airports from Seattle to Burbank.

Mary shipping the Bluebird

After a long weekend in Vancouver, Mary was back in the cockpit of her Bluebird, ready to fly to Victoria for a luncheon reception at the invitation of Robert Bruce, the Governor of British Columbia. As she prepared for take-off, a huge Standard Oil Stearman monoplane landed beside the Bluebird, ready to take on Mary's luggage. 'It was a marvellous-looking machine,' she wrote, 'painted red, white and blue—a great monster beside my little Bluebird. One of the company's crack pilots came with it; he turned out to be a most charming fellow.' He was Captain Hans W. Looff, who would be Mary's escort for much of the Pacific Coast portion of the trip.

They took off from Vancouver's muddy airfield and headed west across the Strait of Georgia toward the provincial capital, Victoria, on the southern tip of Vancouver Island. Mary followed the Stearman, and Looff soon developed the habit of looking over his left shoulder to see the little Bluebird. They had not been aloft for long when Mary smelled something burning. When she throttled down the smell seemed to disappear, and she flew on, somewhat uneasily.

There was a big reception at Victoria's airfield, including members of the Women's Aeronautic Association of Canada holding up a huge British flag as a greeting. In the excitement and rush of the moment, Mary could not find a mechanic to whom she could relay her concerns about the possible engine trouble. She rode with General Bruce to Government House, where she was his guest at a luncheon. It was a hurried affair; she was concerned about leaving as soon as possible, because a telegram had arrived from Seattle informing her that 18 planes would be waiting to escort her into the United States.

Mary with Hans Looff

Back at the airfield—having foregone the after-lunch coffee in their haste—Mary and Looff took off again; this time she was in the lead. Still uneasy, she decided to make one complete circuit low over the field before striking off across Puget Sound toward Seattle. It was the luckiest thing she ever did, she claimed. Before the circuit was complete she began to smell smoke again, so she opened the throttle and began a second circuit—reasoning that it would be better to expose and solve the problem while directly above an airfield, rather than midway through a water crossing.

Smoke and suffocating fumes poured into the Bluebird's cockpit, and the heat of the rudder bar burned Mary's feet. She guessed that the Bluebird was on fire. With no parachute aboard, a rapid landing was her only chance. She switched off the engine and glided to the runway; grabbing her Pyrene fire extinguisher, she climbed from the cockpit. With the engine cowling removed she could see the damage: the front half of the firewall was burned away; the fuel tanks were hot and the woodwork was smouldering. The fire was quickly controlled, and Mary stepped back to consider the situation.

She knew at once what the source of the trouble was. She remembered the small stream of exhaust that she had seen on her long flight over the Yellow Sea, when the change in the sound of the engine had stood her hair on end. That small hole in the exhaust pipe had enlarged, and the pipe had broken. Neither the mechanics at Yokohama nor Vancouver had noticed or repaired it. Hot exhaust fumes had poured out, causing the smoke and putting the Bluebird in jeopardy.

Mary was assured that excellent repairs could be made overnight at the nearby Yarrows, Ltd. shipyard. The yard's manager had come to make the offer personally, saying that his mechanics would work through the night to fabricate and install a new exhaust pipe for the Bluebird. Mary sent a telegram to the welcoming committee in Seattle explaining the delay, and returned to Government House. The women of the local aviation community greeted the news of Mary's unexpected delay in Victoria with delight, and promptly arranged a dinner for her that evening. While her record-breaking flight was of interest to everyone, it was invariably women who cheered the loudest when Mary related her adventures.

The flight to Seattle the next day was a scenic treat. The great expanse of Puget Sound, dotted with islands dark with pinewoods, stretched before her, with the snowcapped peaks of the northern Cascade Mountains rising as a backdrop. As the Bluebird and the Stearman approached Seattle, several big airplanes met them. The little Bluebird was quickly surrounded, and Mary narrowly escaped disaster when one large Ford Trimotor cut in front of her. The Bluebird fell into its slipstream, tipped onto its side and began a spin. Wrestling for control, Mary pulled it out of the spin—and thereafter maintained a cautious distance from the other planes.

The Mayor of Seattle presented her with the ceremonial key to the city at a civic reception, and Mary was a guest of several different clubs and organizations during her short visit. She caught up on correspondence there, including a telegram from the De Havilland Aircraft Company, manufacturers of the Bluebird's engine, which said: 'Understand oil consumption still excessive. Fully prepared to carry out complete overhaul and rectification at our Toronto factory. Sincere congratulations on your achievement so far; your airmanship has our great admiration.' Toronto was definitely not on Mary's itinerary; she set the telegram aside.

On 20 December Mary flew out of Boeing Field in Seattle, followed by Captain Looff in the Standard Oil Stearman. She circled over the state capitol building in Olympia, at the southern end of Puget Sound, dropping a British and an American flag. She had been told that Charles Lindbergh had dropped an American flag there the previous year, and that hers would be displayed next to his.

The mountain peaks of the Cascade Range pointed the way south, and Mary admired their snowcapped splendour as she flew. She found them as striking as Fujiyama, although Japan's sacred mountain, standing in splendid isolation, seemed more dramatic to her than the Cascades, following one after the other as far as she could see.

Portland—Oregon's 'City of Roses'—was proud of its new airport on Swan Island in the Willamette River. Mary was suitably impressed both with the field and with the scenery around the city. 'The cultivated valley land was most picturesque,' she wrote, 'and the rows upon rows of apple trees looked liked giant checkerboards from the air.' The Women's Aeronautic Association honoured her at a dinner that night, and Mary was pleased to see how many women were enthusiastic aviators. Among the guests was one young woman whose specialty was aerobatics; she was, Mary learned, the only woman in the world who had flown an outside loop.[1]

The Pacific Coast weather, which had allowed Mary such splendid views on her flight from Vancouver, deteriorated as Mary prepared to continue south. She had hoped to spend Christmas in San Francisco, and she and Looff weighed the forecast of heavy coastal fog against the calendar. They agreed that if the fog, which lay thick and close to the ground, became too severe, they would turn back to Portland. Mary was reassured, knowing that Looff's Stearman had a radio by which he could enquire about landing conditions at Medford, their destination.

Mary had the Bluebird's fuel tanks topped up and she and Looff took off into a grey sky. As they flew, they saw no sign of the rich farmland below; thick clouds covered everything except the snowcapped peaks of the Cascades and an occasional clump of trees 'peeping up through the dense fog like little islands in a vast ocean.' Mary quickly learned to rely on Hans Looff, who flew this route regularly for Standard Oil. He jokingly told Mary that he knew every tree that stuck up by name.

Three hours' flying brought them to the valley where Medford lay, some 30 miles north of the California border. The fog had thinned a bit, and Mary spotted the airport on the north side of the small city. An old friend of Mary's from her school days was waiting there to greet her, and Mary was full of anticipation as she followed Looff on the descent.

The approach was smooth, but then disaster struck in what Mary later called her 'Christmas crash'. 'I glided in, but as I touched the ground something snapped in the undercarriage,' she wrote. 'Immediately the right wheel collapsed and the airplane was shot forward onto its nose and turned a complete somersault, ending up with its wheels pointing skywards. I found myself upside down hanging from my straps, and was unable to extricate myself. The thought of fire was in my mind, and I could see the petrol from the overflow pipe dripping onto the newly installed exhaust pipe. I struggled violently. I could hardly breathe in this upside down position, with the straps pressing tightly against me and the blood all rushing to my head. Nearly a minute and a half must have elapsed before I was able to undo my belt, which had become caught up in my coat. I heard someone cry "Mary! Mary!" It was my old school friend in a frenzy of anxiety. Then I fell out, only to roll onto the hot exhaust pipe and burn my hands.'

The Bluebird was badly damaged; pieces of the propeller were strewn about. The plane was overturned, its wings damaged. Determined to show a brave face, Mary smiled and waved reassurances as the welcoming crowd rushed forward. "But surely you didn't think I would be hurt!" she laughed, as she hugged her childhood friend and surveyed the Bluebird's damage. "After coming all these miles, what did I do? Well, she's mendable, easily mendable. I'm not hurt at all," she said. "I had just strapped my safety belt; lucky thing for me!"[2]

Looff had watched the Bluebird cartwheel on the runway from the cockpit of his big Stearman as he taxied to a stop.[3] He leapt to the ground and raced to Mary's side. Relieved to find her injuries minor, he turned his attention to practical solutions to the problems. Mary had planned no more than an overnight stop in Medford; now she would need accommodations for some time. Her school chum and her husband lived 85 miles away in Dunsmuir, California—too distant for Mary to oversee arrangements for the Bluebird's repair. Fortunately Looff's wife's parents lived in nearby Grants Pass; they would be happy to offer her hospitality. Looff would stay there also, and his wife and young son would arrive from Seattle on Christmas Eve.

It was a frustrating delay for Mary. It became apparent that the damage was too extensive for repairs at Medford's little airfield, and the Bluebird could not be flown until the undercarriage was rebuilt. Frequent landings on poor terrain and takeoffs with heavy loads had evidently weakened the bolt that gave way. The Bluebird would have to be lifted onto a truck and transported to a proper repair facility, but the nearest was at the Boeing factory in Seattle, five hundred miles north. In a newspaper interview she speculated on the cause of the accident: 'The whole thing was caused by a rusted or missing bolt in the landing gear. We don't know whether it was gone before I landed, but it was at least rusted. I think maybe they left it out the last time it was serviced. So you see I was bound to crash someday. And I'm rather glad it happened here. It's the first rest I've had since I left London.'

Her cheerful public face concealed her true feelings. The novelty of flying and the adrenaline rush of record-setting had paled in the day-to-day routine—nearly drudgery, she felt—of pressing forward toward her goal. She spelled out her inner thoughts in a letter to a friend: 'Because I have crashed I have a chance to write. The only chance I have to get my hair cut or write is when I crash. Everybody works me to death at every town I arrive at, and I am so tired sometimes I can hardly fly. This journey down the west coast at this time of year is terrible. The rain freezes on the wings of your machine, forms ice, and then you crash. I shall be thankful when I get over these mountains to San Francisco.'

On Christmas Eve, Mary telephoned home from Grants Pass. She was embarrassed to recall afterward that her first words to Victor were "Hello! Listen, before I get cut off! It's important! Please send 200 pounds immediately; I've bitten the dust with Bluebird." Then she asked how he and Tony were. She was delighted to hear that Tony, on holiday from his school in Eastbourne, was earning honours in geography. The minutes flew by and she, conscious of the mounting cost, finally concluded with "Goodbye! I'm broke!" after nine minutes of nine-thousand-mile conversation.[4]

It was Monday 29 December before Mary could arrange transport to the Boeing factory. The Bluebird made the trip north by truck that afternoon, and the next day Mary took a commercial flight from Medford to Seattle to oversee the repairs. The Boeing mechanics went to work on the Bluebird immediately, mending the metal spars that formed the framework of the little plane's wings. The job went smoothly, and Mary made a successful test flight on the morning of New Year's Eve, wearing a parachute for the flight at the insistence of the Boeing management.

Mary turned down an invitation to a party that evening in favour of restful solitude in her hotel room, wondering what the New Year would hold. While she was looking forward to visiting San Francisco, she longed to have the whole flight behind her. She wrote: 'Perhaps in three weeks I should actually be home in England. Oh, how I wished the flight was over! I was so tired of flying, flying, flying. For the last three months I never had a chance to forget it. When I wasn't flying then I had to be talking about it, and when I wasn't doing either of these, then I was dreaming about it.'

Cold and cloudy weather greeted Mary on New Year's Day, but she was determined to cover as much distance as possible. She would have to begin the trip south alone. Two days earlier an airmail pilot had gone missing during a sleet storm over the Cascade Mountains in central Oregon. His last radio transmission had reported ice forming on his wings. Other pilots—including Captain Looff— were searching for him. Two hours after her solo departure from Seattle, she landed in Portland for a weather update. There was sleet and snow in the Siskiyou Mountains beyond Medford, she was told. She opted to head for Medford at once, and was off again quickly.

The snowy peaks of Mt. Hood and Mt. Jefferson—the two highest mountains in Oregon's Cascades—stood out above the clouds as Mary flew south. No doubt regretting the absence of a radio, Mary landed again at Eugene for more weather news, the Bluebird's wheels sinking deep into snow on the runway. The news was not encouraging; more sleet storms were moving in from the south, but still she was anxious to log a few more miles. Back in the air again, she pressed on.

Her mother would have shaken her head as Mary used up one more of her nine lives. Within sight of Grants Pass, with just one ridge of mountains between her and Medford, Mary encountered a snowstorm. She opened the throttle, determined to get through at all costs. To her dismay she saw a thin film of ice gradually forming on the windscreen and wings of the Bluebird. Below were terrifying gorges, with the icy-cold Rogue River winding and twisting in and out of rocky passes. Mary wrote that, of all the tense moments she'd had on the trip, the appearance of this ice was the worst.

The Bluebird began to lose altitude: the weight of the ice was bringing her down. 'I pressed on the throttle,' she wrote, 'and tried to get the last ounce of strength out of the little engine, but the weight kept on increasing and I found myself slowly sinking'. In the distance she could see Medford's valley; could she stay aloft until she reached it? The Bluebird flew lower and lower, nearly touching the tops of the trees until suddenly Mary saw and felt a change: the layers of ice began to melt and drop from the Bluebird's wings. What seemed like a miracle was simple science: the lower altitude meant a warmer temperature. The ice was gone as she made a flawless landing at Medford.

The ground crew at Medford was incredulous. The airmail flight had not been able to get through that day; how had this tiny woman in an open biplane made it? Mary, feeling that she must push the limits of her skill and the Bluebird's endurance, had seen no alternative. She had to get past more mountains to San Francisco before she lost her nerve.

The blizzard barred any thought of continuing that day; Mary was driven once again to Grants Pass, where she waited for word from Captain Looff. Two days later he appeared, elated by the news that the missing airmail pilot had been found safe after a crash in the Cascades. Looff and the other searchers had experienced their own problems with icing during the search, and he was relieved to hear about Mary's successful flight over the mountains.

On 8 January Mary and Looff took off again from Medford in cold but clear weather; San Francisco was finally within reach. The crossing of the Siskiyou Mountains was uneventful and Mary noted with pleasure the warmer air as they flew down California's great Central Valley. She was impressed with the clearly marked landing strips that formed a string down the valley—signals for the airmail pilots of maintained runways and refuelling facilities. Eagerly awaiting her first view of San Francisco, she recalled stories her mother had told her of her school days there.[5]

The welcome at San Francisco exceeded Mary's expectations. She landed at Mills

Field, several miles south of the city. After seeing the Bluebird safely into a hangar, she was taken to an Air Ferries, Ltd. flying boat for the short flight to their wharf on San Francisco Bay near the centre of the city. A crowd waited on the Embarcadero, led by Mayor Angelo Rossi.[6] Mary was introduced to the welcoming officials, bouquets of roses were presented, and press photographers recorded the scene. A motorcade of 30 motorcycles, sirens wailing, led the way to the Mark Hopkins Hotel, at the top of San Francisco's Nob Hill. It was Mary's first experience with an American luxury hotel, and the view from the sixteenth floor was spectacular. She was thrilled to be given the keys to a new Nash Eight automobile for her use while in San Francisco.

Telegrams were waiting for her, too. Not surprisingly, Victor—after more than three months of bachelorhood—was anxious to have her home. She was pleased to hear from officials in her mother's hometown, New Albany, Indiana, who were preparing a gala celebration for her arrival later that month.

Mary and Hans Looff had four days together in San Francisco, and by now their friendship had apparently ripened into something more than the camaraderie of pilots. Mary's marriage had been strained by the months-long separation. Although Victor never publicly complained, it must have been a source of some annoyance

Mary arrives in San Francisco

that he was left behind to manage their home (and Mary's son Tony, too) while she flew off alone on the adventure of a lifetime. Captain Looff was understandably smitten with this exotic and adventurous sprite who was so at home in his element, the sky. The two flyers recognized each other as kindred spirits, and they made the most of their last days together.

But San Francisco was the end of the road for them; Looff had to return to his home base, Boeing Field in Seattle, while Mary set out for Southern California. Standard Oil assigned another pilot for the second half of her Pacific coast journey. Mary and Looff said goodbye, but not before they made plans to meet again in Paris, two years hence. The promise of a reunion was something to look forward to, particularly for Looff.

The pair exchanged letters and telegrams for several months. Looff called Mary 'My dear little Bluebird' and signed his letters 'Your Golden Butterfly'. He wrote: 'I returned from a trip to Portland today and instinctively looked back time after time. Just now everything seems hopeless and disappointing but I know everything will turn out all right in the end. The thoughts of you, warm blue skies, the sea and clean white sands will always spur me on. You may expect me to visit you within two years. When I do make my fortune I shall not give you up. You are on my mind constantly. At any rate I am filling an engagement at LeBourget two years from this coming June regardless of what happens. Am rather lonely tonight, wish I could look over my left shoulder tomorrow and see the Bluebird bravely coming along. I am so tired tonight, must go to bed and dream about Paris in less than two years. Good night, Bluebird . . . I am your Golden Butterfly.'

18 Crossing America

Hollywood drew Mary like a flame draws a moth. Not only had she inherited her mother's dramatic bent, she was a great movie fan as well; a visit to Southern California was a must. The Los Angeles suburb of Burbank boasted what Mary declared 'the finest airport in the world'—and it is a fair assumption that she had seen more of the world's airports in the previous four months than any other pilot. Among the crowd gathered to welcome Mary were Bobbi Trout and Edna May Cooper, two American women who had just set an impressive air endurance record of one full week, demonstrating the feasibility of mid-air refuelling.

From her suite of rooms at the luxurious Ambassador Hotel, Mary played the role of Los Angeles tourist with gusto. She was disappointed not to meet her favourite movie star, Mary Pickford, who had sent a telegram saying that she would not be able to entertain Mary because she had been called to New York suddenly. On a tour of the Warner Brothers movie studio Mary watched several films being shot. After three hours, she wrote, she felt like she had made a second trip around the world: Eastern scenes, jungles, deserts, oceans, palaces, mountains, skyscrapers—the studio was a world of its own.

When Mary was introduced to Los Angeles Chief of Police James E. Davis,[1] she told him of her forced landing in the Southeast Asian jungle, when she had a revolver but not the skill to use it. He insisted that she come to the police shooting range for a lesson in gun handling. The Chief did a little showing off first, shooting two revolvers at once and hitting bull's-eyes with both—and then put on a blindfold and did it again. Mary was properly impressed, and intimidated as he handed her a huge Colt .38. She shrank from it, whereupon he said "You want confidence, that's all. I'll soon put you right," and led her toward the targets. He offered her a cigarette, declaring that he would shoot the ash from the end as she held it in her mouth! Her protests that she was not a smoker fell on deaf ears and, cigarette between her lips, she waited with dread while he retreated twenty feet, took aim and shot. The shot missed both the cigarette and Mary, and the

Chief said, "It's all right! Better luck this time!" She was about to lose her nerve and refuse when someone thoughtfully provided a cigarette holder. With a little more distance between her head and the target, she recovered her bravery and stood waiting. Another Bang! A shower of ash resulted, and Mary and the Chief were both relieved. 'Nevermore was I to be thrilled with tales of William Tell,' she wrote, 'and I left the revolver range feeling a better and bolder woman.'

At the shooting range with Chief James 'Two Gun' Davis

She was given a tour around Beverly Hills, and shown the homes of Charlie Chaplin, Mary Pickford, Harold Lloyd, and John Barrymore. American movie stars were well known in England, and Mary was suitably impressed by the beauty and grandeur of their homes. She admired the lavish gardens, ablaze with colour in the bright January sunshine, so different from England in the winter.

San Diego was her next stop, and Mary was flattered to see two squadrons of military aircraft flying toward her as she approached the city. She was used to being met by aircraft now, but this was a particularly impressive reception. As she neared the landing strip she could see a huge mass of soldiers standing in smart ranks along the runway. Thrilled with the extraordinary greeting, she wanted to express her delight and greet the crowd in a memorable fashion. She swooped down low in the Bluebird, flying just a few feet above the heads of the officials. As she pulled up she spotted the General, and dove a second time right over his head. He stood at rigid attention as Mary flew around a third time—nearly knocking off his hat. Belatedly, Mary noticed her Standard Oil escort pilot waving to her frantically, motioning her away from what she thought was her impressive welcoming committee. Perplexed, she followed the bigger plane across town to another landing strip, where a more modest civic reception committee waited for her—leaving behind the military review and air show that she had inadvertently disrupted.

January was the month for the Monte Carlo Rally and this was the first time in six years that Mary would miss it. As much as she always enjoyed the Rally itself, relaxing in the sunshine of the French Riviera and gambling at the casino were the icing on the cake for her. As a consolation, she took a side trip from San Diego to the posh Agua Caliente resort in Tijuana, Mexico. Built at the height of the Prohibition era, the opulent seven million dollar playground drew a wealthy and sophisticated clientele with its gambling, thoroughbred horse racing, luxury hotel, restaurants, and entertainment.[2] Mary marvelled at the swimming pools, marble terraces, and lavish gardens.

Eating lunch in a courtyard beside a lily pond sparkling with bright goldfish, she was serenaded with lively tunes by a Mexican *mariachi* band. Asked if she had any musical request, she replied "Oh yes; please play something Hawaiian." The bandleader's cold look and her hostess's quick "You're getting a little mixed up with your countries, my dear!" exposed her *faux pas*. Anxious to make amends, Mary only made things worse with her next request, "Oh! Then 'The Toreador'!" Evidently the bandleader found a selection from a French opera to be as inappropriate as Hawaiian music. He was nearly apoplectic, and the whole band seemed to quiver in sympathy with him as he seized his fiddle and began to play the Mexican national anthem.

The pleasant days in the sunshine of southern California were her last leisure time before the cross-country flight, and Mary was soon back to her early-rising habits. Her route east from San Diego took her over the Colorado River and across the mountains and deserts of the American southwest. 'Never have I seen such country,' she wrote; 'huge, stern hills and river beds dry of water. It was particularly interesting to me, for my great-grandfather and great-grandmother trekked across this same country to California in covered wagons in the great gold rush, and now today I was flying over the very ground in a little aeroplane.' At the insistence of well-meaning friends in San Diego, Mary wore a parachute for this leg of the flight. She smiled as she looked down at a far-reaching expanse of giant cacti, envisioning a parachute descent into the spiky stems below.

She landed in Phoenix, staying just long enough for a luncheon with members of the local women's aeronautic association. Pilot and plane refuelled, the journey eastward continued over more flat and barren territory. A strong headwind slowed her progress, and she was chagrined to find herself in a race of sorts with a train. It was travelling around 70 mph, she figured—a speed that the Bluebird could easily exceed ordinarily. But the 30 to 40 mph headwinds slowed her speed severely. She passed the train when it stopped at a station but soon it overtook her again. She was flying very low, and watched as the passengers leaned out their windows to wave to her.

As she flew over the Rio Grande at El Paso she was thrilled to realize she had reached Texas, the heartland of the storied American West. Hollywood westerns were popular in England and movie fan Mary craned her neck, scanning the west Texas vastness in vain for a sign of cowboys or Indians. There were none to be seen; she saw instead mile after mile of oilfields: tanks, drilling rigs, and pools of black oil on the ground. Beyond Dallas there was more interesting scenery as she crossed the Ozark Mountains of Arkansas and Missouri, coming at last to the broad Mississippi River. Since childhood she had heard her mother's stories of journeys up and down the river, and the sight of the wide ribbon of water below thrilled Mary.

Industrial smoke clouded the evening air above St. Louis as Mary circled, looking for the Curtiss-Wright airfield. At every airfield across the United States, Curtiss-Wright had put its mechanics at Mary's disposal; they had serviced the Bluebird since Seattle, and Mary was looking forward to thanking the company's directors personally.

She had intended to fly to her mother's hometown the next day, but a message was delivered to her in St. Louis from the directors of the Standard Oil Company in Chicago, suggesting that she pay a visit there. It was the politic thing to do, she decided, since Standard Oil had provided her fuel for the trip across America—to say nothing of the escort plane that still accompanied her, carrying her excess baggage.

At noon the next day, 22 January, she left for Chicago, once again flying along the railway. It was freezing cold, and she shivered in her open cockpit. A blizzard was blowing across Lake Michigan, Mary wrote. 'How I stood the journey is beyond me; I just froze. I couldn't feel my hands and feet, and I was terrified that I should not be able to land the machine.' It was, in fact, a hair-raising landing. A queue of airliners circled above the busy airfield, waiting their turns to land. Mary circled for half an hour, miserable in the bitter cold. 'My head had become so cold,' she wrote, 'that my brain refused to work; I nearly landed 20 feet too soon. The machine dropped and I just saved myself by putting on the engine at the last minute.'

Interviewed in Chicago, Mary was described as 'a chic, slender girl with the immortal light of adventure still shining in her eyes,'[3] a description which surely appealed to her flair for the dramatic. She kept to herself her low opinion of the city (she later called it 'Hell-with-the-lid-off'). A reporter quoted her as saying "Such a foggy day! I haven't seen anything quite like this since I left England," and was surprised to learn that what she was seeing was mostly smoke and not fog. Sometime during her overnight stay in the city, Al Capone[4] visited the airfield and added his signature to the hundreds already decorating the Bluebird. Across the tail he wrote 'Hurrah for Prohibition! Al Capone.'

Mary picked up still more baggage in Chicago, but she was glad to have it; she was able to borrow fur boots and a warm flying suit for the trip to the Curtiss-Wright airfield at Indianapolis. There were now two Standard Oil planes escorting her, with her luggage distributed between them. They took off in a snowstorm, gradually leaving behind the bitingly cold weather as they flew south, away from the Great Lakes. In mid-afternoon they landed at Indianapolis, where she was given a hearty welcome by the Governor of Indiana. Mary was burning with excitement, about to reach what she considered the pinnacle of her trip around the world: a visit to New Albany.

A reception was planned there for the next day, a Saturday. There were crowds at the Indianapolis airfield to see her off on this exciting leg of her trip. South she flew, tense with excitement. She circled low over New Albany, then crossed the Ohio River to land at Louisville, Kentucky, the nearest airport. Another throng of well-wishers awaited her and, with a bouquet of American Beauty roses in her arms, she was escorted to an automobile and driven, with motorcycle police escort, across the river to New Albany. The town's mayor, C.B. McLinn, waited with a welcoming committee and another motorcycle escort.

Mary had heard dozens of welcoming speeches during her trip, but none touched her more than Mayor McLinn's: "Mrs. Bruce, you are at the gates of New Albany. We are proud to welcome you. We have never before had a great person who has ridden the air and encircled the earth to visit us, and we marvel at the spirit of love and of courage which has brought you to us. You have had honor and praise in the great cities of the world. We give you honor and give you also the kindly welcome of home folks and friends who knew your mother and your people and who would be friendly to you. We have looked for your coming—we want you to be one of us while you stay. The city of New Albany presents you with an air photograph of our city with your mother's birthplace marked. Take it to her, and may it recall old memories for her and remind you of the little city which cradled the mother and, with open arms, received the daughter."

Mary is greeted at the entrance to New Albany, Indiana (Photo courtesy of Stuart B. Wrege Indiana History Room, New Albany-Floyd County Public Library)

A motorcade carried Mary through the streets lined with townspeople, between buildings hung with British and American flags. She was driven to visit the house in which her mother was born, and was introduced to a 95-year-old lady who had been a childhood playmate of her grandmother's. She was given a letter from a man who had known her mother and her uncles when they were children.

At a public reception following a dinner party in her honour at the local hotel, Mary was presented with an American flag and a letter from Mayor McLinn, which she was to deliver to the American Ambassador to Britain, Charles Dawes. It read: 'Mrs. Victor Bruce has been our guest in her round-the-world flight. The idea of coming to this city, the birthplace of her mother, prompted her dramatic and adventurous flight in a small plane from England over Europe, Asia, and our own continent. She will drop tomorrow on her mother's old home an American flag carried all the way from England, and I am sending, by her, to you, another flag with the cordial greetings of our city. We feel very near to England today with this ambassadress of goodwill, and citizen through blood ties, in our midst.'

Mary spent the night in New Albany and was driven the next day back to the airfield at Louisville. She took off in the Bluebird at noon, with three bunches of flowers and her mother's American flag. She had weighted the flag with two spark plugs, hoping to prevent it from blowing too far from the house. The roof of her mother's old house had been marked with a big white cross, to make it easy to spot from the air. Circling very low, Mary dropped the weighted flag on the target.

Reports vary as to just where it landed. Mary wrote first that it landed on the ground in front of the house; years later, in her autobiography, she claimed it had fallen squarely on the roof. A New Albany newspaper wrote at the time that the flag, weighted with the spark plugs, had landed on the owner of the house, 'laying her out.' The victim was reportedly 'honored by the assault.'

Mary flew low over the New Albany town cemetery and dropped the bouquets of flowers in honour of her ancestors buried there, then turned east toward her next destination, Columbus, Ohio. In Columbus she again received a telegram suggesting a detour, and this one proved even more disastrous than the miserable flight to Chicago. She had planned to fly to Washington, D.C., but a telegram from the Glenn Martin Aircraft Company invited her to Baltimore where, she was assured, a large National Guard detachment would be available to escort her to Washington. Plans were quickly changed; her escort planes were notified.

Just as she was ready to take off from Columbus Mary noticed, to her dismay, that the St. Christopher medal, given to her by the priest in the village of Lakhon, had been torn off the Bluebird's dash. She had relied on that medal, and was devastated by its loss. She considered delaying her departure until she could get another like it, but the pressure of her schedule and the people waiting for her convinced her not to change her plans. Reluctantly, she concluded that she must go. 'I felt as I took off from Columbus that day that I was not going to reach New York,' she wrote.

She was correct. Almost from takeoff, things went wrong. Her map blew out of the cockpit, and she was left with only a compass for navigation. The weather was stormy, with such poor visibility that she could see neither of her two escort planes behind her. The terrain below was hilly, and it was with relief that she sighted the Potomac River. Relief was immediately replaced with panic, though, as her eye fell on the Bluebird's fuel gauge; the needle was on the red mark. She had ordered extra fuel in Columbus, but she was running on empty after only three hours. She knew she had to land at once—but where? Thankfully she spotted one of her two escort planes. She waggled her wings and motioned frantically to her fuel tank. The pilot understood, and joined her in searching for a spot in which to land. Mary saw him descend, landing in a small field. It looked reasonably dry, she reported, but there were deep cart tracks bisecting the field. The escort plane cleared the ruts and landed on the other side; Mary followed, and was safely down.

Mary and the escort pilot[5] walked a mile to the nearest farmhouse, where they learned that the nearest source of fuel was forty miles away. The farmer offered them some gas from his car, but all he could spare was nine gallons. It was getting dark, and Mary and the escort pilot accepted the farmer's invitation to spend the night. They telephoned the airfield at Baltimore to explain their predicament, and settled down to wait for morning.

The nine gallons of fuel were enough to get the Bluebird up and away, and Baltimore's heavy smoky haze soon enveloped the planes. Mary's escort pilot had told her that he knew the exact position of the airport, but she saw him circling again and again, obviously searching for it. She had been counting on him to lead the way; instead his plane disappeared into the smoke over the city.

Mary had a map this time, and eventually she spotted a large factory complex marked 'Glenn Martin Factory' and flew toward it. But there was no landing strip in sight—only a patch of muddy ground. She decided to try to make the landing, since she had been told to land where she saw the factory sign. The wheels of the Bluebird sank deep into the mud and Mary thought she would nose over into the muck, but she managed to keep it steady, rolling to a stop on the muddy surface. She was met by Glenn Martin and a party of guests, who escorted her to a luncheon arranged in her honour.

Over lunch, Mary expressed her concern to Martin about taking off from the muddy field. American aircraft had generally much more powerful engines, she knew, and the Bluebird was overloaded and underpowered by most standards. But she had just been handed a telegram from the British Embassy in Washington, reminding her that a 3 p.m. reception had been arranged; the National Guard troops were waiting to escort her. Already behind schedule, she did not want to delay any longer.

The decision was costly. Deep, thick mud coated the runway. Two men steadied the wings, trying to keep the Bluebird straight as Mary taxied. Unable to gather enough flying speed, the Bluebird rose a bit, then suddenly dropped and rolled over in the mud. It was a terrifying few seconds for Mary: 'I seemed to be turning over and over for endless ages and the noise of the splintering wood and crashing wings was terrific. Something struck my head and my left leg, and I found myself, for the second time in my life, hanging upside down.'

Mary extricated herself and jumped out, dazed. This seemed to be the end of the road; so close to her final goal, and now the Bluebird lay in pieces in the mud, seemingly broken beyond any hope of repair. Mary's flying goggles had lacerated her forehead when she hit the windshield. Bloody, frustrated, and disappointed beyond words, she sat down in the mud beside the little plane and cried in despair.

At the Glenn Martin factory, Baltimore

The members of the press who were present evidently saw things in different ways. One story called it 'a slight accident but neither she nor her Blackburn Bluebird was seriously hurt. She will be continuing her flight almost immediately to Washington and thence to New York.' Another reporter, seeing blood running down her face from the cut on her forehead immediately assumed disaster and filed a story that she had been seriously injured, and the Bluebird wrecked beyond all repair, an account that was unfortunately delivered to Victor at midnight.

After she had a good cry, Mary wrote, she got up out of the mud and inspected the damage. Both wings were wrecked; the engine was torn out of the fuselage; the rudder was bent, the propeller shattered. She photographed the wreckage, and turned to her luncheon host, Martin. He would have his mechanics inspect the Bluebird, he told her, and he would see her in the morning. She was driven to the Lord Baltimore Hotel, where a doctor attended to the cut on her eyebrow. She ordered room service and spent the evening in her room, so as not to have to repeatedly explain the lump on her head and the unexpected change of plans.

In the morning she returned to the Glenn Martin factory and found the Bluebird right side up in a hangar, surrounded by workmen. Dozens of new names had been added to the Bluebird; she noted that the tail was a wreck, and Al Capone's signature was in danger of being destroyed. Glenn Martin appeared as she was inspecting the wings, and together they met with the head engineer to discuss what could be done. Martin assured her that they would completely investigate the damage that afternoon and give her a report in the morning.

Mary passed another night at the hotel, and wrote a letter to Victor. She was in the position of grateful supplicant to Martin, but privately she was seething. 'I am most annoyed about this accident,' she told her husband, 'as the people here had no right to invite me to their landing field as it was in a disgraceful condition: soft, foot-deep in mud, and has been condemned by the airline here as unsafe. The Glenn Martin factory, whose field it is, wanted to have me here for publicity for themselves. The Standard Oil Company was furious with the Glenn Martin Company for letting me come here, and have told me I should not pay for the repair, and they are going to take the matter up for me.'

Feeling, perhaps, that with Victor she could speak her mind freely and not have to put on a cheerful front, she continued, 'I have not made a penny in this country and see no hope of doing so as everybody is broke here at the moment. I am tired to death of the flight and strain and shall be thankful to be back. I have no money left to pay my passage home so I do not know what is going to be done about it. Anyhow, I expect I shall get back somehow within the next two weeks and shall probably land at Cherbourg in France.'

Mary visited the Glenn Martin factory every day, watching as the repairs were made, and assisting as she could. The wings were mended, and the signature-covered fabric was carefully re-stretched over the newly mended wings.

The weather had turned cold and dry, and the runway was in much better condition as the time for departure neared. Glenn Martin and several hundred of his factory employees watched as Mary pushed the stick forward, and the Bluebird rolled smoothly down the track and lifted into the air. She made two circuits of the field, waggled her wings to say all was well, and flew off toward Washington, just 30 miles to the south.

Mary admired her brief aerial view of Washington, calling it 'one of the nicest-looking cities I have seen in the east of America'. But there was no time for a visit; she was eager to get to New York. She was short of money and short of patience, and very anxious for the flight to be over.

She had been told to watch, as she approached New York, for an airborne welcoming committee of some 25 military planes flying in formation. This time they would really be for her—not as in San Diego! But a heavy cloud cover prevented the planned airborne reception, and Mary was left to find her way to her destination, Glenn Curtiss Airfield.

Forced low because of the cloud cover—she was flying just one hundred feet above the water when she spotted the Statue of Liberty—Mary had a close call when a skyscraper suddenly loomed up before her. She flew up and down the East River for forty-five minutes, and as she finally spotted the landing strip, she also saw the only two airplanes of the United States Army Air Corps welcoming committee that had not become lost in the fog. Mary and the Bluebird touched down at Glenn Curtiss Airfield on Long Island on the sixth of February, 1931.

New York was second only to Hollywood in terms of glamour and excitement for Mary; she was wide-eyed as she was driven to her room at the Ritz-Carlton Hotel. New York struck Mary as a very sophisticated and stylish city. She was impressed by the Holland Tunnel beneath the Hudson River, by a visit to a speakeasy, and by the dazzling display of bright lights on Broadway.

Although Mary wrote of visiting the Empire State Building in both her account of her world flight[6] and in her later autobiography,[7] the details are vastly different. In 1931 she wrote of a 102-story ascent by elevator, to an office where 'there were office girls working their typewriters and calculators above the clouds'. More than forty-five years later, she wrote that she flew around and around the skyscraper as she arrived in New York, close enough to see waving hands from the top story— and that she was met by police when she landed and scolded but not arrested. In the second telling, a later visit to the top floor of the building included a meeting with the women who had waved, one of whom claimed she had seen the colour of Mary's eyes. Both accounts are fanciful: the building was not officially opened until May 1931, when President Herbert Hoover pressed a button in Washington, D.C., turning on the lights. And according to the Empire State Building press office, there were no occupants in February 1931, and no offices have ever been located above the 80th floor.

Mary's visit in New York was short. Anxious to be home, she had arranged to sail on 9 February on the modern liner *Ile de France*. The Bluebird, insured for £525, was again shipped with her. Mary was impressed with the continental atmosphere aboard the ship, and enjoyed the company of several other celebrity passengers. Spanish dancer Antonia Mercé, known as 'La Argentina', was on board, as well as Frank Edison, son of inventor Thomas Edison. Mary was particularly thrilled to meet French aviation pioneer Robert Esnault-Pelterie, whose chief claim to fame was the invention of the joystick design for airplane controls. He was a contemporary of Louis Bleriot, and had a long career as an innovative designer and builder of airplanes and engines. He had just published *Astronautics*, a groundbreaking treatise on the prospects and problems of space travel, which he foresaw as the next great frontier for flyers. He gave a shipboard lecture on the possibility of rocket travel to the moon, and Mary was chosen to introduce him. 'No doubt everyone thought I would be the most likely person to test his wonderful rocket car when it was ready,' she wrote.

Mary was sound asleep when the *Ile de France* docked at Plymouth early in the morning after the six-day Atlantic crossing. She planned to sail on to LeHavre, disembark there with the Bluebird, and fly the final leg home to England. She had not, however, planned for the surprise appearance of her husband at her stateroom door. Needless to say, excitement prevailed. Victor couldn't get a word in edgewise, as Mary started immediately to tell him about her experiences.

After a brief glimpse of England from the deck, Mary and Victor sailed to Le Havre, where they oversaw the unloading of the Bluebird before being driven to their hotel. A few days in Paris followed; the official reception in England was not scheduled until the 20th of February. The weather was stormy; sleet and snow made Mary wonder if she would be able to fly home after all. The two returned to LeHavre, and on the 19th Victor took a boat back to Southampton while Mary set out to fly north across the English Channel alone.

The weather threatened to defeat her, as it had so many times on her journey. She picked up her Dictaphone and recorded: "I have been flying for half an hour and it is impossible to see forward at all. The only line I can follow is the white foam on the coast. I can only tell my bearings by the time I am taking, and it is impossible to distinguish any landmarks. I am flying low, about twenty feet above the water. I fear it will be impossible for me to get across the Channel today."

She would land, she decided, at a small field near Calais—but after searching for an hour, she could not locate the airstrip. Instead, she climbed above the clouds and, consulting her compass, struck off toward England, giving herself 15 minutes of flying time before she would descend through the clouds.

Once again, a tense descent through a cloud cover was rewarded with a happy sight. Even better than the railroad tracks that led her to Hanoi after the terrifying flight over the Annamitic Range, the white cliffs of Dover sent her heart soaring. "Hurrah! Hurrah!" she exclaimed on the Dictaphone, "England at last, after nearly five months of flying. It is too good to be true!"

The little Bluebird touched down at Lympne Airfield near Folkstone on the morning of 19 February 1931. A formal reception was scheduled for the next day at Croydon, some 50 miles to the west, but Mary had decided to take no chances that the winter weather might delay her flight from France. Cautiously, she had chosen to get home in plenty of time for the celebration. Still, it must have been something of a letdown to arrive at Lympne to an absolute absence of cheers.

Mary shut down the engine and jumped out of the Bluebird, striding up to the lone mechanic in sight. "Shake hands with me!" she exclaimed. "I'm back!"

"From where?" he asked, having no idea who she was.

"From the world!" she exulted.

A taxi was called for the short drive to an inn a few miles away in Hythe, a seafront town overlooking the Strait of Dover. A full English high tea was the first order of business, although it was barely noon. News of Mary's arrival spread quickly, and the afternoon was occupied with telephone calls from friends and from the press. Norman Blackburn and his entire staff arrived to pepper her with questions about the performance of the Bluebird, her experiences and her thoughts. "Have you heard?" joked Blackburn, "Scotland Yard are going to take your machine away tomorrow; they want Al Capone's fingerprints!"

Winifred Spooner and Amy Johnson were on hand at Lympne the next morning to greet Mary. The three were undoubtedly the best-known women flyers in the British Empire, and Spooner and Johnson would escort Mary to the triumphant conclusion of her flight at Croydon. A flight of Bluebirds and other airplanes followed in their wake as they took off on the stroke of eleven. Nearly ill with excitement, Mary led the procession over the familiar and welcoming English countryside. She spied the landing strip at Croydon, and flew one low circuit around the huge airfield before she throttled down and glided to the earth one last time.[8]

Surrounded at once by a throng of welcomers, Mary spotted familiar faces all around. Victor rushed forward to greet her, with her son Tony and her father. Ten-year-old Tony scolded her, "Mummy, you're late! You should have been here half an hour ago!" Years later he recalled that she laughed and answered, "I'm glad to be back anyhow, whatever time it is!"

20 February 1931: Mary with Amy Johnson (left) and Winifred Spooner

There was a formal welcome by the Undersecretary for Air, Mr. Montague, and a happy confusion of smiles and shouts of approval, all recorded by newspapers and newsreel cameras. Huge bouquets of flowers were pressed on Mary as her friends and family shared her delight at being home again. Among the crowd was her old housekeeper whose announcement of the leaky water heater had sent Mary to Burlington Gardens for some window-shopping on that fateful day the previous summer.

"How are things at home?" Mary greeted her.

'Her smiling face grew serious,' Mary wrote. 'Looking 'round to make sure that nobody could hear, she whispered in my ear: "There's been a tragedy! That water heater's leaking again!"'

19 Back from the World

The welcome Mary received at Croydon was warm and enthusiastic—but distinctly low-budget. She was acutely aware of the absence of the exuberant outpouring of enthusiasm and the shower of monetary reward that had greeted Amy Johnson after her flight to Australia less than one year earlier. Mary's compensation—the newsreel cameras, bouquets of flowers and formal speeches—paled in comparison to the £10,000, new automobile, and two new airplanes that Johnson had received.

Mary never complained publicly, but there is no doubt that she was bitterly disappointed. Johnson had, after all, merely flown a route already pioneered by a man, Bert Hinkler. Mary had set several brand new records: the first flight from England to Japan; the first air crossing of the Yellow Sea; the first Briton and the first woman ever to fly solo around the world.[1]

Just after buying the Bluebird, Mary had written optimistically to her mother, 'I am told I shall make a fortune if I reach America.' She had gradually realised, however, in the course of the flight, that she was flying in a new economy. In a letter to a friend written during the dark days following her Christmas crash in Oregon, she wrote, 'I have made no money yet, and am nearly broke. I have really gotten so worried about the finances that I sometimes hardly have the heart to go on. The publicity here is wonderful but when it comes to getting any money for your story or lectures, they change their tune immediately.'

The 1920s had been a decade of extravagance and expansion, both socially and financially. The essence of those years was the testing of limits. Financial limits were reached, then breached, with the collapse of the stock market. The Wall Street crash of October 1929 put a match to the fuse of worldwide financial meltdown.

The ensuing Great Depression saw a radical change in society. The exuberance of *Makin' Whoopee* gave way to *Brother, Can You Spare a Dime?* as unemployment lines grew, soup kitchens appeared, and families everywhere gave up luxuries for

An Enthralling Story

will be told by

THE HON. MRS. VICTOR BRUCE

entitled

"Flying Alone Round the World"

Mrs. Bruce will tell the story of her remarkable adventures whilst flying through twenty-three Countries and across three Continents. The tale of her crash on a lonely stretch of Persian Desert on the borders of Baluchistan alone should hold any audience spellbound apart from the many other adventures that befel this brave little woman in the jungles of Burma and Siam, and the pirate infested regions on the Coast of China.

Illustrated with Lantern Slides, and with Films in addition where desired bare necessities. 'Getting by' was the new norm.

It was clear to Mary, upon her return, that the economic and social climate in England that spring of 1931 was dramatically changed; with the stubborn determination that was so basic to her character, she searched for another route to financial success.

In a move that helped to keep her name before the public, the Bluebird was put on display in the lobby of the Charing Cross underground station, where passers-by marvelled at the autograph-decorated little plane that had circled the globe.

Within a month Mary embarked on a lecture tour. She appeared, often several times a week, all over England, telling of her adventures. She was much in demand at community clubs, civic organizations, aviation groups, and Ladies' Society meetings. She developed a standard presentation, illustrated with dozens of lantern slides. Mary had taken most of the pictures herself, but she added some press photographs and maps showing her route.

Victor joined her on the tour, operating the slide projector and sometimes answering the recurring question about how it felt to be left at home while his wife went adventuring. One reporter enquired as to why a man would let his wife go off on such a long trip. "The very idea of my letting her do anything is humorous," Victor declared, as he described her stubborn and determined character. "Some people would call it pig-headedness," he said, "but it is the quality which has been her greatest asset."

Mary's standard presentation was titled *Flying Alone around the World*, and her lectures were well advertised in the newspapers and on handbills posted in advance of her appearances. Newspaper interviews often preceded these events, raising interest and increasing attendance.

There was plenty of curiosity about what kind of a woman would buy an airplane and fly off alone around the world, leaving husband and child at home. Mary was constantly quizzed about her motives; she always had a ready answer for the question. In an article titled 'Not All Done for Fun', Mary made the rather self-righteous assertion that her world flight was primarily to secure financial stability for her family. She had been hurt, she told the reporter, by hearing it said that women condemned those of their sex who forsook their homes and their children to go off gallivanting around the world in a plane. "It is time that the truth were told," Mary declared. "It is time that other women realise we do these things because our exploits lead to ways of earning money. I have a little boy to think of, and these are hard times."[2]

Mary embraced her new role as aviator, and set about to extol the virtues of air travel for the common person. She was a frequent participant in air pageants and races like the annual King's Cup Air Race. Interviewed in August, she sent up a trial balloon for a proposed non-stop Pacific flight. She was disheartened, she told the reporter, at the apathy shown by British air concerns, while flyers from other nations were setting new records nearly every week. She proposed to fly the Pacific Ocean from Tokyo to Seattle, a distance of 4,000 miles, within the year. "The Americans are desperately keen on being first to fly the Pacific," she said. "Meanwhile Britain sits still and does nothing! If anybody is prepared to finance me I will do my best to show that Britain can still lead in the air world."

No one stepped forward to offer the financing, and two months later Mary watched as the record for the first Pacific crossing went to American flyers Clyde Pangborn and Hugh Herndon, who flew a Bellanca CH-400 non-stop from Tokyo to Wenatchee, Washington in October, 1931.[3] Also watching—and undoubtedly sighing with relief—was Standard Oil's pilot Hans Looff. In nearly every letter Mary received from him she was admonished not to take any risks such as transoceanic flights. 'What is this I read?' he wrote to her. 'Please don't consider it. You have done quite enough, and much more than any other girl flyer. Have a long rest where things are quiet. Be a good girl and don't take any more chances. I don't want you to fly anymore, but if you must—be careful!'

Never shy about publicity, Mary's activities were the subject of several newspaper stories. She and fellow aviator Winifred Brown[4] plotted a six-part, 500-mile marathon race around Britain. The plan was to race from Hyde Park to the Thames by horse, race upstream a few miles by speedboat, then change to bicycles and motorcycles for the short run from the river to Brooklands, make several laps of the track in automobiles, and finish the race by flying to Manchester and back.

Several changes of plan and date were made, and eventually a local pundit wrote 'No doubt these mixed events will soon become the rage, and at any moment I may issue a challenge to anyone to race me to Bootle on a scooter, thence to Blackpool by bicycle, and then to Aberdeen on a donkey. The journey from Aberdeen to Pitlochry must be made on roller skates, from Pitlochry to Peebles on crutches, and from Peebles home on a brewer's dray drawn by four army mules suffering from the staggers. It is only by experiments such as these that modern means of transport can be brought to that pitch of perfection.'

Whether it was the ribbing in the press or the distraction of other activities, the great race never came off, but Mary's schedule was full enough without it. It was not only lectures and flying that occupied Mary that summer and fall. She returned to speedboat racing, winning the *Daily Telegraph* Cup in a race at Poole Harbour in August. The next month, in her new role as aviation booster and celebrity, she was chosen to hoist the newly designed Civil Air ensign in London.[5]

Women were increasingly active in the world of aviation. To celebrate their new visibility in the field, the first all-women's flying meet took place in September. It drew a diverse and impressive assembly of pilots who joined in a memorable event.[6]

To complete the triple play of planes, boats and cars, October found Mary competing in a special race for women on the track at Brooklands, driving an Aston Martin in a field of ten of the fastest women of the day. Two months later Brooklands announced that women, having 'proved themselves capable of competing with men in the longest and most gruelling contests,' would be eligible to take part in regular racing there beginning with the spring season.

The tempting thought of crossing an ocean by air—either the Pacific or Atlantic—continued to intrigue Mary. She was convinced that she could do it, but also knew that her navigational skills were insufficient for a solo attempt.

Mary broadened her flying expertise by becoming the first woman certified in instrument flying. Her course at Hamble Aerodrome, on the Solent, finished with the final test: a flight over a triangular route, with the cockpit of the plane covered by a canvas hood. With no view of earth or sky, Mary flew by instruments alone. When she estimated she had returned to her starting place she raised the hood and was greatly relieved to find that she was indeed above Hamble and not out in the middle of the English Channel. Even more difficult than the absence of horizon, she said, was the hypnotic effect of the dashboard instruments; the dials and pointers so captured her attention that she found it took great effort to interpret the information from each.

Mary was soon back at the Brooklands School of Flying for lessons to prepare for her B licence, allowing her to fly for hire. If there really was a future in aviation, she knew, the way to turn a profit was not merely to make a flight—however spectacular it might be—and then go on the lecture circuit. Commercial aviation would be the moneymaking wave of the future, and that would require a commercial licence.

Mary's tale of her adventurous world flight not only made for an entertaining evening at the lecture hall; it translated successfully into a book published in London in the fall of 1931 by Chapman and Hall. *The Bluebird's Flight* was illustrated with dozens of maps and photos, many taken by Mary, and included a transcription of some of the Dictaphone notes from the trip. She re-recorded several excerpts from her original Dictaphone messages. Released by Columbia Records, the recording enjoyed modest popularity for several months.

She continued to write for magazines and newspapers, too, although her focus had shifted from automotive topics to promotion of aviation for the public.

'Comfort at the Controls—Three Important Points' included the advice that hobble skirts were not a wise choice when flying, nor were loose flying scarves. 'Emergency Landing Grounds' suggested signposting visible from the air for pilots looking for safe places to make unscheduled landings. Together with receipts from lectures, income from her book and articles contributed to Mary's growing financial stability.

There were still aviation records to be established, though, and May 1932 saw one of those records set by American aviator Amelia Earhart, who flew the Atlantic non-stop from Newfoundland to Ireland. Earhart was the first woman pilot to cross the Atlantic, and she set the fastest time ever. She was received in London with great acclaim; the King and Queen sent a telegram of congratulations. She was the houseguest of American Ambassador Andrew Mellon, and was the hostess for a tea party at his home in honour of English airwomen. Mary was among the guests, and had a long chat with the American aviator. The conversation undoubtedly turned to the topic of Mary's circumnavigation—a feat Earhart would attempt five years later, with tragic results.

It may have been the tea with Amelia Earhart that reignited Mary's competitive spirit, or perhaps she was just itching for action again. Within weeks she had found another challenge.

20   The Sky's the Limit

Nineteen-thirty two saw dramatic expansion of commercial and private aviation. Route mileage for scheduled air service throughout the world totalled nearly a quarter million miles, up from a mere 9,700 in 1920. Britain's Imperial Airways, already the largest airline in the world, expanded its service to 22 countries, carrying more than thirty thousand passengers per year to India, Egypt, and South Africa, in addition to European destinations.

Because limited fuel capacity necessitated multiple stops on long-distance air routes, techniques for mid-air refuelling had been explored on both sides of the Atlantic. One early refuelling pioneer was Wesley May who, in 1921 over Long Beach, California, strapped a five-gallon can of petrol to his back and jumped from the wing of one plane to another to refuel it in flight. The procedure was quickly refined, with the US Army Air Corps taking an active lead in the process. Lieutenant Lowell Smith[1] developed the technique and equipment needed. In 1923 he and Lieutenant John Richter set an endurance record by staying airborne for 37 hours with mid-air refuelling. Six years later American brothers John and Kenneth Hunter surpassed that record, staying aloft over Chicago for 533 hours—more than three weeks.

Mary always watched American flight progress, taking each Yankee advance as a direct and personal challenge. Mid-air refuelling was no exception, and she was determined to win the flying endurance record for England. She and Victor began planning their course of action, along with RAF Lieutenant John Pugh. Even before they located a suitable airplane for the attempt, they began practicing night flying and rehearsing the transfer of fuel from one airplane to another. The three set up a private company called Luxury Air Tours, registering it with initial capital of £100 and a stated object of 'manufacturing and dealing in aeroplanes, seaplanes, and aircraft of all kinds'.

At the end of May 1932, Mary flew to Gibraltar with pilot Stuart Douglas Scott and a mechanic from the Saunders Roe Company, manufacturers of a Saro

Windhover seaplane that was available for charter by the week from Gibraltar Airways, Ltd. It seemed the perfect aircraft for a refuelling attempt; it had three powerful engines, a large fuel capacity, and a roomy interior that would be comfortable to live in for—they hoped!—several weeks. On the first of June they left Gibraltar, flying seven hours to Málaga, on Spain's Costa del Sol; the next day they made Alicante, south of Valencia. But the next day, shortly after takeoff, Mary knew that another of her nine lives was on the line: one of the Windhover's engines cut out, followed in seconds by a second, and then the last.

The pilot, Captain Scott, was at the controls. He turned quickly toward the sea, anticipating a safe water landing on the pontoons, but the heavy plane was losing altitude too quickly. With three dead propellers, it was clear they were about to crash. Mary wrote: 'I saw a cottage and a woman and some chickens running; one sees everything so vividly on such occasions. It looked as though we were going to hit the cottage. Captain Scott just kept the Windhover on a straight downward course. Then about fifty feet from the ground he turned the plane, and missed the cottage by a few yards. We ploughed through an olive grove, leaving a piece of wing in a tree, then over a road and into a wall. There was a shower of bricks in my lap, but we were unhurt.'

The airplane, in pieces, was trucked back to Gibraltar, where Mary found a telegram from the Bibby Shipping Company waiting for her, offering to ship the Windhover, free of charge, back to the Saunders Roe factory in Cowes, on the Isle of Wight. Clearly Bibby and others shared Mary's eagerness to see Britain take the air endurance record away from America.

Throughout July, while the flying boat was being repaired, Mary and Victor and the other crew members rehearsed the refuelling process. Mary bought a Bristol Fighter for the fuel supply plane and both it and the Windhover were fitted with auxiliary 100-gallon fuel tanks. The supply plane was to fly above the Windhover and it would be Mary's job to catch the dangling fuel line and pass it to the refuelling crew. With practice—and with the assistance of a third plane, a Gipsy Moth, to make capturing the fuel pipe easier—the technique became routine and they could soon transfer a hundred gallons of fuel in just five minutes.

The press had a heyday with the preparations, dubbing the Windhover 'The Flying Bungalow' and speculating on how married life for the Bruces would play out at three thousand feet. In an interview, she said, "From a woman's point of view it is the ideal air-house deluxe, with bathroom, larder, and the cutest of kitchenettes." Christened *The City of Portsmouth*, it also contained dining and sitting rooms. A spring mattress was fitted into the hull, on which Mary, Victor, and John Pugh would take turns sleeping.

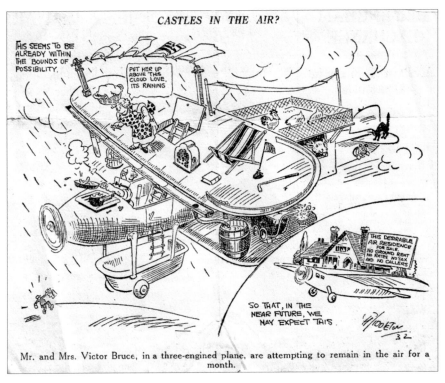

CASTLES IN THE AIR?

Mr. and Mrs. Victor Bruce, in a three-engined plane, are attempting to remain in the air for a month.

(From the Birmingham Gazette)

Advertisers took advantage of the opportunity to put their names before the public. During the flight Mary, it was said, 'on the recommendation of two medical advisors will be sustained and refreshed by Fox's Glacier Mints, the finest peppermint in the world—equally good for you—buy some today!' A magazine article described in detail the items to be used on the flight, including Dunlop tyres, Pyrene fire extinguishers, and flying clothes by Burberry. The larder would be stocked with Ovaltine, Ryvita Crisp Bread, Smith's Potato Crisps, and Crosse & Blackwell's tinned foods and marmalade—in addition to those Fox's Glacier Mints.[2]

By the beginning of August, planes and crews were ready. As the mechanics completed the fuelling of the big Saro Windhover, Mary gave one last interview to the swarm of reporters present. "This is going to be a flying holiday in a flying bungalow," she smiled. "The cost of it? Don't ask me! I am financing it myself and I think a very considerable hole will be made in £10,000 before we come down. It is not a crazy-brained scheme merely to gather laurels but a definite move towards making Atlantic flying safer." The Windhover got a gala send-off on 2 August as newsreel cameras rolled. The cameras were absent when it landed just one hour later; excessive water temperature had caused a short circuit and the first attempt was aborted.

A few days later the threesome was in the air again, but this attempt also ended prematurely when the starboard engine overheated. Discouraged, they landed for repairs and decided to make one more try. At noon on 9 August the Windhover went up for the third and last time. Refuelling runs by the Bristol Fighter came every few hours, and at last they settled into a routine. Night fell and they flew on, circling slowly over the south coast of England. It was impossible to refuel in the dark, and the second auxiliary fuel tank was called into use as the crew hand-pumped its contents into the main tank.

The Wednesday morning supply plane brought the daily newspapers in addition to fresh fuel supply; Mary and Victor read about themselves over their orange juice and coffee. The day passed, interrupted only by the refuelling routine, and another night passed as the pilots and crew took turns sleeping in the roomy cabin.

The Bristol Fighter refuels the Windhover

Thursday dawned, and Mary was filled with optimism. The refuelling went smoothly, and the weather cooperated beautifully. But by late afternoon there was trouble. Lieutenant Pugh discovered that the oil pressure on the starboard engine—the one that had overheated and brought them down on the second attempt—had dropped to zero. The engine was shut down—one big advantage of the Saro's three engines was that altitude could be maintained with only two engines—and Mary took the controls. John Pugh attached a safety line, picked up his tool kit, and climbed out onto the Windhover's wing. Positioning himself under the big Gipsy engine, Pugh went to work on the problem. The remaining two engines hummed satisfactorily, but Mary knew they could not hope to break the American record of 533 hours in an airplane that was working at only two-thirds of its capacity.

Pugh crawled back into the cockpit at last, and Mary could read his face: it was not good news. The main oil line to the starboard engine was ruptured and could not be repaired; the flight was over. They landed at 7 p.m. on 11 August, after a 55-hour flight.

They had failed to beat the American Hunter brothers' non-stop flying record, but they did at least improve on the existing British record of 50 hours. That mark had been set in 1929 when a Fairey Long-Range Monoplane flew non-stop from England to India, covering 4,130 miles in 50 hours and 48 minutes without refuelling.

The Saro Windhover was clearly not up to the challenge of a weeks-long flight, but Mary chose not to start all over with another plane. She had proven her point, she claimed, that British determination and talent could make refuelling flights a reality.

By the end of September 1932, Mary had earned her commercial pilot's licence, and the way was clear for flying for profit. There were many opportunities in aviation, and she considered each one. Her days were increasingly devoted to flying; it was clear to her that flying would be the key to making her fortune.

Mary spent many hours away from home, and away from Victor. Perhaps in an attempt to regain the closeness they had once felt when their common passion was auto racing, Victor signed up for flying lessons at Stanley Park Aerodrome in Blackpool. It did not help; the marriage was disintegrating. Their final joint public appearance in the record-setting arena, where together and singly they had scored so many successes, was an automobile refuelling record set in the spring of 1933.

Frivolous as it seems now, there was interest in the concept of non-stop driving. The need to stop for fuel periodically comes as a welcome break to most modern drivers, but the idea of refuelling 'on the fly' captured the fancy of the motoring public. To prove the feasibility of the scheme—and to generate another record and more publicity—Mary and Victor drove a Jowett Kestrel saloon non-stop for three days on the track at Montlhéry, logging 2,772 miles at an average

38 mph. At intervals, the driver would slow the car to a walking pace while the passenger hopped out and refuelled the car from a 100-gallon tank trailer towed behind the Jowett. The press reported the feat, and the Bruces were honoured at a civic reception in Bradford, the Yorkshire industrial city where the Jowett was produced. Not surprisingly, no one took up the challenge of beating that quirky record.

Jowett Kestrel auto refuelling record – Montlhéry, 1933
(Courtesy of Wiltshire Swindon Archives)

It would be decades before Mary again made the news in an automobile; her eyes were now firmly fixed on the skies. Always eager to share her enthusiasm for aviation, she performed with a travelling air show, the British Hospital Air Pageant, which featured aerobatics, wing walking, and flying demonstrations. A holiday atmosphere prevailed whenever this 'flying circus' came to town. The public turned out for a chance to see an airplane up close, to watch the daring dives and formation flying, and for the chance to take a ride (for a fee) with one of the pilots. Proceeds went to support charities.

In May 1933, Mary bought a Miles Satyr, a tiny plane well-suited for aerobatics.[3] Her second purchase was a Fairey Fox bomber, rescued from an aircraft scrap yard where it was awaiting demolition. Admired for its grace and style, the Fairey Fox had been a stalwart of the RAF during the late 1920s, until it was replaced by the faster Bristol Bulldog fighter. Mary spent a grand total of £14 for the Fairey Fox and its Rolls-Royce engine. Nearly twice the size of the Satyr, the Fox[4] boasted impressive speed and power as well as passenger space for joy-riders.

John Pugh, who had piloted the Saro Windhover during the previous summer's refuelling marathon, usually flew the Satyr in the pageant while Mary flew the Fairey Fox. A newspaper columnist described Mary's performance at one pageant, 'I saw the Hon. Mrs. Victor Bruce at Hanworth, throwing herself about in an aeroplane in the most abandoned manner. She looped the loop, slow rolled, and flick rolled with perfect skill.' He reported that Mary told him laughingly that the chief attraction of aerobatics for her was that it enabled her to keep Victor in order when an argument arose between them while he was her passenger.

Whether or not there were airborne arguments, a rift was widening between the Bruces. They maintained their relationship, partly for the sake of Mary's son; Victor had been a father figure since Tony was five years old, and he continued to fill that role for the teenager. Victor and Mary drove together to pick up Tony from his boarding school for holidays, and when Mary was otherwise occupied, it was Victor who watched over Tony.

And she was increasingly 'otherwise occupied'. In July 1934, using capital accumulated from the sale of her books, proceeds from her lecture tours, and payments from the flying circus, as well as the trust fund from her Aunt Maud, she began purchasing airplanes and established the first of several commercial air companies. Air Dispatch, Ltd., carried newspapers between London and Paris. Flights left Croydon, the 'Air Port of London' south of the city, before dawn each day, in order to have newspapers on the breakfast tables of English readers in the French capital. Mary was the Managing Director; other directors were Viscount Scarsdale, Norman M. Poole, and RAF pilot Eric Edward Noddings. Chief pilot was Johnny Pugh; Victor's name did not appear on the registration papers.

Just one month later Mary registered Commercial Air Hire, Ltd., with co-directors Sir Maurice Bonham-Carter and Viscount Scarsdale. Their chief pilot was Flight Lieutenant S.W.A. Scott, whose brother Charles Scott was also a well-known pilot and a friend of Mary's from her days in the flying circus. Commercial Air Hire flew a route from Croydon to LeBourget, Paris's major airport, where Charles Lindbergh had landed after his solo Atlantic flight just seven years earlier. Mary operated the two Croydon-based companies simultaneously, quickly expanding the range of services to include freight and air ambulance services.

As Managing Director of Air Dispatch, Mary was closely involved in all aspects of the business—supervising personnel, acquiring aircraft, and making most of the vital decisions affecting day-to-day operations. She had exactly the right temperament and drive to succeed in business: determination and careful attention to detail were second nature to her, and the businesses flourished from the beginning.

She reserved some time for private flying too. As usual, she looked for something unusual. Intrigued by the thought of another flying frontier to conquer, she purchased an autogiro, a conceptual forerunner of today's helicopter.[5]

Mary had her first autogiro flying lessons in September 1934 at Hanworth Aerodrome, a few miles southeast of present-day Heathrow. She abandoned her fixed wing flying for weeks, logging dozens of hours in the new craft. She was soon confident enough to try for a new record—the first autogiro flight to South Africa. On 25 November she departed from Lympne Aerodrome near Folkstone, where she had first touched down on English soil after her world flight. Three days later she crashed while landing at Nîmes, France, with significant damage to the autogiro and bruises and cuts for herself.

Within two weeks the damaged autogiro was shipped back to England. On 10 December Mary was at Tilbury, on the Thames east of London, to watch the unloading of the autogiro. She would make another attempt within a fortnight, she told a reporter—but she never did. She logged a few more hours in the autogiro in January 1935; there was no further mention of it in her flight record.[6]

With the press of business, Mary's personal flying had to be mostly set aside; the last entry in her flight log was made in February 1935. She continued with occasional performances with the British Hospitals' flying circus, enjoying their recreational aspects as a counterpoint to the more structured pressure of her airline businesses. In one of her last outings with the Air Pageant she made a bet with Johnny Pugh as to who could land on a field in the shorter distance. She misjudged her altitude and ploughed into some telephone wires at the edge of the field. The plane fell 15 feet, but she emerged with only a bump to her head. She made her way to a nearby telephone box and, knowing that news of the mishap would spread quickly, tried to call Victor to report that she was uninjured. She couldn't get through, and finally reached an operator to whom she complained bitterly about the telephone service. The operator was very apologetic—explaining that 'some silly fool' had just flown an airplane into the telephone wires.

In April 1935, Mary's Commercial Air Hire established an 'Inner Circle Route' connecting two of London's busiest airfields with four flights a day. During one early week they flew 47 passengers to and from Heston and Croydon. Flying short-haul commuter routes around the city, the service was quickly dubbed the 'Tube of the Air'. Among its first regular passengers were two schoolchildren whose family had just moved to Croydon. Their mother wanted them to remain in their former school near Heston, so instead of a two hour commute by automobile they took a daily flight of five minutes in each direction—with a weekly ticket costing just over £1.[7]

In the summer of 1935 Commercial Air Hire—whose flights to France had previously been limited to carrying newspapers, mail, and freight—began offering passenger service between London and Paris. Commercial's workhorse was a twin-engine Avro 642, equipped with an autopilot, with a cruising speed of about 135 mph. It originally had 16 seats, but most had been removed to make room for the bales of newspapers. Why not offer the remaining seats to passengers, Mary reasoned, and collect some extra revenue? The flight left Croydon each night well after midnight, carrying the London morning newspapers for delivery to English readers in Paris at daybreak.

Undoubtedly ticket sales were helped by the romantic name given this new service: the 'Paris Dawn Express'. Theatre-goers in London could see a show, the advertising pointed out, make their way to Croydon for a cup of hot coffee before departure, fly the Channel in the dark and arrive in Paris at daybreak, with plenty of time for a bath and breakfast before starting the new day. To appeal to the budget-minded, the original ticket cost was calculated according to the weight of the passenger. That short-lived scheme was stopped by the International Air Travel Association after a complaint from rival Imperial Airways. Commercial Air Hire employee Ken Crofts wrote: 'A pity; it might have encouraged dieting and an end to obesity for air travelers.'[8]

To emphasize the luxurious nature of this flight—and to blunt any negative response to the unattractive departure time—the airline advertised for a hostess to serve champagne, smoked salmon, and caviar to passengers. Since nearly all the passengers were men, Mary knew that an attractive hostess would be a great asset; she advertised for models. Dozens applied, but all lacked the aptitude for the job. As Mary walked through the Air Dispatch office one day, her eye fell on an attractive and vivacious typist named Daphne Kearly. "Why am I wasting all this money advertising?" Mary exclaimed. "You'll do!" Daphne was hired on the spot, at a salary of £3 per week, as the first air hostess in Britain.[9] It was the beginning of a lifelong friendship; Mary and Daphne became close friends and confidantes.[10]

A news article in September 1935 chronicled 'the latest smuggling racket', selling war planes to Abyssinia, then under threat of invasion from Italy.[11] An embargo was in place, supported by Britain and other western powers, against the sale of war planes to Abyssinia. The article suggested that commercial aircraft—specifically four Fairey Foxes—were being shipped without a licence from Britain

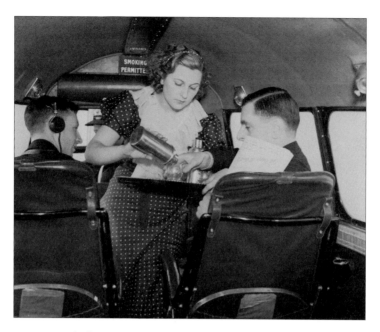

Britain's first stewardess, Daphne Kearly, serves the pilots
(*Woman Magazine*, 27 May 1972)

to an unnamed neutral country, converted to bombers and fighters, and then sent to Abyssinia. It claimed: 'This airplane smuggling was started by an enterprising young Englishwoman who began operations during the Bolivia–Paraguay war.[12] By means of a number of aliases she bought up all of the second-hand aircraft and their component parts that were on the market. The problem was to find a secret storage place for these aircraft and ultimately she used the vaults of a disused church in the southern counties. There the machines were stored until they were ready for shipment to South America. In this way she was able to evade the embargo.'

Mary sued Odhams Press, Ltd., publishers of the magazine, alleging that the article was meant to refer to her, and that it accused her of the criminal offence of smuggling in defiance of the embargo. The defence protested that nowhere in the article was any name mentioned, nor did it contain any information that would make anyone believe it referred to the Hon. Mrs Victor Bruce. Nevertheless, in May 1936 Mary received a formal apology in court from Odhams Press.

21 Gathering Clouds

By the mid-1930s, Mary and Victor were leading essentially separate lives, and neither showed any interest in maintaining their relationship. Years later, asked about her marriage, Mary said "I married a motorcar. The only thing we had in common was cars: that was all we talked and lived for."

Mary had fallen in love with Eric Noddings, her airline business partner. Noddings was newly married, with a baby already on the way, when he met Mary in the spring of 1934. Ten years younger than Mary, Eric shared her love of aviation. Their common passion echoed the fascination with speed and automobiles that Mary and Victor had shared a decade earlier. While Mary continued to live with Victor, she and Eric were spending as much time together as possible. Mary was generous with gifts for Eric. In a November 1935 visit to a Bond Street tailor she ordered a riding outfit for herself—cavalry twill jodhpurs with buckskin strappings—and a Christmas gift for Eric: a blue-grey cashmere lounging coat, vest and trousers.

Noddings and his wife Ada divorced in 1935; their infant daughter, Theodora, lived with her mother in Cambridge while Eric's usual base of operations was the Aerodrome Hotel at Croydon. A skilled pilot and Mary's most trusted business partner, Eric quickly became indispensable to her in those unsettled days.

Commercial Air Hire was formally merged with Air Dispatch in 1936, although both names continued to be used. Service was expanded to include Portsmouth, Bournemouth, Torquay and Plymouth. With a dramatic increase in miles flown there was, unfortunately, a parallel increase in misfortune. Two of the company's De Havilland Dragons crashed that year—one in January and one in March—and two Monospar ST4s crashed in May. The first fatality, however, was not recorded until January of 1937. An Airspeed Envoy operated by Commercial Air Hire crashed on a hillside early one morning, soon after it took off from Croydon. It was a freight run, and the two crew members—pilot and wireless operator—were killed on impact.

With Mary increasingly occupied with air pageants and her ventures in commercial aviation, Victor's frustration grew. There was little of the home life that he craved. When he and Mary were younger and wrapped up with auto racing, Victor had found it exciting to live with a woman who shared his love for speed and adventure. Now, with his fortieth birthday approaching, Victor was looking for hearth, home, and family—and that sort of thing was not on Mary's agenda. "Victor just got lonely because I was never home, and he drifted away to marry someone else," she told an interviewer years later.

Victor turned 40 in April 1937, in a world undergoing political and social upheaval. Civil war raged in Spain,[1] and the repressive regimes of Hitler, Stalin, and Mussolini threatened European stability. At home, King Edward VIII abdicated England's throne to marry the American divorcée Wallis Warfield Simpson. Parliament had passed the Matrimonial Causes Bill, which facilitated divorce by expanding the grounds to include desertion, eliminating the need to prove adultery or physical cruelty.

By July 1937, Mary and Victor's marriage had run its course. Late that month she asked him to leave Mole Cottage, their home in Cobham, south of London. Victor moved to nearby Inglenook Cottage, close enough that he could continue assisting Mary with Tony's upbringing.

On 23 September Victor drove seventeen-year-old Tony to Downside, his boarding school near Bath, for the fall term. Four days later Victor had his first date with the woman who would become his second wife, Charlotte Margaret 'Peggy' Beechey. They had met months earlier in Holne, Devon, where Victor was taking part in a hill climb. He had motored to the Dartmoor village with Mary and Eric Noddings; Peggy was staying at the same hotel. She was the driver for Colonel C.M. Jickling, a veteran of the Boer and First World Wars, who had lost his left arm in combat. The Beechey and Jickling families both lived in rural Norfolk. Peggy helped the Colonel and his wife with their horses, and served as chauffeur on long drives.

In Peggy, Victor once again found a woman who shared his appreciation for the automobile. However, Peggy was different. Driving was a job for her, and she enjoyed it—but it was not a passion, as it had been for Mary. Peggy was part of a warm and lively family who enjoyed each others' company, and Victor was soon drawn into their circle.

At first, Peggy's parents were sceptical. Although Victor and Mary were living apart, he was still a married man when he began courting Peggy. In addition, he continued to fill the role of father to Tony, and he spent a great deal of time with the lad during school holidays. By the time Tony turned 18 in March 1938, however, Victor was spending every free moment with Peggy.

Mary, meanwhile, was now living alone in Chipstead, south of London, close to Croydon. She had rediscovered her childhood fondness for horses, and divided her time and energy between her various airlines and a riding stable she established. Renting paddock and pasture from the vicar of the local church, she bought several horses and began giving riding lessons.[2] She shared this love of horses with the daughter of one of Air Dispatch's pilots; Mary gave riding lessons to young Georgina Alexander, whose father flew a Dragon Rapide between Croydon and Paris. Georgina remembered Mary as a kind but firm instructor who insisted that the ten-year-old girl get right back on the horse when she fell off. Georgina's pilot father transported newspapers for Air Dispatch, and later carried passengers as well, in the short-lived Paris Dawn Express venture. That was not the only cargo, according to Georgina; at Mary's request, Alexander also smuggled home French champagne for her in his flying boots.[3]

Europe's political climate continued to deteriorate in the late 1930s. England was well aware of its vulnerability, and while a policy of appeasement was adopted by the Chamberlain government, attention was being paid to preparation for homeland defence as well. As the threat of war grew, Mary watched over her airlines and wondered what the future would bring. The fleet of Air Dispatch comprised 23 planes, mostly Avro 642s and De Havilland Dragons and Rapides. If England was plunged into war, her fleet would certainly be conscripted for military service. She prepared for that eventuality, trying to blunt the possibility by involving Air Dispatch in defence preparations.

In October 1937, Air Dispatch was awarded a contract by the Air Ministry for 'army co-operation flying'. Mary's pilots made night flights so that ground troops of the Territorial Army could practice spotting planes with their searchlights and sound-locators. Air Dispatch continued contract flying until 1939, although relations with the Air Ministry were not always cordial. Mary had to fight for safeguards for her pilots, and she lodged strenuous objections when their assignments involved dangerous conditions such as inadequate air traffic control, unlighted landing fields, and shortage of ground-based wireless operators to maintain communication with the pilots.

By 1939 war seemed inevitable. Conscription began in April of that year, and defence planning proceeded at every level—from high-level governmental planning in Whitehall to London neighbourhood evacuation schemes and the recruitment and organization of aircraft spotters in tiny villages. Even Mary's younger brother Roderick, whose only occupation was selling newspapers, became a neighbourhood 'Civil Defence' worker.

It was understood that civilian air traffic would come to an end if war began. Mary, along with all other airline owners and operators, had been informed by the Air Ministry of its plans for nationalisation of aircraft in that event. She had been given sealed orders that were to be opened only upon further instructions. For months the envelope lay locked in the Air Dispatch safe at Croydon.

On the morning of 31 August 1939, Mary received the first of three dispatches from the Air Ministry: 'Get ready to stand by'. The Air Dispatch pilots and radio operators who had been assigned to searchlight flying in the Midlands and Wales were recalled to Croydon. The following morning, as German troops began their invasion of Poland, the second dispatch was delivered: 'Stand by'. All 23 aircraft of the Air Dispatch fleet were lined up on the field, and the engines were tested every hour. Bulldozers began digging defensive trenches around the Aerodrome Hotel, and a blackout was in effect. At home that evening Mary's telephone rang. Her trusted chief engineer Keith Vickers gave her the news: another message had arrived. He slowly spelled out the one word message: 'Lascelle'. It was the signal to open the sealed envelope.

22   The War Years

Rushing back to Air Dispatch headquarters at Croydon, Mary took the envelope from the safe. She tore it open and read the instructions. The war was on; her fleet was now under government control. Her patriotic spirit could not entirely overcome her unease about the future. She had poured her time and energy into her commercial air enterprises; countless hours of hard work had resulted in a well-run and flourishing organization. Her niche in Britain's commercial aviation community had been secure; would she lose everything she had laboured for?

Ten of her planes left within an hour for RAF bases in England; the remaining 13 were flown to Cardiff, which was to be the wartime base of operations for Air Dispatch. The airport lay on the eastern side of the city on the Bristol Channel, and would be a less likely target for bombing than London and environs.[1]

For the first few months of the war, the primary duty of Air Dispatch was ferrying RAF personnel and cargo between Cardiff and Paris. As Managing Director of Air Dispatch, Mary needed to remain closely involved with the day-to-day operations. There was no reason for her to remain in Chipstead. She sold her cottage there and moved farther west.

Eric Noddings had left Air Dispatch to return to active duty with the RAF. He was commissioned a Flight Lieutenant and assigned first to a Flight Training Squadron based at Sywell in Northhamptonshire. In his early thirties, Eric already had years of flying experience, which served him well in his capacity as instructor to the RAF's young novice pilots.

The love affair between Mary and Eric continued. In March 1939 he wrote a new will, leaving his entire estate to her. She gave him a lavish gift that summer, a Rolls-Royce Phantom III, with a Hooper Sedanca body. Painted in two shades of grey with a blue and grey interior, it was a magnificent piece of machinery.[2]

Together with Keith and Daphne Kearly Vickers, Mary and Eric rented a house called Tanglewood, set in five acres at Lisvane, Wales. For Mary, Keith, and Daphne, it was conveniently close to Air Dispatch in Cardiff; for Eric, it was a relatively easy drive from his new RAF base in Gloucestershire. But Mary—who treasured privacy, in spite of her love of publicity—divided her time between Tanglewood and an elegant country home in the Wiltshire hamlet of Upper Seagry. Sprawling Seagry Manor had numerous outbuildings and fine stables, and all of her horses made the move from Chipstead with her. There were gardens and a tennis court, and plenty of room for her dogs to run. Mary filled the house with lovely furniture and accessories.

Between the German invasion of Poland on 3 September and the invasion of the Low Countries and France in May 1940, there was an uneasy lull in military activity in Europe.[3] The period was termed the Phony War, and although war had been declared and mobilization was occurring all around, some aspects of routine life continued with little change. During the winter of 1939-1940, fox-hunting clubs even held hunts as they always had, and Mary rode in several.

Eric's squadron, 9SFTS, used auxiliary airfields for training purposes, and he was stationed at a Relief Training Ground at Babdown Farm, a small airfield near Westonbirt, Gloucestershire. Mary was not far away at Seagry Manor, and Eric was a frequent visitor there. They enjoyed riding together and relaxing on the large terraces of the manor house, but when the property adjacent to Babdown Farm came up for sale, Mary bought the 517-acre Down Farm Estate[4] for £16,000.

Acres of farmland and orchard surrounded Down Farm's handsome manor house of honey-coloured Cotswold stone; several outbuildings provided not only stable room for her horses but also storage for a most unusual investment. At the outbreak of the war, manufacture of luxury automobiles was abruptly halted in favour of production of wartime goods and machinery. Mary realised there would be a great demand for such automobiles as soon as peace reigned again, but it would take time to retool the factories and resume production. Always a shrewd businesswoman, Mary went to London Rolls-Royce dealer Jack Barclay and purchased his entire floor stock: six brand new Rolls-Royce saloons at £1,000 apiece. She stored them throughout the war on raised blocks in outbuildings at Down Farm and turned a nice profit when she sold them in 1945.

It was becoming clear that the war might not be won quickly. As the Phony War continued, Mary worried about the future of her airlines and the security of her employees. She searched for a way to make Air Dispatch essential to the war effort. RAF aircraft would be damaged, Mary reasoned, and parts would need to be remanufactured and installed. As early as February 1940, Mary and her engineers were accumulating spare aircraft parts and equipment. Civilian airports were closed and there was a ready supply of material sitting idle in hangars. Air Dispatch bought stock and parts from small airports like the one at Shoreham, where she dealt with local landowner Stephen Easter—who had been her lover so many years earlier.

Within months, all of Mary's planes had been requisitioned for the RAF. When German troops entered Paris in mid-June 1940, the Air Dispatch flights across the Channel stopped abruptly. Only military planes were in the air; there were no civilian flights. Thanks to her foresight, Mary was ready with a proposal that would guarantee the continued existence of Air Dispatch and keep its civilian employees safely at work in Cardiff. Their location in south Wales, an area rich in steel and coal for industry, helped provide the answer.

Mary approached the Air Ministry with her plan for repair and rebuilding of damaged RAF aircraft. Air Dispatch had the facilities, manpower and a stockpile of parts and supplies.[5] Mary had a reputation as a canny businesswoman of boundless energy and drive. The government contract was hers; Air Dispatch, in this new guise, would survive the war—but Mary's marriage would not.

After three years of living apart, Victor filed for divorce in December 1940, charging desertion. Mary was anxious to speed up the process, and appealed to Victor to hurry things along. She and Eric planned to wed, and the sooner the better. But Victor insisted on waiting until he and Mary had lived apart long enough so that the charge of desertion would go unchallenged, preferring those grounds to the potentially embarrassing alternatives of adultery or cruelty. He refused to accelerate the process, and early spring 1941 found them still married, albeit in name only.

Eric Edward Noddings: 13 June 1906 – 22 April 1941
(Photo courtesy of Julia Driver and Linda Naidu)

Mary was at Down Farm, with Eric stationed nearby at Babdown Farm. They spent as many hours together as they could, riding horses over her farm, playing with Mary's dogs, and making plans for life after the war. 'My own little darling lovebird, I am longing to be with you again,' Eric wrote. 'I miss you terribly, Dear, and wish this silly war would come to an end soon.'

Spring in the English countryside is breathtakingly beautiful, with clouds of yellow daffodils covering the hillsides and lining country roads. March and April 1941 were as lovely as ever, with lilacs scenting the air as it warmed from winter's chill. As the days lengthened, England's gardens bloomed in spite of the chaos in the world. At Babdown Farm the trainee pilots studied and practiced their manoeuvres, and as one of their instructors, Eric Noddings got in plenty of flight time.

At dusk on 22 April 1941, Eric took off from the airstrip at Babdown Farm with student pilot J.A.B. Day at the controls. According to a witness, the Miles Master training plane simply 'flew right into the ground' shortly after takeoff. Both pilots were killed instantly. Mary was devastated. She telephoned Victor, who wrote in his journal 'ERIC KILLED'.

Six weeks after Eric died, Mary and Victor's divorce became final. Within days, Victor and Peggy Beechey were married. Mary, still overwhelmed with grief, went through the motions of daily life. Air Dispatch required her guidance. Her 21-year-old son Tony was away, serving in the RAF.[6] Her friend Daphne Vickers, by now an essential assistant and close friend and confidante, stood by her and offered what comfort she could.

In Cardiff, Air Dispatch maintained an 80-hour week, with more than four hundred employees working under government contract. Damaged RAF planes arrived daily; Mary's crews kept their output high. She concentrated on the business, putting in long hours of work.

While her business life was going well, her personal life was anything but happy. Her older brother Louis died in 1942. He had lived in South Africa for many years, a self-imposed exile due to struggles with alcohol. He never married; he and Mary maintained a somewhat distant but friendly relationship. Later that year their beloved Aunt Maud died; her financing had made possible the record run at Montlhéry, as well as Louis's long-ago purchase of the Matchless motorcycle. In June 1943 Mary's mother Jennie died after many years' confinement in a sanitarium; she, like Louis, had been alcohol-dependent.[7] And Mary's father, always one of her most enthusiastic boosters—and a courtly and charming gentleman, according to Daphne Vickers—died in the spring of 1944. "Mary called him Dada," Daphne said; "He was a dear old soul."

Mary's immediate family was now reduced to Tony and her brother Roderick, known in the family as 'Buzzy', who lived in London with a companion to look after him.[8]

Two earlier loves in her life—Tony's father Stephen Easter and her former husband Victor—both were busy with new families. Stephen Easter's first wife, Alice Gibbings, died in June 1942; six months later, at the age of 68, he remarried. He and his new wife, Claire, began a family.

The kind of home life that Victor had missed in his marriage to Mary was his at last. He had grown up with six older brothers and sisters, the baby of the family. Now Victor and Peggy were happily welcoming babies too.

Both new families showed the underlying optimism and determination of the British people during the war years. Stephen Easter and his new family were living in Shoreham. Victor and Peggy lived at Cobham; his engineering firm, Bruce & Holroyd, was involved with war production. They were close enough to feel the effects of German attacks on London.

Beginning in mid-June 1944, Germany hurled thousands of V-1 rockets at London. The death toll was high, and property damage extensive. Graham Cloake was ten years old that summer; his father, W.H. 'Jimmy' Cloake, was Mary's stockbroker. As Londoners reeled from the battering of the V-1s, parents feared for their children's safety. Down Farm, nestled in rural Gloucestershire, seemed like a safe retreat. At Mary's invitation, young Graham Cloake was sent to stay with her, part of a great exodus of children from the dangers of the capital city.

Mary drove to Cardiff several times a week to oversee the aircraft repair work, and Graham was left in the care of her companion, Anne Watkins. He played with a boy named Richard who lived in a cottage on the farm, and they soon became accustomed to watching RAF fighter planes land in one of Down Farm's big fields. The planes were concealed under trees for camouflage, at the far end of what had formerly been a polo field. Cloake recalls those days with affection. 'One was taught manners and discipline,' he wrote. 'One did not speak at the table unless spoken to and you were punished if you misbehaved. I once ran through the stables and was sent to my room without supper and was told always to walk, not run, so as not to disturb the horses.'[9]

In May 1945 the long war in Europe ended at last; there was no further need for aircraft repair in Cardiff. Air Dispatch's government contracts were completed, but no more would be forthcoming. Much to the dismay of Mary and the other pre-war owners of airlines—whose equipment had all been commandeered by the government in 1939—the Labour Party landslide in the election called just two weeks after V-E Day spelled the end of their businesses.

In spite of Churchill's inspiring leadership through Britain's darkest hours, his personal popularity was not enough to overcome the rising sentiment for a welfare state and nationalisation of key industries, including aviation, and his Conservative Party was routed. Labour's view—that public transportation should be controlled by the government—prevailed. There would be no return to private ownership of airlines. The government agreed to pay the owners, including Mary, for the aircraft and other property it had acquired. But there was outrage when compensation was offered only for the tangible assets, and nothing for the loss of goodwill or customer base.

Lobbying and long wrangling ensued before a settlement was reached. Imperial Airways was chosen for conversion to the government-operated BOAC; all other operators were excluded entirely. Not even freight charters or short-hop commute lines were allowed as private ventures; the government would henceforth control all aviation, commercial as well as military.

This was a stunning blow for Mary; she had built her airline businesses with the passion of a true believer in aviation for all, and it galled her to see the government monopolise the skies. She fought the new order fiercely, to no avail. A news item about Mary reported that the 'pioneer woman flyer and founder of one of Britain's oldest plane services' was planning to leave Britain and settle in South Africa, 'in search of freedom'. She was disgusted, she said, "at the Socialist attempt to quench all spirit of adventure, all attempt at initiative, with the Civil Aviation bill."

With no possibility that Air Dispatch could resume its pre-war activities, Mary once again looked for a way to sustain her company. She felt a keen obligation to her employees, many of whom had been with her since before the war. The Air Dispatch facility at Cardiff was equipped for the repair and rebuilding of aircraft; the raw materials and the workforce were in place. But with private commercial flying no longer an option and no further need for aircraft repair, how could these resources be utilised?

The answer was vehicles of a different sort: buses. Throughout the war years the maintenance and repair of the nation's fleets of buses had been deferred, with all raw materials, time, and labour being devoted to maintaining military equipment. Air Dispatch reinvented itself once again, this time as a renovator of buses.

In November 1945, the first big contract was awarded, for the refurbishment of ten buses for the Cardiff Corporation. The work was successfully completed within seven months, and more contracts followed. Mary's concern was for the survival of Air Dispatch and jobs for its workers; that seemed assured. But buses never held the same allure for Mary as did automobiles or airplanes. When Tony came home from military service and joined his mother in Cardiff, she happily relinquished control of Air Dispatch to him.

23 Fantasia

Mary's years of concern and effort with Air Dispatch and the associated airline companies were over. For the first time in two decades, she felt herself at loose ends, without a passion. She had her automobiles, including the treasured Rolls-Royce she had bought for Eric, but her airplanes were gone, and the political situation did not allow for the kind of free enterprise she so enjoyed. In her early fifties, Mary had just received a substantial payoff from the government for her 23 aircraft. She was ready to begin enjoying the fruits of her labour—not that she had ever really held back from doing so.

In October 1945 Mary sold Down Farm[1] and moved into London. She had inherited property there from her father, and lived at several different addresses during the late 1940s.[2] She undertook the remodelling and furnishing of a large and elegant home at 20 Hanover Terrace, near Regent's Park. She had always loved quality furniture and accessories, and she haunted the auction houses and fine boutiques, buying whatever took her fancy. She bought several portraits, including one attributed to the Dutch painter Sir Peter Lely. She found some luxurious satin fabric she admired, and ordered window-seat cushions to be covered in it for the large bay window in the dining room. She purchased three pairs of red Utrecht velvet curtains and a long Persian runner, and ordered replacements for the wrought iron gates and grilles that had been given up for the war effort. She kept stacks of receipts for her purchases; every delivery, characteristically, was labelled 'Urgent'.

The excitement of the business world continued to entice Mary. In Cardiff she had met Raymond Boulton, a retired Army captain who was a member of a glove-manufacturing family. At his urging she purchased the firm of Holman Byfield, a glove manufacturer in Warminster. Mary assumed control as Managing Director; she maintained a home, Regency House, in that small Wiltshire town in order to be close to the business. The Boulton family glove factory was in nearby Westbury, and Raymond Boulton and Mary became friendly, exchanging advice and sharing experiences.

Mary maintained a balance between business and pleasure. The keen appetite for speed that characterized her earlier years had ebbed, but the travel bug was as strong as ever. Her top three hobbies, she told an interviewer during a visit to South Africa in 1946, were motor racing, speedboat racing, and flying—although in fact she had done little if any racing or flying since before the war. However, she declared, her next venture would be in a much slower mode of transportation: a motor yacht. She planned to return to England, she said, and then sail to Durban, South Africa, and settle there.[4]

In January 1947 Mary purchased a 53-foot harbour defence motor launch that had become surplus naval equipment. She hired a captain and had the ship sailed from its anchorage at Milford Haven, Wales,[4] to Sittingborne in Kent. She named the vessel *Fantasia*, and hired well-known marine architect Arthur C. Robb to design and supervise the conversion of the launch into a luxury yacht. Robb was given a free hand and a generous budget; he produced a yacht whose appearance bore few traces of its military origins.

The engine room, with twin 150 hp diesel engines, remained unchanged, but significant revisions were the rule everywhere else. An owner's cabin and salon were designed, with a separate small cabin to accommodate a maid. In addition, there was a guest cabin and quarters for four crew members. A spacious salon on the bridge deck was panelled in teak salvaged from HMS *Cornwall*. Plum-coloured upholstery and beige carpeting served as a backdrop to the focal point of the salon: panelled mirrors which surrounded a commissioned oil painting of the yacht by marine artist Winston Megoran.[5] Mary was closely involved in careful selection of fittings and trim. The furniture was teak, with mahogany pieces in the lobby. Custom-made horizontal sliding triple-glazed windows were installed. Brass handles with flanges in a Florentine bronze finish were ordered, along with a dinghy, awnings, clocks, and dozens of other items.

Almost from the outset, Mary suspected that *Fantasia* might never really suit her. Two months into the project she wrote to the captain she had hired, giving him two weeks' notice of termination of employment. She had thought over the matter, she wrote, and decided that she would sell the yacht as soon as the conversion was completed, and buy a small ketch instead.

But *Fantasia*'s metamorphosis continued through the spring of 1947 and Mary spent lavishly, with little apparent consideration of the return. By May, with the conversion only half done, the bill from the Sittingbourne Shipyard was well over £2000. She decided to try to get her money's worth out of the venture, and hired another Captain at a yearly salary of £1500. In June she was elected to membership in the Royal Motor Yacht Club, and acquired the club's blue ensign to fly from the yacht. It was just the sort of status symbol that appealed to Mary, and she flew it proudly.

The work on *Fantasia* dragged on through the summer; by the end of August the shipyard's bill was nearing £5000; Robb's fees and the costs for the lavish furnishings were mounting even faster. She had been advised to sail *Fantasia* to the south of France. There were a lot of wealthy people there, she was told, particularly Americans, who would want to charter the yacht—or perhaps even buy it. Mary planned the itinerary for the maiden voyage with that advice in mind.

She loved the Mediterranean, and decided to sail there by way of one of her favourite cities, Paris. The route would take *Fantasia* across the Channel to the mouth of the Seine at Honfleur, then inland through the French countryside. A visit in Paris would be followed by a leisurely journey through the canal system linking the two great French river systems, the Seine and the Rhône, then south past Avignon and Arles to the Mediterranean.

With characteristic forethought, Mary had reminded Robb of the obstacles she might encounter on this itinerary. In his remodel of *Fantasia*, he designed the wheelhouse with a removable top, to allow easy passage under the low bridges of the French canals. Tony, now 27 and still unmarried, accompanied her, as did Raymond Boulton and his teen-age niece Jill.[6]

Fantasia *on the Thames* (Courtesy of Wiltshire Swindon Archives)

It was a grand scheme, but the travellers never got farther south than Paris. By mid-September they had made their way across the Channel to Le Havre, where they stopped to stock *Fantasia*'s bar with extra dry Taittinger Champagne,

Beaujolais, Riesling, and Perrier. A week later they dropped anchor at the Quay de la Plaisance in Paris—and there they stayed. Optimistic at first that they could reach the Mediterranean through the canals, Mary shopped in Paris for a chart of the Rhône and a French dictionary. But extremely low water levels that year made canal travel impossible for *Fantasia*, with its four-and-a-half-foot draught. Mary and the others made the best of it—an enforced stay in Paris was no one's idea of a hardship anyway. They spent nearly four weeks at anchor in Paris, sightseeing and shopping. The younger contingent, including Boulton's niece Jill, made a habit of sneaking out at night to sample the Parisian nightlife until Mary, who retired nightly by 9 p.m., remarked seriously one morning at breakfast, "You know, I must get a cat. I think we have rats aboard this ship; I heard them scampering across the roof of my cabin last night!"

By mid-October the goal of reaching the Mediterranean was abandoned, and *Fantasia* returned to England. The yacht sailed up the Thames to a berth at Burgoyne's Shipyard at Kingston upon Thames, west of London. The passage upriver did not go unobserved; a week after their return Mary was served with a notice from the Thames Conservancy that 'On 22 Oct *Fantasia* was navigated on the Thames at Teddington Lock whilst unregistered and unlicensed' and that a penalty of £10 would be imposed if she did not immediately register the yacht. Two days later she paid the £8 registration fee, as *Fantasia* sat in the shipyard at Kingston. Mary would never sail it again.

In the same mail with the notice from the Thames Conservancy came a terse letter from Donald Robinson, *Fantasia*'s first mate. 'Dear Madam,' he wrote, 'I was surprised to hear from your captain Kerr that my services terminate on Friday 1st. I left a good steady job to come to *Fantasia* as I understood it to be a six-month guaranteed job. Also that if I did not get a uniform I would be paid in lieu of same. I would be much obliged if you could let me have your comments on the matter. Yours faithfully, Donald M. Robinson.'

There was more mail for Mary: a new bill from the Sittingbourne Shipyard showed a balance due of more than £6,600. She began searching earnestly for a buyer for *Fantasia*, setting the price at £20,000. It was clear that her brief venture into the world of luxury yachting had been a folly, an extravagant expenditure of time and money that had produced scant return for her investment. *Fantasia* was, in fact, the single worst investment of her life: the sort of imprudent undertaking that perpetuates the cliché that 'a yacht is a hole in the water into which one pours money'.

Within a month Mary lowered the selling price to £17,000; by December, 1947, it was down to £14,000. There were enquiries, but no offers. She placed an advertisement in the London *Times* in January. Her debt to the Sittingbourne Shipyard was finally paid off in March 1948, and they offered to try to find a buyer for her. Burgoyne's Yard at Kingston was trying to help too, and eventually a physician from Wales purchased *Fantasia* for the bargain price of £6,500.

When extensive decay was discovered in the hull, *Fantasia* was moved directly to another shipyard for repairs. In a letter to A.C. Robb, the naval architect who had done the conversion of the yacht, Mary wrote that she was shocked at the condition of the boat, and wondered if the yard at Sittingbourne, where the original conversion had been carried out less than a year earlier, might also bear some responsibility. The sum of £500 had been withheld from the purchase price, by prior agreement; when she learned the extent of the damage, she wrote 'I am beginning to think I am lucky to have got anything for it at all.'

Two months after she sold *Fantasia* she resigned from the Royal Yacht Club. They accepted her resignation and requested the return of the Admiralty warrant authorizing the use of the blue ensign for *Fantasia*. A month later the Yacht Club repeated the request for the warrant. It had been lost, Mary reported; would the club kindly explain that to the Admiralty?

With Tony running the coachworks in Cardiff, Mary immersed herself in the business of glove manufacturing. That was proving to be a challenge as well. She found herself in conflict with another Wiltshire glovemaker, Boulton Bros., Ltd., owned by a branch of Raymond Boulton's family. She was accused of hiring away one of Boulton's managers, and of trying to lure Boulton clients to her company. Mary's appetite for adrenaline highs—no longer fed by racing automobiles or flying tiny aircraft—now was satisfied by a good row. She immediately fired off a counter charge to V.C. Boulton, accusing them of trying to steal one of her employees. 'I propose to go to the Labour Exchange about this,' she wrote; 'It is regrettable that this lack of cooperation exists between our two companies, but you must admit that you were the first to adopt this attitude!'

Mary sold some of her antiques—a Persian rug, a wing chair, a diamond bracelet that fetched £1,850—and considered selling one of her Rolls-Royces. She booked a spring cruise on the *Queen Elizabeth* and then cancelled it. She dusted off her glass slides and gave lectures about her world flight. It had taken place less than 20 years before, but intervening events—the war, the growth and collapse of her airline businesses, her love affair with Eric which ended in such heartbreak— made it seem nearly another lifetime.

In addition to Regency House in Warminster, Mary kept a home in London. The property she inherited from her father included two houses in Bryanston Square, near Marble Arch. She formed her own building company and undertook their conversion into flats, acting as architect, builder and foreman. She hired workers from the Labour Exchange and took an active part in the actual work. She wrote in her autobiography that her family suggested that remodelling buildings would be a safer occupation than getting back into automobile racing. She noted ruefully that, having survived at least three airplane crashes without the need for medical treatment, she found herself in the local A&E twice within her first week as a contractor. A workman's sledgehammer fell on her foot, and days later she stepped on a board with an exposed nail, driving it into her foot. Which was the more dangerous occupation, she wondered?

24 Winding Down

Over the years Mary had masterminded a long string of business successes but she seemed to be losing her Midas touch. *Fantasia* was a spectacular failure, and the bus-body coachworks, under Tony's direction, was a losing concern nearly from the beginning. The name Air Dispatch was changed first to Air Dispatch (Coachbuilders), Ltd. in 1947 and then to Bruce Coach Works in 1948. There were several orders for repairs and rebuilding, and they won a few contracts for new bus bodies for Cardiff and other municipalities, but their financial ground was always shaky. In 1948 an officer at Lloyds Bank wrote that he was pleased to have had the opportunity to discuss with Mary and Tony the affairs of the coachworks. However, his records showed, he mentioned politely, approximately £14,000 of debt. Could Mrs. Bruce please furnish him a list of the orders for buses that had been placed with the company? And would she advise him regarding the number and identity of the company's debtors?

Orders for bus bodies were becoming infrequent, and the company slid further and further into the red. Banks extended credit, due primarily to Mary's reputation as an astute businesswoman. At one point the debt to Lloyds Bank exceeded £20,000; the credit limit was raised repeatedly. Tony assured the bank that orders were brisk and there were several invoices outstanding.

Mary's corps of loyal employees—several of whom, like Keith Vickers, had been with her since the early airline days at Croydon—had little confidence in Tony's competence or the company's prospects. They shared Mary's affection for airplanes rather than bus bodies; one by one they drifted away to other employment, many returning to the aviation industry at Croydon.

Bruce Coach Works faced increasing debt as contracts for repairs decreased and orders for new bodies declined. Tony lacked his mother's keen business sense and her instinct for survival. He did not inspire confidence or enthusiasm among his workers, and his inexpert management was a major factor in the fading fortunes of the company. His dealings with the bank were a constant game of cat and mouse: checks were deposited without signatures, the account was regularly overdrawn; the books were never quite in order for inspection by auditors. More than once Mary wrote cheques from her personal account to cover the company's shortfalls. Eventually the banks lost confidence in the business and, in spite of Mary's reputation and her repeated bail-outs, they withdrew their support. By the end of 1951 there were no more contracts to be had. In December the last of the 161 bus bodies produced by Bruce Coach Works left the factory; in April 1952 the Works closed.

More financial dealings plagued Mary. Her friend Raymond Boulton was irresponsible with money. She bankrolled his habit of betting on horse races; he was not a lucky gambler. He spent lavishly on liquor as well, and was remembered by Mary's grandson as 'always drunk'. Notes from Boulton's banks, co-signed by Mary, were called in. He had promised to repay her from his share of profits when the Boulton glove business was sold, but he never did; she was on the hook for several thousand pounds. A settlement from Stephen Easter eased the financial pinch; Easter had never been stingy in his support of his son or Mary.

Tony had met and married Marcelle Magneron, whose parents operated Cardiff's Windsor Hotel; two sons were born: Philip in 1949 and Michael in 1952. After the closing of the coach works, the young Easter-Bruce family moved to London. Tony began assisting his mother with the management and renovation of her growing inventory of London real estate; large townhouses were being divided into flats and apartments. Tony became immersed in the business of property management, an undertaking much more suited to his interests and talents than bus body manufacture.

Mary divided her time between London and Wiltshire. In the spring of 1950 she bought The Rise in the old wool town of Bradford-on-Avon, a few miles north of the Holman Byfield glove works in Warminster. Traces of an Iron Age settlement date to about 500 BC, with subsequent occupations by Roman, Saxon, and Norman settlers, all of whom left their marks. In the centre of the town a bridge built in the thirteenth century spans the Avon. The prosperity brought by the wool trade is reflected in the ranks of spinners' and weavers' cottages on the surrounding hills and the large woollen mills beside the river—although they are long since abandoned as mills. In the nineteeth century the textile trade moved north, and Bradford-on-Avon became the hub of the rubber industry.

The Rise comprised a row of seventeenth century weavers' cottages overlooking the historical town. Given her experience with renovating houses, Mary enjoyed the challenge they presented. She remodelled them into a single, handsome three-storey home, with panoramic views over the town and the river below. Beside the house a long flight of steps provided a path to the centre of the town; close by was a priory, and she chose the name Priory Steps for the house. A sturdy garage of Cotswold stone stood just beyond the steps, and Mary equipped it with locking doors and a heating system to keep the temperature warm enough to prevent damage to her precious Rolls-Royces.[1]

Priory Steps, Bradford-on-Avon (Courtesy of Andrew Eberlin)

Furnishing Priory Steps was a treat for her. She haunted auction houses in Bath and London, selecting furniture, fabrics, carpets, and accessories. She had a special fondness for antique oak furniture, selecting several tables, chests, and beds. She indulged her expensive tastes: silk was a favourite fabric, and she collected artwork as well. Horses were a frequent subject of nineteenth century painter John Frederick Herrick; two of his oils hung in her home. Red-flocked lampshades, garden statuary, a gilt fire screen with a needlework panel, an alabaster and ormolu lamp, a Hungarian elm games table: the acquisitions piled up as Mary spent freely.

Much as she was enjoying her new home, the wider world still called to her. With *Fantasia* gone, Mary did her sailing only on cruise ships. The chill of England's winter motivated her to travel south every December. The memory of post Monte Carlo vacations was a factor—the annual escape to the sunny beaches of the Riviera had been a highlight in her racing years. But now instead of the Mediterranean she sailed regularly to Ceylon, a favourite destination. She frequently carried with her samples of the work from her Warminster glove factory, characterizing the trips as business-related, but recreation and pleasure were her primary reasons for the trips.

In July 1951, ten years after Eric Noddings' sudden death in the field at Down Farm, Mary received a communication from the Air Ministry. Eric's service medals were to be sent to his heirs. As executrix of his will, she received them. Several months later the Noddings name came up again. Eric's daughter Theodora reached her eighteenth birthday in early October 1952. Under the terms of the May 1942 settlement that Mary had made with Eric's former wife Ada, monthly payments from his estate were to be paid to Theodora until she was 18. A London bank had made the transfers regularly, at the rate of £42 per year. No one noticed that the girl's birthday had passed, and two more payments were made before Mary caught the error. She fired off a letter to her solicitor; the payments stopped.

At age 56, twice a grandmother, Mary's inborn need for an adrenaline rush came to the surface again. Commercial jet aviation was a hot topic in 1952; BOAC launched its first regular jet service, from London to Johannesburg, using a De Havilland Comet. Mary announced to the press that she intended to buy a jet aircraft of her own and break BOAC's speed record. "When you've got it in your blood," she told a reporter, "there is always that one last record bid."

It proved to be only an extravagant daydream, although at least one columnist was prepared to take it seriously. 'It sounded a little wild,' he wrote, 'until my informant told me that it was Mrs. Victor Bruce. She's one of those rare people who have only to hear of something new—a land, an invention or an experience—and it will be off she goes. In the 1920s her name was on every lip, and now the new jet age has roused the devil of adventure in her.'[2] It was the money that stopped her. Accustomed as she was to spending freely for what she fancied, the price tag of a half million pounds for a Comet was enough to cool her enthusiasm.

Glove manufacturing, conversion of London houses into luxury flats, and travel occupied Mary for the balance of the 1950s. Having touched Europe, Africa, Asia, and North America in her earlier years, she now checked off two more continents: winter cruises took her to South America one year and Australia another. She was exploring export and trade possibilities for her glove manufacturing concern, she told a reporter in Buenos Aires, although she used the leisure time aboard ship to write her memoirs. That was a recurring theme over the period of several years, although it would be years before her autobiography was ready for publication. She was too busy living, she explained, to stop and write it all down.

Mary had settled into a comfortable relationship with Raymond Boulton, but marriage was not on her agenda. She had always enjoyed male companionship, although Boulton seemed an odd match for Mary, whose lively interests had scarcely diminished with age.

Mary as drawn by caricaturist Ralph Sallon of the 'Daily Mirror'

Boulton was a former military officer whose major interests, according to Mary's grandson Michael, were gambling on the horses and drinking. Mary provided Boulton with small amounts of cash to support both habits. He was remembered with some fondness by Michael, who called him 'Uncle Raymond'.

According to one news story of the 1960s Mary was living an 'unfettered existence with four old family retainers, including an 81-year-old housekeeper, an old married couple and a 71-year-old manservant' (Boulton). Presumably the writer thought describing him as a manservant was preferable to exposing the fact that an unmarried couple were sharing a home. Two Cairn terriers were also a part of the household, along with an African grey parrot named Smokey.

Smokey would roar with laughter, and was quite a talker. Mary told one interviewer that she was coaching the 19-year-old parrot in French. "I plan to spend six months in the south of France writing my memoirs," she said, "and as

Smokey is coming with me, I thought he ought to speak the language." Whether or not he ever learned French, Smokey did pick up a lot of salty language. People would telephone to hear the parrot swear, and Mary made a tape recording of some of his worst language and played it for callers.

Smokey was only a small factor in the larger-than-life reputation that Mary enjoyed in Bradford-on-Avon. She was often seen speeding around the countryside in one of her two vintage Rolls-Royce saloons. The rationing of petrol during the Suez Crisis in the late 1950s did little to slow Mary down. A young policeman stopped Mary one day and demanded to see the papers for the car; not knowing who she was, he was unprepared for what followed. Mary handed him registration papers; he returned them, saying they were not in order. She glanced at them and exclaimed "Oh! Wait here!" She sped away and returned with the proper papers—which had been inadvertently stored in her other Rolls-Royce.

Mary expressed an interest in the conservation of Wiltshire's historic architecture; she joined her local preservation society. Her motives, however, might have been less than altruistic. An early crusade was opposition to a building scheme next door to Priory Steps. She wanted to preserve her unobstructed view of Bradford and its fine old Saxon church.[3]

In her seventies, Mary still dreamed of setting a speed record: in 1968 a reporter noted that her 1929 record for crossing the Channel in an outboard motorboat still stood. Mary's comment was, 'I only wish someone would break that record; it would be an incentive for me to try it again.'

Tony and his wife Marcelle lived in London, where he carried on his property management business; their sons were away at school. Michael, the younger son, was at Downside School near Bath, where Tony had been enrolled years before. Mary saw Michael several times each term; the routine seldom varied. She would drive to the school in one of her Rolls-Royces to pick up the teenager, then take him home to Priory Steps, some twenty miles away. The two would chat over a lunch prepared by the housekeeper, and then Mary would retire to her room upstairs for a nap. Michael would sneak down to his grandmother's pantry and raid the liquor cabinet for whisky—and enjoy a mellow bus ride back to his boarding school.

25 Last Laps

The 1970s found Mary restless and unsettled. She gave occasional radio and press interviews, most memorably with the late Russell Harty; the glove manufacturing business ran well without much close supervision. She and Raymond Boulton divided their time between Priory Steps and the home she maintained near Regent's Park in London, close to Tony's home. She saw her family only occasionally; she was not fond of her daughter-in-law. Her grandsons were not particularly close to her, although she secretly admired their rebellious natures. "One is a queer and one is a hippie," she told a visitor.[1]

She maintained her keen interest in speed, and attended auto races regularly. New racing venues had succeeded Brooklands, among them Thruxton, Brands Hatch and Silverstone. At a racing event at Silverstone in the spring of 1974 Mary met driver Peter Wardle. The two talked about her racing days, reigniting Mary's passion for speed. She sat in Wardle's formula racing car and was hooked again. "That was it," she told an interviewer; "I thought I really must get back into racing." She was 78 years-old.

A speed trial was arranged; she requested the use of one of Ford's hot new racing cars, a Ford Ghia Capri saloon. The event was scheduled at the Thruxton course for the end of April. Mary prepared for the trial in her 1937 Rolls-Royce Phantom III. "I tried it out, double de-clutching from top to third at 60 miles an hour. It's like riding a bike," she said, "it's something you don't forget. The track record is 120 mph, I believe; that's not very high, but I'm not making any promises. I shouldn't think it will take me very long to get the feel of the car and the track."

The press loved the story. To Mary's delight, the Thruxton event was well attended by the media. It had been over forty years since her last race, but Mary had not been forgotten in automotive circles. Camera crews and still photographers recorded every moment, and she basked in the praise and attention. She rode the first lap as a passenger with Ford test driver Stuart McCrudden, listening attentively as he made comments on the course and suggested strategies; then she took the wheel herself.

The pit crew fitted her with the required crash helmet. She put it on backwards at first, but once it was turned around she was on her way. She had paid close attention to McCrudden's advice, and settled into the rhythm at once. Shifting smoothly through the corners, she ran the Capri's speed up and up, until in the homestretch she set her personal lifetime speed mark of 110 mph.

78-year-old Mary's test-drive at Thruxton

As she approached the finish line in front of the grandstand, she worried that she was going too fast and might have to use the escape road. Determined to avoid what she felt would be a humiliating conclusion to the trial she downshifted to third gear, then second, and finally down to low gear. Tyres squealing, she came to a smooth stop in front of the clubhouse. Turning to McCrudden, she said, "You are brave to go round this track with a vintage driver like me; were you afraid?"

With no further opportunities for racetrack adventures in sight, Mary looked for excitement closer to home. She had always enjoyed a good argument; confrontation brought an adrenaline rush not unlike speeding. "I always have to be doing something exciting," she once told a reporter; "If I'm not involved in something dangerous, then there's nothing I like better than a good row with a big organization like a Council."

She went head to head with the West Wiltshire District Council, whose responsibilities included safety and building design in the city of Warminster. She owned a large building of rental flats near the Holman Byfield glove factory. The Council required the installation of fire escapes, a safety measure that had Mary's enthusiastic support. But the building had historical and architectural value; the Council wanted to preserve the façade in its original state, placing the fire escape at the rear. Mary was all in favor of historic interest and architectural beauty—but she wanted the fire escape to run down the front of the building, pointing out that placing it at the back would deny two of the five tenants access in case of fire. Threatening to take the cause clear to the House of Lords, she snapped, "Hitlers, I call them! The Council is putting beauty before safety and I will not give in on this one."

She developed the habit of scrutinizing insurance policies, studying the small print, and picking out errors and discrepancies. She wrote dozens of letters to insurance companies, demanding changes in her policies to suit her. She owned a block of 12 luxury flats in London's Bryanston Square. The policy insuring them for £500,000 was revised and reworded to her satisfaction. "I don't know what the insurance brokers think they're doing," she told an interviewer, "very few brokers seem to inform their clients. My present ones are all right; in fact they offered me a job. I've made such a full study of these policies that my broker said 'Come and work for us anytime Mrs. B.' but I am far too busy to take him up on it."[2]

As it had for the previous ten or fifteen years, one project that kept Mary busy was the writing of her memoirs. 'It won't be an autobiography,' she claimed, 'more a racy story of speed.' Pelham published *Nine Lives Plus* in April 1977. A plan was hatched to publicize its release: she would have a brief refresher course in flying at the airport in Bristol and then, accompanied by a pilot, take the controls of a small plane for the first time in more than forty years.

Pelham was delighted with the stunt; it was sure to boost sales. Mary's son Tony, however, was aghast. "He was very shocked when he heard about it," she said, "and he told me that it was ridiculous at my age. He chose the wrong word. After that I just couldn't wait to get into the air. I told him that if he simply asked me not to fly again, I wouldn't, so he did." She was, after all, 81 years-old.

She drove to Bristol in her Rolls Phantom III and was pleased to see that the escapade would be well-covered by the press. She climbed into the cockpit with the pilot and amid waves and cheers, they took off. Mary did not disappoint her admirers: her short flight included a neatly executed loop-the-loop. On the ground, the approval from the spectators was music to her ears. Out of the spotlight for so many years, she drank in the admiration and played to her audience. "What a lark!" she exclaimed, "It's knocked 50 years off my life!"

In deference to Tony—and because of course she had never intended to take up flying again—it was Mary's last flight. Her autobiography had been properly launched; she returned to her quiet life in Bradford-on-Avon.

Victor died the following year, leaving his wife and three grown children. Mary's name had never been spoken in their household; Peggy had to grit her teeth on the numerous occasions when, being introduced as The Honourable Mrs. Victor Bruce, new acquaintances would exclaim "Oh! The famous Mrs. Bruce! Didn't you fly around the world alone?"

Mary had never seen the necessity of giving up the honorific title after she and Victor divorced. She was widely known as The Honourable Mrs. Bruce; her five books[3] had all been published under that name. No doubt she enjoyed the hint of elevated social status the title conveyed.[4] The fact that there was a second Honourable Mrs. Victor Bruce was of no concern to Mary. Victor and Peggy's children inevitably learned about the famous woman to whom their father had been married, but they kept their questions to themselves out of love and respect for their mother.[5]

After Raymond Boulton died, Mary sold her house in London and lived only at Priory Steps with her housekeeper and companion, Louise Winter. And when Louise died in the early 1980s, it became apparent that Mary could no longer manage living alone. She sold Priory Steps and her beloved Rolls-Royces, and at the age of 90 she reluctantly consented to move to London to live with Tony and Marcelle.

Mary lived in a separate wing of the home; a live-in maid helped with her care. Mary would often join Tony's family in the evening for dinner, but daytimes were largely taken up with receiving visitors.[6] Mary and Tony appeared together on a television interview program[7] just four months before her death. The interviewer asked what had been her motivation for the automotive and aviation records she had set. "I wouldn't have done it if there was no publicity, that's quite sure," she told him; "I wouldn't do it just for pleasure, no, I admit that, but as there was publicity—I did it for that, because then I knew I'd make my fortune! And I did make my fortune! I've lost most of it now, but I did make my fortune!"

In May 1990, Mary Petre Bruce finally ran out of her own personal fuel, adrenaline. The spirited and determined woman who had helped create the aviation history of Britain and who had been such a bright and lively presence in the world of racing in the 1920s, died at the age of 94.

Afterword

The story of Mary Petre Bruce's adventurous life provides an engrossing look into a bygone era, when a barely trained pilot—a woman no less—would dare climb into the cockpit of a tiny open airplane and set out to fly solo around the world.

Mary held her own against all comers: Monte Carlo Rally competitors, bandits in the Syrian desert, rival airline companies in the 1930s. She met every crisis with a practical intelligence, a very British wry sense of humour, and, above all, bravery that would now be considered almost foolhardy; she always did what she felt was the right thing to do. The phrase 'she's an inspiration' is apt: actions of a fearless woman like Mary may instill confidence in a timid person; her determination and drive could inspire action where hesitation has prevailed.

Mary Bruce was fiercely independent and self-assured. She was also given to dramatic declarations and gestures. "She was a great actress," said her closest friend, Daphne. "She could have taken it up if she hadn't been so keen on flying." When Mary wrote her autobiography it was clear that she meant what she had said earlier: "That is the beauty of writing a book. You can say whatever you like without being corrected at every turn by people who will be so painfully precise."

Painful precision was not my goal in writing this book. My objective was to learn everything I could about her extraordinary adventures, and share her story with others. It was a labour of love. How I wish I had known her.

Ken Crofts' Remembrances

In 1935, about to leave school, I was interviewed by Johnny Pugh, chief pilot and director of Air Dispatch at Croydon. The job for which I was applying was that of Air Traffic Clerk. To my delight I was accepted and was told to return in a few days time in order to be taken up to London to be measured for a uniform. During this time Mrs. Bruce was away somewhere so that by the time she returned I had joined the firm, resplendent in my new naval-type clothing. Thus packaged, I was then presented to Mrs. Bruce for her approval and possible use. I had very little idea what my duties might be but it turned out that Mrs. B apparently considered that they should be very many, sometimes odd, and certainly varied.

My association with the Hon. Mrs. Victor Bruce was therefore, at this time, very much on a "Yes, Ma'am" basis. The term 'dogsbody' comes to mind, and a very junior one at that. It might give a little insight into her rather wild character if I list a few of the tasks she expected me to carry out; bear in mind that I was then only a teenager.

Driver

The Company had an ancient Bullnose Morris motorcar which was used for communication between officers in the main airport building and the hangar on the north side of the airfield. The cinder track which connected them ran past the rear of the Aerodrome Hotel, the distance probably being almost one-quarter mile. One of the mechanics had shown me what the pedals and levers did in the old car and I had literally taught myself to drive on this private roadway—that is, after a fashion!

One day I was summoned to the office and Mrs. B said, "Kenneth," (she always called me that) "I want you to take the car and go to my house in Cobham and pick up some paperwork." I felt obliged to point out that I had no driving license. "Oh, never mind," said she, "I've seen you driving around the airfield—you'll be all right; don't be long!" I can't remember how far it is between Croydon and Cobham but it seemed like an awful lot of one-quarter miles. Of course, there was not so much traffic in those days or police patrol cars; even so!

Ballast

During the summer there suddenly appeared a Cierva Autogiro in our hangar. I never really knew the truth about this aircraft. I presume that it belonged to Mrs. B and it had been rumored that she had attempted a record-breaking flight to the Cape, but had been forced to land somewhere in the Pyrenees. This would not have been 'box office' so maybe hence the mystery. I do know, however, that the Autogiro had just been converted from a single-seater to a two-seater aircraft. This modification was carried out by the Chief Ground Engineer Mr. Hancock. Mister Hancock was a huge and intimidating man and was therefore only addressed as 'Mister', even by Mrs. B.

On this sunny morning I was standing on the tarmac with my mind many miles away when characteristic rapid footsteps and a prod in the back brought me to earth. There was Mrs. B complete with flying helmet and string of trademark pearls making for the Autogiro. "Come along Kenneth," said she, "I need some weight." Obedience and youthful curiosity had me in the second seat for a very memorable 20-minute flight under the then-unusual rotors. Later in life I may have declined this kind offer, but even so I seem to remember some slightly aching jaw muscles at the time.

Riding Shotgun

Hillman's Airways, during my employment with Air Dispatch, had the misfortune to develop a hole in the floor of one of their DeHavilland Dragons, through which they inadvertently jettisoned several boxes of gold coin. I have no doubt that they were very sorry about this but as far as Mrs. B was concerned it was pennies from heaven. In her usual way she managed to talk the underwriters and bullion merchants into the idea that Air Dispatch could carry their gold a lot more safely! This all happened rather suddenly and in spite of all the assurances and promises, there was much improvisation in the early days of this contract. For example I remember accompanying Mrs. B from Croydon to Johnson Mattheys in London in her AC coupe with two boxes of gold ingots hidden under a blanket in the dickey seat.

Another time I was sent up to London on the bus carrying a pencil box-size container of platinum. I think I was 17 at the time. I don't remember what the platinum was worth but I'm sure it was worth a lot more than the bus.

Later the floor of the Avro 642 which was to fly the bullion was reinforced and a Ford V-8 Utility Van (half-timbered!) was purchased to convey the gold between Croydon and London. Screwed to the front inside passenger door was a leather holster which carried a Webley handgun and for a while I was given the job of 'bullion courier'. This whole affair seems ludicrous in the light of today's standards, but I should say I never remember any ammunition being supplied for the gun; it was obviously only for brandishing in an emergency! Luckily there never was an emergency apart from a roadside wheel change on one occasion, when we had to politely declined help from a curious passerby. In these times life seemed a lot safer although there was a bullion robbery at Croydon airport, fortunately nothing to do with us; even this was carried out in a very gentlemanly and nonviolent manner.

User of Initiative (failed)

The newspaper run to Le Bourget (Paris) every morning meant that returning aircraft often had freight space and any payload was very welcome. On one occasion one of our aircraft arrived back at Croydon with a large bale of printed matter which was shown on the manifest as 'film magazines'. The consignment was been loaded onto a hand truck when the Duty Customs officer produced his clasp knife and tore away the brown paper covering the top of the bale. Yes, there were film magazines printed in sepia. Becoming a little more curious he then ran his knife down the spine side of the pile only to reveal that the folded edges of the publications had developed streaks of color. Becoming even more curious he then pried out a copy midway down the stack. This one turned out to be anything but family film fun and he promptly impounded the load and had it wheeled off to some dark place of safety. At this point I felt I should seek the protection of senior management; I was told to go and see the appropriate Senior Customs Officer and 'use my initiative'. Having found the office I fearfully knocked and entered; I found myself in the presence of a very large gentleman who peered at me over half-rim glasses and bawled "Yes?" I quickly stated my business as best I could. He walked over to his desk and returned with one of the offending articles, which he slammed down on the counter in front of me. "How would you describe these?" he said.

"Physical culture?" I meekly offered. An unforgiving knuckle rapped the centerfold.

"Physical, yes!" said he; "culture, no!" Totally defeated I returned to senior management, hoping for sympathy and forgiveness. Suddenly everything to do with this event went very quiet and I am sure Mrs. B, with her usual persuasive manner, convinced everyone that it was all an innocent mistake.

Farmer (?)

Air Dispatch used a 16-seater aircraft Avro 642 to take the early morning newspapers to Paris. Most of the seats were stripped out to give floor space for the 40 kg bales of newspaper. However there was some seating available and Mrs. B. had the bright idea that these seats could be sold to passengers. This service was romantically called the Dawn Express—'See the dawn rise over the Channel'. As a further incentive passengers were to be charged 'livestock freight rates', i.e. so many shillings to the pound or kilogram. For a very short period it became my job to weigh each passenger, charge them accordingly, shepherd them out to the aircraft and seat them amid the stacks of newspaper. We even supplied in-flight entertainment in the form of complementary newsprint—the distributors always supplied loose papers in order to prevent the bales being vandalized by the crew. Needless to say this innovation did not last very long. Imperial Airways quickly alerted IATA, who threatened legal action. Even Mrs. B. was not able to talk her way out of that.

Pump Boy

As I mentioned, with freight capacity available on the return runs from Le Bourget, no cargo was refused, however strange. On one occasion we were asked to transport a herd of seahorses which were destined for the zoo in Regents Park. It was specified that this tank must be accompanied at all times; the reason, at the time, was not quite clear. "All right" said Mrs. B. "Kenneth can do that." We waited on the tarmac at Le Bourget and eventually a van marked *Zoologie* appeared, with a fair size tank and a very enthusiastic, rapidly-speaking Frenchman. He did not speak any English and my French was of rather recent school standard. The tank of seahorses was loaded onto the aircraft and the little Frenchmen finally made me understand—I think—that although there was some sort of warming device for the tank water, present technology did not extend to an aeration system. This was achieved by periodically squeezing a rubber bulb—"*Comme ça!*" I remember spending the entire flight back to Croydon worrying about whether I had fully understood about the frequency of *Comme ça*-ing. These seahorses might either be dancing for error or suffering with a bad attack of wind. Anyway the tank was duly collected at Croydon and the fish successfully corralled in their new home. Much to my relief we received no complaints so we all must have survived the journey without harm.

I was later to have a further experienced at the handle of a pump involving auxiliary fuel tanks and a relatively long distance flight, but since I believe that was not completely legal, perhaps I better not commit the episode to print.

Postscript

After the war, having left the RAF, I applied for a job with Rolls-Royce at Church Broughton on their flight experimental establishment. I found I really needed a civilian reference of some sort. Since the only job I ever had before the war was with Air Dispatch, I decided to spend the day in London in the hope of tracking down Mrs. Bruce. After phoning around many of the clubs and addresses I thought might know of her whereabouts (some of whom wanted to know if I was a creditor!), I eventually discovered that she now lived in Grosvenor Square near to the American Embassy. I found and phoned her number and she said, "Come on up". She greeted me very well and typically asked what I would like her to say in the reference! I had spent much of the war years in the Far East so there was quite a lot to talk about. There seemed to have been a party going on in the adjoining room and eventually her son in an Army uniform came in to see what had happened to her. I believe his name was Tony. So I arrived back in Derby with a glowing reference and got the job!

Acknowledgements

A chance reading of Mary Petre Bruce's 1990 obituary in the San Francisco Chronicle set in motion a fascinating process of discovering, sorting, and assembling a huge jigsaw puzzle of bits of information. As the pieces fell together, they began to reveal a picture of a remarkable life. The more I learned, the more I wanted to know. At each step I was blessed with great good fortune.

In those early days of the internet, a search for 'Hon. Mrs. Victor Bruce' led to a news story from Salisbury about an auction of some of her possessions. Weeks later another search revealed the name and home town of the winning bidder, Caroline Gough-Cooper. Fortunately she lived in a village, and a letter addressed to her in care of the local postmaster reached her.

Caroline was the key to the story. Visiting at her Hampshire cottage, I learned the name that opened the doors wide: Carey Chapman, whose enthusiasm and support have been endless. After Carey and his wife Diana purchased Mary Bruce's former home, Priory Steps in Bradford-on-Avon, they uncovered boxes of news clippings that chronicled Mary's extraordinary past. They had expanded the trove of memorabilia and, yes, I was welcome to come and visit—which I did, again and again. I knew the story had to be told, and Carey's generous sharing of ideas, information and contacts has been a constant source of immeasurable value.

The phrase 'without them this book could never have been written' is absolutely true of Carey and Diana Chapman and Caroline Gough-Cooper. I am greatly in their debt.

I am very grateful to the children of Victor and Peggy Bruce: Wendy Grimmond, Jill Hope, and the late Colin Bruce, who warmly welcomed me into their lives, sharing their memories and experiences.

I thank Carey Chapman, Wendy Grimmond and the late Colin Bruce for permission to reproduce illustrations and pictures from their collections.

More puzzle pieces fell into place with the kind assistance of many new friends made in the process, including:

Mary's only surviving relative, her grandson Michael Easter-Bruce;

Stephen Easter's granddaughter, Annabel Easter-Davis;

Eric Noddings' granddaughter, Linda Naidu;

Julia Driver, who graciously provided a copy of one of Mary's own photo albums;

John Pulford and Julian Temple of Brooklands Museum, who have cheerfully answered my questions for over 15 years;

and the staff of the superb Wiltshire and Swindon History Centre.

Thanks are due as well to Mary's friends and acquaintances who offered personal reminiscences: Daphne Kearly Vickers Watson, Jill Forster, Ken Crofts, Georgina Alexander, Graham Cloake, Stuart McCrudden, Hazel Bolton, and Mary's daughter-in-law Marcelle Easter-Bruce.

I learned still more from archivists and reference librarians on two continents, and from experts who graciously shared their knowledge in subjects ranging from aviation to race cars to early London theatre to bus bodies and a dozen other fields.

A great deal of material in this book comes, of course, from Mary's own writings. Her detailed accounts of her Mediterranean trip and her world flight are well worth searching for.

I am grateful to Roger Jones of Ex Libris Press for patiently shepherding this neophyte through the publication process.

I owe particular thanks to author Alexandra Pratt, who shared the dream of telling this story, and who provided generous advice and boundless encouragement.

I am incredibly fortunate to belong to a family of smart and sharp-eyed readers, and I am deeply grateful for the expert editing done with such lovingly 'painful precision' by my brother Denis Wade; my daughter Melinda Feinstein; and my husband, Tom Wilson.

There is of course the certainty that some reader will have one more titbit of information, one more anecdote about Mary Bruce that should have been included in this book. That's life.

NOTES and REFERENCES

Chapter 1: GROWING UP

1. Family History: Mary's father, Lawrence Petre, was a member of a prominent family, which numbered among its members Sir William Petre, a secretary of state under four monarchs: Henry VIII, Edward VI, Mary, and Elizabeth. Tact must have been his strong suit; a devout Catholic, he served both Protestant and Catholic rulers. Among the duties he performed for Henry VIII was confiscating the keys from convents and monasteries, an awkward assignment for a staunch Catholic. He kept his position during the unsettled years of Edward VI, and through most of the reign of Queen Mary, winning her loyalty when he favored her marriage to Philip II of Spain, a match of which Parliament disapproved. Petre resigned his position in 1557, near the end of Mary's reign, but later performed some duties for her successor, Elizabeth. He died in 1562.

   Another ancestor, the fourth Baron Petre, was denounced as a papist and arrested in the 'Popish Plot' of 1678; he was imprisoned without trial in the Tower of London for six years, dying there in 1684. Yet another ancestor, James Radcliffe, the Third Earl of Derwentwater, went to the executioner's block on Tower Hill for his participation in the 1715 Jacobite Uprising. As Mary related the story in her 1977 autobiography, he did not go without objection. He complained that the block upon which he was required to lay his head was too rough for his neck, and insisted that it be smoothed first. When the block satisfied him, he then gave instructions that the blade was not to fall until he had said 'Jesus' three times—another request which was granted. After the earl was beheaded, his body was spirited away by his supporters and taken north for burial in the chapel at Dilston, his estate in Northumberland. His execution and the return of his body to his home coincided with a particularly brilliant showing of the Northern Lights, and a rumour sprang up that they were a sign of heavenly outrage at the death of this well-loved young Earl. For many years, the aurora borealis was known in the north of England as 'Lord Derwentwater's Lights'.

   In marked contrast to the Petre family, Jennie's family was very New World: bold, adventurous, and unconventional. Jennie, encouraged by her brothers, was just a teenager when she left Indiana for London. Mary wrote with pride—and probably a colossal dose of exaggeration—about her intrepid maternal great-grandmother, a member of a party of Indiana adventurers who trekked across the American plains in the 1849 gold rush to California. According to Mary, calamity struck when an attack by Indians coincided with the birth of a child—Mary's grandmother. Allegedly the baby was born beneath a covered wagon, while the labouring mother fired at the Indians through the spokes of a wheel. Baby delivered and Indian attack defeated, Mary's great-grandmother finished the trip as leader of the party, whose numbers had been reduced from 122 to 21.
2. *Pall Mall Magazine*, Vol. X1V, January 1898.
3. In later years Mary identified her first car as an Enfield Allday.
4. The Royal East Kent Regiment, one of the oldest regiments of the British Army.

Chapter 2: GEARING UP

1. Two pace cars, with teams of drivers, accompanied Edge on the track, which was lit by lanterns during the nighttime hours. Edge carried a passenger, but he drove the entire 24 hours.
2. In 1909 at Lea Valley, A.V. Roe became the first Englishman to fly a plane of his own design. With his brother Humphrey Verdon Roe he formed A.V. Roe & Co. in 1910; their best known product was the AVRO 504 bomber.
3. Only two Rallies were run before the First World War—in 1911 and 1912—and they were

won, respectively, by the French driver Rougier in a Turcat-Mery and Beutler of Germany in a Berliet. Suspended during the First World War, the Monte Carlo was reinstated in 1924. French automobiles and drivers maintained their dominance until Victor Bruce's 1926 win in an AC. In subsequent years the Rally became a truly international event, with drivers and automobiles from all over Europe competing. Italy scored its first win with a Fiat in 1928, although French national pride remained intact, since a French driver was at the wheel. The following year, Dr. Sprenger Van Euk of Holland won the Rally driving an American car, a Graham-Paige. The 1930s saw entrants from a variety of countries, with the French Hotchkiss, Peugeot, and Renault automobiles dominating the top spot.

A competitor's starting point choice was subject to the approval of the Rally officials, and every start had to be recorded by official observers. Athens was the most distant sanctioned starting place— 2,333 miles from Monaco—but the terrain and winter weather made that route particularly hazardous. Scandinavia attracted many entrants, with automobiles leaving from Stavanger, Norway, as well as Stockholm and Sundsvaal, Sweden.

Entrants followed a strict timetable, with pre-arranged checkpoints and times. Points were subtracted for deviations. The contestants traveled day and night; relief drivers were allowed, but the primary designated driver had to cover the entire route.
4. Brunell was a lifelong fan of motor vehicles of all descriptions, frequently competing in races and rallies in addition to photographing them.
5. Brunell cautiously retained the copyright on the photo album.

Chapter 4: ACROSS NORTH AFRICA AND HOME
1. Still a five-star hotel, its classic Moorish architecture and magnificent detail has made it a UNESCO World Heritage site.

Chapter 6: MONTLHÉRY ENDURANCE RECORD
1. Maud Petre, Lawrence's older sister, was a prominent Catholic activist and writer.
2. In her autobiography *Nine Lives Plus* and in later-life interviews, Mary claimed this drink of petrol occurred during her solo 24-hour run at Montlhéry in June 1929, offering the mishap as a reason for not attaining an even higher total mileage. However, she related the incident in an interview published in the *Ceylon Observer*, Colombo, 28 January 1928: 'One night, after leaving the wheel, I mistook a bottle in the darkness and took 2 large gulps of petrol instead of water; it made me very ill.'
3. New records were set for 5,000, 10,000 and 15,000 miles, and for 10,000, 15,000 and 20,000 kilometres.

Chapter 7: THE LEGEND GROWS
1. Campbell was inspired by a production of Belgian playwright Maurice Maeterlinck's *The Blue Bird*, a fantasy about the search for happiness. He used the name Bluebird for every automobile and boat he raced thereafter.
2. Donald Campbell, son of Sir Malcolm Campbell, followed in his father's footsteps as a racer, setting multiple records before his tragic death at the age of 45 while attempting to set a new water speed record on Coniston Water in Lancashire.
3. Born in Baltimore to an American mother and an Irish father, Segrave was just Mary's age. Beginning in 1919 he raced at Brooklands, and was a member of the driving team for Sunbeam Talbot Darracq, along with Malcolm Campbell. In 1923 he became the first Briton ever to win a French Grand Prix. In 1927 he set a new land speed record at Daytona, breaking the 200 mph speed barrier, and in 1929 he raised the mark to 231 mph—an effort for which he was knighted. Like Mary, Campbell, Kaye Don, and other racers, Segrave took

his love of speed to the water, and on 13 June 1930 he set a new record of 101 mph in his boat *Miss England*. After two runs the boat was refuelled and he went back for a third run, hoping to boost the mark just a bit higher; he died when *Miss England* hit a submerged log, flew into the air, hit the water again, and sank.

4. 'Count on a woman,' wrote one reporter, 'for a spectacular double-crossing.'

Chapter 8: THE LITTLE LADY AND THE BIG BENTLEY

1. An AC racing team member, Gillett was Victor's passenger in his first Monte Carlo Rally in 1925.

2. Mary also set 2,000 mile and 3,000 kilometre records at the same speed. Twenty-four hour endurance runs continue to attract attention in the racing world, most notably at Le Mans each June. The first Le Mans was run in 1923, but none has ever been a solo effort. Teams of at least two drivers compete there and at the annual 24-hour race at Daytona. While there is a big difference between the oval banked Montlhéry track and the 10+ mile Le Mans circuit, it is notable that Mary's mileage of 2,149.68 and her average speed of 89.57 were not surpassed at Le Mans until 1951, when Great Britain's team of P. Walker and P. Whitehead covered 2,243.9 miles in their Jaguar-C at an average 93.5 mph. Her 24-hour solo record, which eclipsed the original mark set by Selwyn Edge and then broken by Thomas Gillett, stood for four years. It was broken in August 1933 by David Abbot 'Ab' Jenkins on the Bonneville Salt Flats in Utah. No woman has ever surpassed Mary's record.

Chapter 9: ON THE WATER

1. It is unclear just which record she actually wanted to beat. Cunard's liner *Mauretania* had held the Blue Riband for the fastest Atlantic crossing for 20 years, but that mark was surpassed by the new German liner *Bremen* in July 1929, with a westbound crossing in four days, 17 hours, and 42 minutes. Cunard's *Berengaria* never held any speed records at all.

2. London *Daily News*, 24 September 1929.

Chapter 10: TAKING FLIGHT

1. The first major air race for women, from California to Ohio, 13-20 August 1929.

2. Judy Lomax; *Women of the Air*; Ivy Books, 1987.

3. For the most part, place names used by Mary during her world flight are maintained here; many have changed in the intervening years (Angora is now Ankara, Siam is now Thailand, etc.) Some are variant spellings (Hanjam or Hengam) for which I have arbitrarily chosen one.

4. Wade was clearly a kindred spirit to Mary, although they never met. In 1925 he and fellow pilot Linton Wells completed the first non-stop trip by car across the U.S., in 167 hours, even changing a flat tyre in motion, using a rolling jack. He later became the first aviator to fly over the Andes.

5. Burberry, for decades Britain's premier outfitter for explorers, provided a gabardine tent for South Pole pioneer Amundsen. In the 1930s Burberry produced specialty garments for many aviators.

6. *Bystander*, 15 April 1931.

7. The Graham Amplion Company at Slough, near Heston Airfield.

8. Elsie M Lang; *British Women in the Twentieth Century*; Kessinger Publishing, 2003.

9. *Illustrated Sporting and Dramatic News*, 4 January 1930.

10. Diary of Victor Bruce, 25 May 1930.

11. Mary's hunger for fame was a sore point with Victor's family, who reportedly told her scornfully, "When you die we're going to have written across your grave 'Publicity!'"

Chapter 11: UP AND AWAY
1. Bradshaw's *Railway Guides*, which began publication in 1839, were an indispensable aid to travellers coping with the myriad rail routes in Britain. Beginning in 1847, a continental edition was also published, which not only served travellers but was also the main reference for Jules Verne's *Around the World in Eighty Days*. The name Bradshaw became so closely associated with rail routes that pilots called following the tracks 'flying by Bradshaw'.

Chapter 12: UNHAPPY LANDINGS
1. In retrospect, Biscoe's suggestion of a fly-by of the navy ships was very ill-advised. Had Mary kept to the eastern shoreline of the Gulf as she flew south, rather than going out of her way to signal the ships off the coast of Hanjam Island, she almost certainly would have avoided the disastrous forced landing in the desert.

Chapter 13: LIFE WITH THE BALUCHIS
1. Brand's Essence: Mary wrote in a letter to a friend: 'The Brand's Essence came in fine, I was most thankful for it. The Baluchi tribesmen finished off the last five tins I had in the desert, and danced a war dance on the strength of it.' Available in beef or chicken flavours, it was a staple for British adventurers. In 2001 the Mallory-Irvine Research Expedition on Mt. Everest found a label from a container of Brand's Essence of Beef at the 26,000-foot-high camp of the 1933 British Everest Expedition.

Chapter 14: DESERT TO JUNGLE
1. The casual nature of Garden's flight was captured in newspaper accounts such as 'Mystery Flyer's Australian Flight', which reported that Oscar Garden's mother made an unsuccessful eleventh-hour attempt to dissuade her son from flying to Australia, saying "He was not carrying a hat and has only a dozen sandwiches. He has no fixed schedule." Like Mary, he was long on enthusiasm and determination and short on flying experience. Like hers, his journey was peppered with near accidents and unplanned landings. Berry, Stephen & Margareta Gee. 'Garden, Oscar, 1903–1997'. *Dictionary of New Zealand Biography*, July 2005.
2. The dirigibles designated R100 and R101 were the keystone of an ambitious program to unite the British Empire by air by providing passenger service to Canada and India. R100, built by Vickers, had made a successful crossing to Canada in August 1930. Tragically, the government-built R101 crashed into a French hillside on its maiden voyage to Egypt and India on 6 October, just two weeks before Mary and Garden reached Karachi. It exploded in flames with the disastrous loss of 48 of the 55 passengers aboard, including the Air Minister, Lord Thompson. That was effectively the end of the British effort to match Germany's Zeppelin program.
3. A Vancouver, B.C., newspaper headlined an account in a slightly more dramatic tone: 'Mrs. Bruce Attacked by Great Vultures On Flight Over Desert'.
4. The nearby West Bengal town of Dum Dum was the site of an ammunition factory where dumdum bullets were first made.

Chapter 15: SIAM TO CHINA
1. The tradition of the pigtail, or queue, for Chinese men was largely abandoned at the time of the Chinese Revolution of 1911, the fall of the Manchu Dynasty.

Chapter 16: THE YELLOW SEA AND JAPAN
1. Now called Ta-ya Wan, Bias Bay harboured pirates until the late 1930s. Its position near the main shipping routes between the Orient and the Indian Ocean made it an ideal base.

2. The British solution was to sell opium from their India colony to the Chinese to balance the trade deficit, a move that at least temporarily met the goal, albeit at huge expense in terms of the health and well-being of the Chinese. When the Chinese government tried to control the trade in the late 1830s, the British began the First Opium War (1839-1842). It was ended by the Treaty of Nanking in which Hong Kong was ceded to the British and trade concessions such as expanded port access were granted.

3. Launched in December 1929, the *Empress of Japan* completed her sea trials in June 1930, crossed the Atlantic to Liverpool, and then continued via the Suez Canal to Hong Kong, where she began her trans-Pacific service.

4. The *tai*, or red sea bream, is often served at weddings and other ceremonies, and is considered the good luck fish in Japan.

5. His moustache, measuring 20 inches from tip to tip, was legendary. When he died two years after Mary's visit, the moustache was ceremoniously clipped from his face by his son, bound with white silk, laid on a satin cushion and buried in a separate grave.

   Besides the prodigious moustache, Nagaoka is remembered for his part in bringing skiing to Japan. As an army officer in 1911, he arranged instruction for his troops by an Austrian army officer who had come to observe the Japanese army.

6. The Imperial Hotel had been designed by American architect Frank Lloyd Wright to withstand the earthquakes so common to Japan. It had sustained some damage in the great Kanto earthquake of 1923, which measured 8.3 on the Richter scale and claimed over 100,000 lives. When the Japanese government wired to inform Wright that the hotel was still standing, he reportedly replied "Of course."

7. 'She had amassed five trunks full of beautiful clothes and pieces of jewellery given to her by people of various countries in which she had landed. They were filled with dozens of exquisitely embroidered kimonos, sheer silk lingerie from Shanghai, woollies from Hong Kong and a valuable string of cultured pearls, the gift of Miki Moto, the Japanese pearl merchant. The trunks were sent on to England by steamer.' Mary G Ferguson, Newcastle *Chronicle*, 5 October 1931.

Chapter 17: TO THE NEW WORLD

1. Also called a 'bunt', the outside loop was first performed by Jimmy Doolittle in 1927. Even in her later days in a flying circus, Mary never attempted this difficult manoeuvre.

2. Mary wrote that she was heartbroken when she crashed, but the local press had nothing but praise for her cheery 'pluck and good humor'. The British press concurred: 'In London aviation circles the highest praise and some astonishment is being expressed for Mrs. Bruce's enterprise and cautious skill as a pilot. Her instructor, Captain H. Duncan Davis, A.F.C., of the Brooklands School of Flying, stated yesterday: 'We knew she was a promising pilot, but she was a mere novice when she set out, and frankly, few of us thought she would ever finish her journey to Japan, which has never been flown before.' *Midland Daily Telegraph*, 23 December 1930.

3. Weeks later Looff wrote a letter to Squadron Leader Claude Ridley in London on the subject of the mishap, saying that Mary was an excellent pilot and that the accident was due more to the gravel on the runway and the extra heavy load of petrol than any lack of skill on her part. 'I do not profess to know all about flying but I know a good landing when I see one. Mrs. Bruce led the way on her journey and not once did I find it necessary to correct her course. Someone certainly gave her good instruction in map reading and navigation. My only object in writing is to give you my version of an unavoidable accident to a stout-hearted little lady who certainly deserves a real cheer.'

4. International phone calls were rare enough in 1930 that a local newspaper devoted a half

column to the event.

5. Jennie was a member of the 1880 class of the Mills Preparatory School in Oakland; she lived in San Francisco while attending the school.

6. Greeting Mary was one of Rossi's first official mayoral duties; he had assumed office just the previous day.

Chapter 18: CROSSING AMERICA

1. Chief Davis earned the nickname 'Two Gun Davis' for his fondness for firearms.

2. Actress Rita Hayworth, born Margarita Carmen Cansino, was 'discovered' while performing onstage at Agua Caliente.

3. Ione Quimby, writing in the *Chicago Post* of 23 January 1931.

4. Or perhaps a practical joker impersonating the notorious gangster.

5. The other pilot flew on to Baltimore alone.

6. *The Bluebird's Flight*, Chapman & Hall, London, 1931.

7. *Nine Lives Plus*, Pelham Books, London, 1977.

8. Mary had flown more than 19,100 miles, crossing 23 countries in 21 weeks.

Chapter 19: BACK FROM THE WORLD

1. Mary's world flight was the first circumnavigation by a woman, but the distinction of 'first solo flight around the world' eluded her by a mere three months. A young German flyer, Baron Friedrich Karl von Koenig-Warthausen, completed a solo circumnavigation in November 1930 in a Klemm monoplane powered by a 20 hp engine. He had set out in August 1929 to win Germany's Hindenburg Cup with a solo flight from Berlin to Moscow but, having accomplished that, he decided to go on a little farther. And a little farther. And then a little farther still. At each juncture—Moscow, Teheran, Bushire—he decided to fly a bit farther. He wrote in his 1930 account of the journey, *Wings Around the World*, that as he waited in Calcutta for replacement parts for his airplane, he 'had the fever to continue'. He flew on to Singapore and sailed to California, with stops for flying excursions in China, Japan, and Hawaii. Crossing the U.S. took five months, including two months' recuperation after an auto accident in Texas. He sailed from New York to Bremen and arrived home 24 November, having flown 20,000 miles in 15 months. The first all-air solo circumnavigation was accomplished by American flyer Wiley Post in 1933, although with a route near the Arctic Circle, he flew only 15,596 miles—a distance that, by modern standards, would not qualify as a true circumnavigation.

2. Newcastle *Chronicle*, 5 October 1931: 'Not All Done for Fun'. Interview with Mary G. Ferguson.

3. The Pacific crossing record was an afterthought for Pangborn and Herndon. They were attempting to break Post and Gatty's June 1931 record for circumnavigation when they were delayed by bad weather in Siberia. Realizing that they could not beat the record, they decided to try for the $25,000 prize offered by a Japanese newspaper for the first non-stop crossing of the Pacific.

4. Also well known as a yachtswoman and ice hockey player, Brown was the first woman to win the prestigious King's Cup Air Race, in 1930.

5. The flag was commissioned after a dispute arose when flying boats of Imperial Airways flew the Union Jack while at anchor. The Navy claimed that only warships had that privilege; Imperial acquiesced and appealed to the Air Ministry for an appropriate substitute ensign.

6. The prominent role played by women in aviation was demonstrated by the first All-Women's Flying Meet in September 1931. Sywell Aerodrome in Northamptonshire was the locale, and the press was full of news of the event. Formally opened by the Duchess of Bedford, a great

booster of aviation, the Meet included a 15-mile air race, an air-ambulance demonstration, aerobatics and formation flying. The buzz of the event, though, was the much-anticipated appearance of two mysterious 'ladies of the Czechoslovakian aristocracy'. Organisers of the Meet had received an envelope containing expensive, heavily embossed note paper, upon which was written in good, but slightly broken English, a cordial letter, signed by two ladies, both keen amateur pilots, who, having heard of the meet, would 'so like to have the opportunity of being present'. Agog at the prospect of titled foreigners attending their meeting, a warm invitation had been extended. The press had been notified that in addition to such well-known British aviators as the Hon. Mrs. Victor Bruce and the Hon. Lady Bailey, spectators could look forward to seeing Baroness Orhonsky and Madame Katunka, who would fly over from Amsterdam in their Moth. Midway through the program the Moth arrived, bearing strange foreign markings. Out stepped the exotic flyers. Eager male members of the Northampton Flying Club immediately escorted the aristocratic ladies to the pavilion, where they were introduced. It was reported that, although they could not speak more than a few words of slightly guttural English, there was soon a general rush to meet the fascinating Baroness and her demure companion. The Duchess of Bedford warmly shook hands with them and rapidly everyone was vying with others in correctly pronouncing 'Orhonsky'.

After hours had passed, flying club officials passed around a commemorative card, which was to bear the signatures of all the lady pilots present. The exotic Czechs demurred, protesting that they were not famous enough for such an honour. Persuaded at last, they signed, 'but with signatures which the officials found it difficult to associate with the calligraphy of continental society. However with tactful good taste they refrained from commenting, writing off the weird inscription as probably an old Czechoslovakian custom'. Suddenly someone wondered aloud about the absence of two of the flying club's most prominent male members: 'Where are Newton and Deterding?' Members looked around and asked again, 'Yes, but where are the Baroness Orhonsky and Madame Katunka?' They had fled. Only then did everyone look at each other, speechless, realizing they had been duped. A hunt began at once to find the missing ladies, and shortly there appeared in trousered triumph Mr. C. M. Newton and Mr. H. Deterding, all the way from Czechoslovakia to take the full toll they deserved of their colleagues' complete mortification.

Chapter 20: THE SKY'S THE LIMIT

1. Smith later gained fame as pilot of the *Chicago*, one of the Douglas World Cruisers that circled the world in 1924.
2. *Popular Flying*, June 1932.
3. Just over six feet high, the Satyr measured 17'8" long, with a 21' upper wingspan; Mary's Blackburn Bluebird's length had been 23', with a 30'wingspan.
4. At 10'8"high, its length was 28'3" and the wingspan was nearly 38'.
5. The autogiro was developed by Juan de la Cierva, a visionary Spanish aeronautical engineer who designed and built numerous gliders and aircraft before World War I. His autogiro replaced fixed wings with a freewheeling rotor to provide lift, although the aircraft's forward motion was powered by a standard propeller driven by the engine. This peculiar hybrid design meant that the autogiro could neither hover nor fly sideways; the rotors turned only in response to airflow, and were not connected to the engine. First successfully flown in 1923, the lack of flexibility was a deficiency that limited the autogiro's appeal, although it served as something of a holding-place until the successful development of a true helicopter. Russian Igor Sikorsky had built an early helicopter, with a rotor supplying both lift and forward power, in 1909. It never left the ground, however, and after a subsequent unsuccessful revision Sikorsky turned to designing fixed-wing aircraft until resuming work on helicopters

in the 1930s 1930.

De la Cierva's invention created significant interest in the rest of Europe. In 1925 the British Air Ministry saw demonstrations of the C6 model and ordered several autogiros for use by the Royal Air Force, which were built by A.V. Roe's aviation firm in Manchester. Design refinements followed, and the usefulness and popularity of the autogiro increased during the next decade.

6. Ken Crofts was hired as an assistant by Air Dispatch in 1935 at the age of 16. One of his unusual assignments was to serve as ballast while Mary flew the autogiro.

7. Roughly £60 in today's buying power.

8. Ken Crofts' Remembrances appear on pages 207-211.

9. Britain's Imperial Airways had employed male stewards for several years. The world's first female hostess was nurse Ellen Church, who was hired in May 1930 by America's Boeing Air Transport, forerunner of United Airlines.

10. Daphne married Keith Vickers, Chief Engineer for Air Dispatch. Mary later said that she quickly changed her practice and began hiring only plain women as hostesses, because pilots and passengers kept marrying all the pretty ones.

11. Abyssinia had fought off an attempted annexation by Italy in the late 19th century, and was admitted to the League of Nations as an independent country in 1923. A border incident in December 1934 between Ethiopia and neighbouring Italian Somaliland was the pretext for Italy's Benito Mussolini to threaten invasion. In the absence of any action by the League of Nations, Ethiopia's Emperor Haile Selassie appealed for international aid. None came, and Mussolini's troops invaded in October 1935.

12. The Chaco War, 1932-35.

Chapter 21: GATHERING CLOUDS

1. Mary sold two of her remaining De Havilland Dragons for use as air ambulances in Spain to a mysterious man who appeared at Croydon one evening with an offer of an immediate cash purchase. Mary quoted a price three times their value; he agreed, and the next morning handed over ten £1000 notes.

2. An old ambition—to win a ribbon at a prestigious horse show—was realized when she took a first prize in the Open Jumping competition at the Royal Horse Show at Windsor in 1939. Earlier that year she had taken second place in the International Horse Show with her grey, Grand Manor, losing the Daily Mail Cup by only half a fault.

3. Personal interview, Georgina Alexander, July 2002.

Chapter 22: THE WAR YEARS

1. Cardiff Airport, whose gala opening ceremonies Mary had attended shortly after returning from her world flight in 1931, was known as Pengam Moors. The site had been reclaimed from seashore flats with the construction of a seawall. The builders were probably influenced by the belief, widely held at the time, that seaplanes would prove to be the primary vehicles for long distance air travel.

2. Hooper & Company's invoice shows a purchase price of £1920; it was put through the Air Dispatch books with a figure of £3000.

3. Significant naval events took place during these months, however, including the October 1939 sinking of HMS *Royal Oak* in Scapa flow by the German submarine U-47 and the scuttling of the German pocket battleship *Graf Spee* in Montevideo Harbour in November 1939.

4. Now the home of the exclusive Beaufort Polo Club.

5. The aircraft parts, according to her autobiography *Nine Lives Plus*, included a consignment

of forty aircraft wings which Mary and her crew transported to Cardiff from Walsall, near Birmingham, in her horse-trailer, which had hastily been altered to a cargo trailer.

6. Tony served initially in the Royal Air Force, and then in the Army Intelligence Service.

7. Perhaps because of her mother and brother's alcoholism, Mary never drank liquor, according to her friend Daphne. Her habits changed, however, in her later years.

8. Roderick died in 1964. He had inherited a house from his mother, and lived on a pension and some earnings from selling newspapers. He never married.

9. Personal recollections by Graham Cloake, 2002.

Chapter 23: FANTASIA

1. Down Farm was divided into several parcels; 168 acres with the main house and outbuildings brought £28,500.

2. 37 Grosvenor Square, 20 Hanover Terrace, 22 Chester Terrace, 7 Cumberland Terrace, and Welbeck House at 16 Wigmore Street.

3. Mary threatened often to become an expatriate, usually in response to some governmental action she didn't approve of. This time it was the Labour Party's post-war refusal to return the airlines to private ownership.

4. One hundred miles west of Cardiff, this seaport—said by Admiral Lord Nelson to be one of the finest in the world—had been a vital Allied naval base during the war.

5. Mary paid just over £8 for the painting—several hundred pounds in today's terms. Its whereabouts are unknown.

6. Mary also wrote to invite Daphne Vickers, but her husband Keith—jealous of Mary's close friendship with his wife—intercepted all of Mary's letters to Daphne and the invitation was never delivered.

Chapter 24: WINDING DOWN

1. Half a century later the effects of the heating system are still evident to the passer-by, in the form of a fully mature date palm tree growing beside the garage. The tree—uncommon in England—has been well nurtured by the heat intended for the Rolls-Royces.

2. London *Daily Mail*, 7 August 1952 ; column titled 'Who Why Where', unattributed.

3. According to Carey Chapman, Mary had hoped to build a garage on an empty lot next door to Priory Steps, but the local chief planning officer applied and got permission to build a three story house, blocking her view toward the Saxon Church. She spent many thousands of pounds taking this matter up to the high court, claiming corruption because he was able to get permission since he was the chief planning officer. She lost, of course.

Chapter 25: LAST LAPS

1. Philip died of AIDS in his early forties. Michael was the self-described 'black sheep of the family'; his early wanderlust led him to America and a successful career as a stage hypnotist.

2. Jeremy Kilbee in the *Western Daily Press & Times Mirror, 27* January 1976.

3. *Nine Thousand Miles in Eight Weeks*, Heath Cranton, 1927; *The Woman Owner Driver*, Illiffe & Sons, 1928; *The Peregrinations of Penelope,* Heath Cranton, 1930; *The Bluebird's Flight*, Chapman & Hall, 1931; *Nine Lives Plus*, Pelham Books, 1977.

4. Mary never corrected anyone who called her, or referred to her, as 'Lady Bruce'.

5. Unable to completely stifle their curiosity, the three gathered what information they could; one even visited Mary at Bradford-on-Avon.

6. Mary's grandson Michael said that Marcelle despised his grandmother, and in the end treated Tony badly as well.

7. 'Adventurous Eves' BBC, 14 January 1990.

INDEX